8389296

RESIDENTIAL LOCATION MARKETS AND URBAN TRANSPORTATION

STUDIES IN URBAN ECONOMICS

Under the Editorship of

Edwin S. Mills
Princeton University

Norman J. Glickman. ECONOMETRIC ANALYSIS OF REGIONAL SYSTEMS: Explorations in Model Building and Policy Analysis

J. Vernon Henderson. ECONOMIC THEORY AND THE CITIES

Norman J. Glickman. THE GROWTH AND MANAGEMENT OF THE JAPANESE URBAN SYSTEM

George S. Tolley, Philip E. Graves, and John L. Gardner, URBAN GROWTH POLICY IN A MARKET ECONOMY

David Segal (Ed.). THE ECONOMICS OF NEIGHBORHOOD

R. D. Norton. CITY LIFE-CYCLES AND AMERICAN URBAN POLICY

John F. McDonald. ECONOMIC ANALYSIS OF AN URBAN HOUSING MARKET

Daniel Feenberg and Edwin S. Mills. MEASURING THE BENEFITS OF WATER POLLUTION ABATEMENT

Michael J. Greenwood. MIGRATION AND ECONOMIC GROWTH IN THE UNITED STATES: National, Regional, and Metropolitan Perspectives

Takahiro Miyao. DYNAMIC ANALYSIS OF THE URBAN ECONOMY

Katharine L. Bradbury, Anthony Downs, and Kenneth A. Small. FUTURES FOR A DECLINING CITY: Simulations for the Cleveland Area

Charles F. Mueller. THE ECONOMICS OF LABOR MIGRATION: A Behavioral Analysis

Douglas B. Diamond, Jr. and George S. Tolley (Eds.). THE ECONOMICS OF URBAN AMENITIES

Alex Anas. RESIDENTIAL LOCATION MARKETS AND URBAN TRANSPORTATION: Economic Theory, Econometrics, and Policy Analysis with Discrete Choice Models

In preparation

Joseph Friedman and Daniel H. Weinberg. THE ECONOMICS OF HOUSING VOUCHERS

RESIDENTIAL LOCATION MARKETS AND URBAN TRANSPORTATION

Economic Theory, Econometrics, and Policy Analysis with Discrete Choice Models

ALEX ANAS

Urban Systems and Planning Program
Department of Civil Engineering
and The Technological Institute
Northwestern University
Evanston, Illinois

1982
ACADEMIC PRESS
A Subsidiary of Harcourt Brace Jovanovich, Publishers

New York   London
Paris   San Diego   San Francisco   São Paulo   Sydney   Tokyo   Toronto

ACADEMIC PRESS, INC.
111 Fifth Avenue, New York, New York 10003

United Kingdom Edition published by
ACADEMIC PRESS, INC. (LONDON) LTD.
24/28 Oval Road, London NW1 7DX

Library of Congress Cataloging in Publication Data

Anas, Alex.
  Residential location markets and urban transportation.

  (Studies in urban economics)
  Includes bibliographical references.
  1. Rental housing--Location--Economic aspects--
Illinois--Chicago Metropolitan Area. 2. Urban trans-
portation--Illinois--Chicago Metropolitan Area--Plan-
ning. I. Title. II. Series.
HD7288.85.U62C43   333.33'8   82-6690
ISBN 0-12-057920-0   AACR2

PRINTED IN THE UNITED STATES OF AMERICA

82 83 84 85   9 8 7 6 5 4 3 2 1

To my parents
with admiration and gratitude

CONTENTS

PREFACE

Urban economics is largely in the debt of William Alonso, whose "bid rent theory" has been in the journals for nearly two decades. Bid rent theory continues to serve as a framework for pencil-and-paper theoretical models, but the econometric estimation and large scale policy application of these models has proved to be difficult, unmanageable, and frustrating. In part because of this, the applied fields of transportation planning and urban modeling—which stand to benefit from urban economics—have remained largely separate from it.

In this book I develop a theory of equilibrium in urban rental housing markets that includes within it the theory of urban commuting and residential location demand. I proceed to formulate and empirically estimate a specific model for the Chicago SMSA based on this market equilibrium theory. I then apply this model to the analysis and evaluation of public transportation finance policy and specific public transportation projects proposed for Chicago.

I wrote this book primarily for urban economists, to show the value of disengaging from deterministic bid rent analysis and focusing on stochastic maximization models. Equally, the book is intended for the growing number of transportation planners and urban modelers, who, thanks to Daniel McFadden's contribution to urban travel demand and stochastic choice modeling, are increasingly receptive to economic theory and econometrics.

I view this book as one of the steps in a series of developments that will seek to unify the currently separate but logically connected subdisciplines of urban economics, transportation planning, and urban modeling. The final chapter contains, in a nutshell, the future steps that follow logically from the developments in this book. Therein lie ideas for research problems that await exploration.

The book is organized to go from a state-of-the-art review to new theoretical developments, then to econometric estimation, and finally to empirical policy analysis. As such, a graduate student may come to grips with all aspects of the transition, from theory to econometrics, to policy analysis.

Throughout, I have taken care to be self-critical, even though rather briefly. The reader and student will undoubtedly find new angles from which to view, discuss, and restructure my findings and conclusions and to pursue my suggestions and conjectures.

ALEX ANAS
Evanston

ACKNOWLEDGMENTS

I completed the research reported in this book during the past few years. Some of the material presented here stems in part from several of my journal articles. The policy themes of the second part evolved from my graduate courses in urban land use planning and urban modeling that I have taught at Northwestern University since 1976.

The theoretical developments that I report in Part I of this book were partially supported by grant SOC77-18264 from the National Science Foundation, and the empirical estimation and policy applications of Part II by research contract DOT-RC-92028 with the United States Department of Transportation's (U.S.D.O.T.) University Research Program. While I gratefully acknowledge the financial support from these agencies, I remain solely responsible for the entire contents of this work and the opinions and policy conclusions expressed.

I am indebted to my students Chaushie Chu and Liang Shyong Duann, whose competent and careful research assistance and dedicated scholarship contributed to the empirical research, only a part of which is reported in Part II of this book. I am also in their debt for choosing to advance aspects of this work in their Ph.D. dissertations. Robert Martin of U.S.D.O.T. made careful and timely comments on the empirical work reported in Chapters 4 and 5. His comments have been helpful not only for the work reported here but also for planned and in-progress extensions and policy applications of the equilibrium model of Part II.

Cheri Heramb and Chris Krueger of the Department of Public Works of the City of Chicago; Anant Vyas and Suhail Al-Chalabi of the Chicago

xiii

Area Transportation Study; and Ashish Sen and Siim Soot of the University of Illinois at Chicago Circle generously shared with me the census and transportation system data used in this study.

I also convey my thanks to Vera Fisher, who did an excellent job of typing the entire manuscript.

INTRODUCTION

Recently, at a small conference on the interactions between transportation systems and urban land use, a colleague made the following comment during an informal conversation: "... if urban modelers must wait for accurate empirical models of cities based on economic theory, it will take forever before we can analyze public policies or make useful predictions of urban change." This statement is a measure of the distance that separates urban economists from the engineers, planners, geographers, and urban and regional scientists working on urban simulation modeling and transportation planning.

Urban economics, urban simulation modeling, and urban transportation planning are three subdisciplines that are linked by logical, methodological, and historical connections. Despite these linkages, research in these areas has followed fairly independent paths, and the common purpose and interests of the three areas has become obscured by differences in the academic affiliations of the scholars working in these subdisciplines. Few urban modelers or transportation planners would deny the importance of economics in applied model building, yet the degree to which economic theory becomes incorporated into applied models is minimal and ad hoc at best. Few economists would deny the importance of building accurate policy analytic tools rooted in economics, yet little has been done by urban economists toward this goal.

It is only recently that hopeful signs for the synthesis of urban economic theory and applied urban simulation modeling have begun to emerge, but these developments have not yet taken root.

1

1. URBAN ECONOMICS: THE BASIC SCIENCE
FOR URBAN SIMULATION MODELING
AND TRANSPORTATION PLANNING

Modern urban economics owes its beginnings to the work of Alonso (1964), who established the foundations of a mathematical model of urban land use that to this day forms the crux of urban economic theory. Urban economics took great strides beyond Alonso's seminal contribution and became an established field through the works of Muth (1969), Mills (1967, 1972a), and others

The chief contribution of urban economics has been the development of a theoretically consistent but simplified model of urban land use and market land prices. This model, known as the "monocentric city," is inspired by the nineteenth century American urban areas that had nearly all of their employment concentrated in their downtown or central business districts, surrounded by residential suburbs. The simple circular structure of the monocentric city, while not entirely realistic, allowed powerful mathematical analysis.

Using the monocentric city as a prototype, urban economists developed partial and general equilibrium models of urban spatial structure. The typical partial equilibrium analysis takes the number of jobs at the central business district as given and analyzes the spatial structure of residential land use around the central business district. The price of land, the density of land use, and the equilibrium locations of different groups of the urban population are determined by the model. Partial equilibrium models have yielded the most robust conclusions in urban economics. The best known of these are the results that land prices and land use densities will decline as a function of distance from the center of the monocentric city and that higher income households will locate farther away from the center than low income households will. This occurs because as income increases, a household's preference for housing, lot size, and suburban public services increases faster than the household's dislike of commuting. Because of this shift in preferences, higher income households are the highest bidders for suburban land while low income households are the highest bidders near the central business district, where, because of the high land prices, they must live in high densities, consuming a relatively small amount of floor space and land per household.

More complex results are derived from general equilibrium models in which the employment, housing, and transportation sectors of a city are analyzed simultaneously. The objective of these general equilibrium models is to determine the size and productive capacity of a monocentric city's central employment, the socially efficient amount of land that must be allocated to road transportation around the center, the optimal degree of traffic congestion, and the quantity of housing that the market will produce at each location within the monocentric city. General equilibrium models of this kind have been developed by Mills (1967), Dixit (1973), and others.

One of the most important achievements of urban economics in the 1970s was the establishment of the correspondence between market equilibrium and social optimum allocation of resources within urban areas. This development coincides with the advent of general equilibrium models. Urban economic analysis confirms the widely held principle in economic theory that a perfectly competitive urban economy in which production and consumption externalities are nonexistent will produce a Pareto efficient market equilibrium, in which the welfare of any one market participant (consumer or producer) cannot be improved without reducing the welfare of some other market participant. This result does not hold when the perfectly competitive market participants generate externalities such as traffic congestion, pollution, and noise or when certain facilities and services must be provided by the public sector. For such cases, urban economists have again succeeded in demonstrating the general economic principle that efficiency requires the levying of appropriate tolls and taxes, the purpose of which is to internalize the externalities by requiring the market participants to pay the full social costs of their actions in the market.

Perhaps the most flexible and complete general equilibrium formulation in urban economic analysis is Mills' (1972b) linear programming model, extended by Hartwick and Hartwick (1974) and Kim (1979). Mills uses linear programming as a framework for determining the socially efficient geographical allocation of urban land and capital within a fixed-coefficient technology. While this assumption is necessary to enable linear formulations, the scope and capabilities of these linear formulations are quite broad. Models thus developed are not restricted to monocentric cities; these models can deal with a number of interrelated primary and secondary employment and population sectors, can decide the allocation of land to roads and other uses, including subways and transit systems, and can determine the most efficient height and capital/land ratio for buildings in each location within the metropolitan area. These linear programming models can also achieve a good approximation of the optimal congestion level in all parts of the road network. To produce a solution, one must input all technological coefficients, prices that are exogenous to the urban system (such as the price of capital and agricultural land), the potential location of export nodes from which urban goods are shipped to other cities, and the general orientation of the road network as a rectangular grid. Interactions of the public sector with the land market and extensions of the basic models can be introduced without departing from the linear programming framework.

The developments in urban economics, summarized above, comprise a fairly complete and coherent body of knowledge that reconciles the predictive modeling of market processes with the development of optimal plans, the corrective pricing of externalities such as traffic congestion and air pollution, and the financing of public services provided by local municipalities. It would appear, therefore, that urban economic theory should be viewed as the basic science upon which applied fields such as urban simulation modeling or transportation planning must rely. Only very few would dispute the validity of this position: the concern of applied fields such as urban modeling and transportation planning is the development of tools that can be used to make sound policy decisions about the allocation of resources in urban space. Economics is the only social science that deals explicitly with the rationale for optimal resource allocation and the study and explanation of market processes for competitive resource allocation. Why is it, then, that economics in general and urban economics in particular do not occupy a central place in urban simulation modeling and transportation planning? The answer is to be found not in the logical connections between these subdisciplines and economics but in the historical development of these subdisciplines vis-à-vis the historical development of urban economics.

2. TRANSPORTATION PLANNING

Transportation planning as we currently know it emerged as an area of research and professional training in the 1950s as an extension of highway design and traffic engineering. Thus transportation planning started groping for a conceptual framework a decade or so before urban economic theory was being developed and disseminated. The early transportation planners approached problems of investment planning and resource allocation from a mechanistic and nonbehavioral viewpoint. Calculation without theory was the accepted way of doing transportation planning. Tools were developed and applied without justification of their behavioral content or predictive validity but solely for their descriptive usefulness and decision-making appeal.

An interesting example of this syndrome in early transportation planning is the gravity model. These models were invented as tools to help the transportation planner balance an origin-to-destination trip table so that the trips predicted to flow from one geographic traffic zone of an urban area to another would be consistent with the trips generated at each origin zone and terminating at each destination zone. The crudest gravity model has the form

$$T_{ij} = G_{ij}[O_i D_j / f(d_{ij})],$$

where O_i are the trips originating from zone i, and D_j, the trips terminating in zone j; $f(d_{ij})$ is the impedance or separation between i and j as an increasing function of the distance from i to j; T_{ij}, the predicted trips originating from zone i and terminating in zone j; and G_{ij}, an "adjustment factor," the value of which is selected to "balance" trips by assuming that $\sum_i T_{ij} = D_j$ and $\sum_j T_{ij} = O_i$ for each i and each j. Gravity models were brought to transportation planning by the engineers and physicists who entered that field. It would not be unfair to say that Isaac Newton's physics was the most influential body of knowledge for transportation planning, or at least travel demand prediction, during the fifties and sixties.

It was not until 1967 that Wilson provided the first theoretically valid derivation of the gravity model from statistical information-minimizing principles. Wilson's work brought elegance, analytical rigor, and a long-awaited sense of closure to the confusion about the interpretability and theoretical integrity of the gravity model. Following Wilson's work, the application of information-minimizing models flourished in Britain and, to a lesser extent, in the United States and elsewhere. Transportation modeling became enhanced by a new generation of gravity models. Many practicing transportation planners were able to correct their previous abuses of the gravity model and to balance their trip tables with a new sense of statistical consistency. While statistical consistency does not imply behavioral or economic validity, more recent contributions have demonstrated that a generalized version of the so-called gravity model is similar (Williams, 1977), indeed identical (Anas, 1982), to a certain subset of microeconomic choice models called multinomial logit models developed by McFadden (1973) for economic travel demand analysis and prediction. After nearly three decades of research, it may be said that the tradition of mechanistic travel demand modeling has come to an end and microeconomic models of travel behavior have become accepted, though still not widely used, tools among transportation planners.

Travel demand modeling is only one concern within transportation planning. The more general concerns of this subdiscipline naturally deal with questions of investment and transportation system design. Thus the analysis of travel behavior and the development of models for predicting travel patterns provides demand-side information for the transportation planner. To complete its mission, transportation planning must synthesize the demand-side models based on microeconomics with the transportation system performance models derived from engineering relationships. Some developments that contribute toward this goal have taken place in recent years and will be discussed later in this introduction.

A shortcoming of transportation planning as a discipline is its self-imposed scope of viewing transportation problems in relative isolation from the more general aspects of society that they impact. This, too, is a limitation that is rooted in the tradition of engineering problem solving. While urban economists have consistently viewed transportation systems as one sector in the multisectoral urban economy, transportation planners have traditionally taken the geographical distribution of urban land uses as given and then addressed the problem of designing a transportation system to serve the demands generated by the given land use. This perspective suffers from two difficulties. First, it ignores the potential for modeling the reciprocal market interrelationships between transportation systems and land uses, and second, it foregoes the opportunity of viewing transportation as a tool for *shaping* urban development and urban land use. Historically, policy issues stemming from a systemic view of the urban economy and the development of tools consistent with this view are the subject of urban simulation modeling and have remained beyond the scope of transportation planning.

3.   URBAN SIMULATION MODELING

Urban simulation modeling emerged as an area of research and a subdiscipline of urban planning in the sixties. Seminal works that are responsible for the birth of this subdiscipline are the contributions by Lowry (1964) and Forrester (1968). Forrester's approach did not attract many followers because his analysis ignored the spatial dimension of urban areas and the resulting spatial interactions among land use, transportation, housing, and employment. Lowry's model on the other hand, became the centerpiece of urban modeling research and has been extended. For a review of the extensions of the Lowry model, see Putman (1979). Interest in the Lowry model grew primarily because of two reasons. First, the Lowry model was the first operational tool aimed at describing the basic spatial interactions of urban form in an intuitively acceptable conceptual fashion. Second, the Lowry model was operational on the computer at a time when the importance of large scale computation for urban policy testing was becoming widely recognized.

The basic concept of Lowry's urban model is the view that urban development is the result of a two-way interaction between employment and population. A given spatial distribution of employment will generate a certain distribution of population and housing as a result of the employees' demands for residences. Conversely, a given distribution of housing and population will generate a distribution of employment as a result of households' demands for goods and services. Because these reciprocal demands are manifested spatially, transportation plays a key role in determining the distribution of housing and employment in urban space.

This basic structure of Lowry's model is akin to the basic notions of urban economic theory. The linear programming model developed by Mills (1972b) and described above subscribes to the same reciprocal interactions embodied in the Lowry model. The key difference between an economic model such as that of Lowry is that the latter model does not include prices and is thus inconsistent with economic behavior and thus unable to explain or predict market adjustments correctly.

Most mathematical models developed in the urban modeling tradition are subjects to the same limitations as the Lowry model. There are essentially two kinds of consistency that are sought in an economic model. The first is *behavioral consistency* and the second is *systemic consistency*. Behavioral consistency is present when the model's basic relationships such as demand equations, supply equations, and the like can be shown to be mathematically derivable from utility and profit maximization, namely from microeconomic principles. Systemic consistency is present when the behavioral submodels such as the demand and supply equations are linked together in an equilibrating or dynamic mechanism that is consistent with economic analysis. Lowry's model did not have behavioral consistency because the model's equations that corresponded to travel demand behavior lacked key variables such as travel costs, travel times, and housing prices. The model also lacked systemic consistency because the absence of price variables prevented a consistent balancing of supply and demand. To find an "equilibrium" solution, Lowry had to resort to arbitrary adjustment procedures such as the uniform distribution of excess demands among the geographic zones of the urban area. Behavioral and systemic consistency problems have not been completely eliminated from extensions of the Lowry model, such as the Projective Land Use Model developed by Goldner (1968) and the Integrated Transprotation and Land Use Package developed by Putman (1974). Putman's extension introduces a transportation network into the Lowry model, thus providing a framework for studying transportation–land development interactions, including traffic congestion levels on various links of the network. In Putman's model, somewhat arbitrary network loading (traffic assignment) procedures must be implemented to achieve an "equilibrium" level of traffic on the network.

A general shortcoming of urban simulation modeling research is that most models in this tradition that are not developed from an economic viewpoint lack appropriate "cost–benefit criteria" or welfare economic benefit measures. Policies must be evaluated by direct examination of a model's predictions or by appending other models that evaluate the cost–benefit implications of these predictions. This is unfortunate since economic theory does provide a rather sophisticated body of knowledge that can be incorporated into these models to improve their cost–benefit capabilities.

Not all urban models lack in economics. The two operational models that are fairly well rooted in economic analysis are the Urban Institute model (deLeeuw and Struyk, 1975) and the National Bureau of Economic Research model (Ingram *et al.*, 1972; Kain *et al.*, 1976). Both of these models are intended primarily as tools for analyzing housing market policies. Both have been applied to examine the effects of housing allowance programs such as income and rent subsidies on the housing consumption patterns of low income households. The NBER model is generally known as the most ambitious long term experiment in the development of economic urban simulation modeling. The NBER and Urban Institute models do have several problems with behavioral and system consistency considerations, but they are far better in this regard than the Lowry and related models. The one serious shortcoming of these economic models is that the econometrics and the data used to estimate the behavioral relationships are very crude. This crudeness is due partly to the extensive aggregation of geographic locations into large zones, partly to the lack of high quality data and, in the case of the NBER model, partly to the complex structure of the model.

It is perhaps ironic that many urban economists view the development of large scale urban models with considerable cynicism. This is an understandable attidude since the difficulties of marrying good theory and good econometrics with the considerable computational problems of urban simulation are amply demonstrated in models such as the NBER. Clearly a great deal of patient research is needed before urban simulation models can become accepted as reliable policy analytic tools. As a result, most urban economists do not have a strong commitment to the large scale empirical application of their theoretical models and are generally satisfied with pencil and paper analyses and simplified numerical testing of these models. There is good reason for this since it can be argued that the theoretical models are sufficient to provide general and powerful qualitative insight into many crucial policy questions. The theoretical models are inadequate, however, when the policy analyst is seeking precise quantitative answers and when specific urban policies and plans must be analyzed in order to settle questions of investment programming and budgeting. It is for these reasons that the development of empirically based large scale models is needed. Unfortunately, most of the researchers engaged in large scale modeling have come from engineering and planning and have not been adequately trained in economic analysis.

4. STOCHASTIC CHOICE MODELS IN ECONOMICS, URBAN ECONOMICS, AND ECONOMETRICS

The distance between urban economic theory and applied urban modeling is also partly due to certain rigidities in the specific mathematical models developed by urban economists. The main problem arises from the fact that while any applied empirical analysis must deal with stochastic distributions and must assume the way in which unobserved information enters into models, theoretical urban economics has remained aloof from these probabilistic considerations. Utility maximization and profit maximization are the central concepts in any economic analysis, but stochastic maximization models, which are the bridge for the transition from the realm of pure theory to the realm of empirical application, are relatively new in economics and urban economics.

Ironically, travel demand theory is one of the first research areas in which stochastic models made a start. This occurred in 1962, when Warner published a pioneering statistical study of commuters' choices between automobile and public transit. This study was the precursor of the logit models that are now widely used by travel demand analysts. Warner's work created a great deal of interest among economists and analytically inclined non-economists interested in studying travel demand. This interest led to a great deal of empirical work, but the multinomial logit model as we know it today did not become firmly rooted in economics until the works of McFadden (1973), Ben-Akiva (1973), and Domencich and McFadden (1975). It is through these works that the connection between logit models, stochastic utility maximization, and related econometric methods was demonstrated. While McFadden's work is of general importance to economic theory per se, the fact that travel demand was the context of McFadden's work has been a great windfall to the applied fields of "transportation planning" and "urban modeling." This interdisciplinary texture of McFadden's work has substantially narrowed the distance between economic theory and the above-mentioned applied fields. Some noneconomists are now actively engaged in economic research, and the use of economic theory and econometric methods is growing in many noneconomic disciplines such as geography, urban planning, and engineering.

Recently, stochastic choice models of demand have been applied in the area of residential location analysis as well. The works by Quigley (1976), Lerman (1977), McFadden (1978), and Anas (1981a) demonstrate the usefulness of stochastic choice models for analyzing the demand for residential location and housing as a problem of microeconomic choice among numerous discrete location or housing alternatives. Although the application of stochastic choice models as demand-side tools is flourishing, there has been little research aimed at investigating the properties of supply–demand equilibration in which the demand side, the supply side, or both are formulated as stochastic choice models.

One area where such equilibration problems have been recently posed and solved is that of traffic network equilibration, an important subarea of transportation planning. Prior to the development of stochastic models of route choice, transportation planners determined the equilibrium traffic on various links of the transport network by assuming that each traveler's minimum-travel-time route can be deterministicly identified. The development of stochastic models enables transportation analysts to identify minimum-travel-time routes probabilisticly. The traffic network equilibration models developed by Daganzo and Sheffi (1977) and Sheffi (1978) solve the problem of traffic network equilibrium by assigning travelers to travel routes via stochastic models of route choice, and by determining equilibrium travel times on each link of the network such that the entire traffic network is in equilibrium.

Another area where stochastic equilibrium problems have been posed and solved is that of rental housing market equilibrium investigated by this author (Anas, 1980b). Traditionally, urban economists determined rental housing equilibria by assuming that each dwelling is assigned to the highest bidding household that can be identified deterministically. Stochastic choice formulations of housing and residential location demand allow for the probabilistic determination of residential location patterns. Simulation models based on stochastic choice formulations of demand and aimed at investigating the impact of transportation–land use policies and urban changes on real estate values have also been developed [see Anas (1979, 1980a) and Anas and Lee (1981)].

Stochastic choice models are an appealing alternative to the deterministic models that historically have formed the basis of urban economic analysis. The appeal of stochastic choice models is both theoretical and empirical. The theoretical appeal stems from the fact that these models include uncertainty and are suitable tools for describing inhomogeneities or dissimilarities in demand- or supply-side behavior. The empirical appeal stems from the fact that the models are directly suitable for empirical estimation and have flexible econometric applicability compared to the deterministic models, which lead to crude and rigid empirical models.

5. THE FUTURE OF POLICY ANALYSIS

In the years to come, urban economics, transportation planning, and urban simulation modeling should approach their common mission of the development of accurate policy-analytic tools and should achieve strides toward a synthesis. Judging from the recent developments outlined above, this process is already underway and can reach its conclusion if the proper place of economic theory in urban models becomes appropriately cultivated and solidly anchored.

Ultimately, a vast array of urban issues and policies ranging from housing market allowances to transportation pricing, to the financing of local public services, and to the suburbanization of employment must be analyzed using the same theoretical basis provided by urban economics. The precise models and analytical tools may not be the same in each case, but the basic theory and conceptual structure from which the models are derived must certainly be the same. Whether such an "ultimate urban simulation modeling framework" can ever be formulated and empirically applied is a question that cannot be answered at this time. The answer depends on whether enough scholars interested in applied issues will choose to learn the lessons provided by economic theory as a basis for improving the capabilities of their models. Equally, the answer depends on whether sufficient numbers of urban economists develop a lasting interest in applied urban modeling, focusing their efforts on empirical analysis and policy application rooted in the best of urban economic theory.

An implication of the "ultimate synthesis" is that a unity of theory and method will come to dominate the interdisciplinary concerns that may be labeled "urban science and policy analysis." It is only after such a unity of theory and method becomes established that urban scholars will be able to successfully defend their analytical tools and models as instruments of policy making in an inherently political world. In contemporary society it is politics, not economics, that governs urban policy making. It is political power, not scientific truth or objectively established principles of efficiency, that guides the allocation of resources and public funds. The ultimate mission of applied social science in general and economics in particular is to achieve the reduction of the realm of politics to the absolute minimum by providing essentially apolitical decision-making tools. Such an ideal may, at present, appear to be no less than a utopian vision. In fact, it may be a reasonable and achievable goal toward which a great deal of progress can be made in the next few decades.

6. THE PLAN OF THIS BOOK

The research that is reported in this book represents a step in the synthesis of urban economic theory with urban modeling and transportation planning. More precisely, appropriate aspects of economic theory are developed and used to design an urban simulation model, which is then applied to the analysis of urban transportation policies and specific transportation plans in the Chicago Standard Metropolitan Statistical Area (SMSA).

The book consists of two parts. Part I reports the theoretical developments, and Part II presents the empirical implementation and the policy-analytic results. Detailed conclusions and summaries are presented at the end of each chapter.

Part I consists of three chapters. Of these, the first chapter is a review of the most salient aspects of "bid rent analysis," the current mathematical centerpiece in urban economics. In addition to reviewing the state of the art in bid rent analysis, this chapter also provides a criticism of the theoretical and empirical aspects of the deterministic bid rent models and paves the ground for the development of stochastic utility maximization models, which form the basis of the rest of Part I.

Chapter 2 is a detailed examination and review that focuses on the basic mathematical structure and assumptions underlying the discrete stochastic choice model of rental housing and residential location demand. Estimation methods and the aggregation properties of discrete stochastic choice models are also discussed. Particular attention is paid to the multinomial logit, nested logit, and generalized extreme value models and their applicability to residential location choice.

Chapter 3 is a multisubmarket Walrasian equilibrium analysis of the rental housing market. Housing and location demand is formulated as a problem in discrete stochastic choice following the logistic models examined in Chapter 2. The chapter is devoted to the derivation of intersubmarket average rents and intrasubmarket rent distributions at stochastic equilibrium by solving the problem of the allocation of households to dwellings. Useful closed form solutions that follow from the convenient analytical properties of logit and nested logit models are derived.

The overall contribution of Part I is the development of an economic equilibrium theory of the rental housing market that incorporates the stochastic utility maximization models of discrete choice on the demand side. This is a logical development within economic theory, first examined in Anas (1980b).

Part II consists of three chapters discussing the empirical estimation, policy application, and future extensions of an urban simulation model rooted in the theory of Part I. Chapter 4 uses 1970 Census data for the Chicago Standard Metropolitan Statistical Area to estimate the demand- and supply-side models. The demand-side model is one in which each household chooses jointly a residential location and a mode of travel for the daily commute, given a particular workplace location. This formulation of demand integrates the current methodology of travel demand measurement with the comparable measurement of residential location demand. The supply-side model is formulated as a stochastic profit maximization model in which each landlord decides whether the dwelling should be "offered for rent" or "kept vacant." Using small geographic aggregations of the census data, the demand- and supply-side models are estimated and evaluated by examining the estimated elasticities and coefficients. In addition to the estimated results, this chapter contains a discussion of the sources of bias generally encountered in the estimation of choice models and of the methodological contributions to the estimation of choice models from aggregated data.

Chapter 5 combines the demand- and supply-side models into an equilibrium simulation model that endogenously determines travel and residential choices, equilibrium rents, and vacancies by geographic zone. This model is intended for the examination of downtown oriented transportation investments and policies. Thus the demands of the downtown (Central Business District) employees receive special attention in the model and their choices among four commuting modes (auto, suburban commuter rail, rapid transit, and bus) are predicted by the model. The model also predicts the choice of residential location by identifying the distribution of households among the 1690 geographical zones that cover the SMSA. Some of the properties of the equilibrium solution predicted by the model are analytically accessible, and these are examined via comparative statics. The chief purpose of this chapter is the application of the empirically estimated model to transportation policy analysis and transportation planning for Chicago's southwest corridor. Following sensitivity analysis on the estimated models' coefficients and comparison of alternative estimated models, one model is selected for policy testing. Specific policy scenarios are focused on the issue of financing urban public transportation systems in the eighties. Policy alternatives include gasoline taxes imposed on automobile users, parking taxes imposed on downtown rush hour commuters, and incremental lump sum property taxes imposed to capture windfall housing value changes created by public transportation investments. Three specific fixed-guideway rapid transit lines that have been proposed for construction in Chicago's Southwest corridor are studied, and their effects on metropolitan commuting, residential location, and housing rent patterns are predicted. One of these proposed projects is the Gulf Mobile and Ohio selected for detailed study, and the sensitivity of the policy results to various assumed external conditions is evaluated.

The policy simulations demonstrate that federal subsidization of the finance of metropolitan transit systems can be replaced entirely or to a very high degree with economically efficient local financing schemes consisting of gasoline taxes, downtown parking taxes, and real estate taxes. For rail rapid transit projects such as the Gulf Mobile and Ohio, incremental taxes aimed to capture windfall gains in existing housing values and caused by these projects within the southwest corridor are estimated to be 14–18% of their total operating plus construction cost. The tax per dwelling needed to achieve this is shown to be small and not to exceed about $20 per month, even for dwellings benefiting the most from the transit project. Terminating the existing bus service to the downtown in the same corridor is shown to reduce rents by about three times the cost of operating the bus service. This suggests that it may be possible to finance an expanded bus system with appropriate incremental windfall taxes on housing amounting to about 5% or less of annualized housing values.

These and other results, interpreted in light of the sensitivity tests and the possible sources of error in model estimation suggest that, contrary to current popular belief, federal cuts in subsidies need not cripple metropolitan public transportation. Quite to the contrary, public transportation can become locally financed if the public authorities and the state and local governments respond creatively in taking advantage of economically efficient pricing and investment–disinvestment options available to them.

On the methodological side, the urban simulation model developed, estimated, tested, and applied in Chapters 4 and 5 is a synthesis of urban economics with the travel demand models used in transportation planning. It is, therefore, a response to the disciplinary fragmentation discussed in this introduction.

Chapter 6 is a discussion of research directions in economic urban simulation modeling. The focus is on how the theoretical and empirical models developed in this book can be extended to many general equilibrium and dynamic formulations applicable to a wide array of policy issues. In this author's opinion, these extensions comprise an agenda of applied research problems for the current decade and beyond.

PART I

PROBABILISTIC DISCRETE CHOICE THEORY AND RENTAL HOUSING MARKET EQUILIBRIUM

CHAPTER 1

AN OVERVIEW OF BID RENT ANALYSIS

This chapter is a critical overview of the standard microeconomic model of housing markets and residential location. We examine theoretical and operational (algorithmic) versions of this model and discuss econometric problems associated with its empirical implementation.

It is fair to say that the concept of "bid rent," or "bid price," forms the crux of modern urban economic analysis and underlies most formal microeconomic models of urban spatial structure. Historically, the concept of bid rent stems from von Thünen's (1826) original model of agricultural land use. Since the early sixties and owing to Alonso's work (1964), the same concept has become the centerpiece of formal models of residential location and urban housing markets. The works of Muth (1969), Mills (1967), and many others have demonstrated that models based on the bid rent concept coupled with the analytics of neoclassical economics provide a powerful tool. The centrality of the bid rent approach may not always be transparent, primarily because "bid rent analysis" is often reworked as "demand analysis" and "utility maximization." A careful prodding of any analytical model developed in the Alonso tradition reveals that the underlying behavior is thought of as bidding behavior. According to this approach, each household is a perfectly informed and efficient bidder "submitting" bids for all available housing units or locations. Each housing unit supplier or land developer is, likewise, perfectly informed about all bids submitted and will auction off the housing unit or land to the highest bidding household. An interesting question is how this bidding and auctioning process unfolds itself in real time. Urban economists have not addressed this question. Instead, almost all attention and effort have been reserved for an analysis of a steady state long run equilibrium outcome in which the bidding–auctioneering process eventually works itself out so that each land parcel or dwelling is allocated to the highest bidder. It has been suggested throughout the literature that if households' mobility costs are negligible, in a steady state situation they would be able to find their equilibrium position eventually, and the speed of adjustment to such an equilibrium will be rapid for a perfectly informed market.

Urban planners have focused on the development of operational simulation algorithms for finding solutions to the bidding–auctioneering process. As early as 1960, Herbert and Stevens proposed the use of linear programming as a method for allocating households within urban areas. The Herbert–Stevens model was based on the concept of bid rent. A research team led by Britton Harris at the University of Pennsylvania in 1966 attempted to apply the Herbert–Stevens model to the design of a new town and to sketch planning for the Penn–Jersey transportation study (see Harris *et al.*, 1966). An important part of this research was a timely attempt to use econometric methods to estimate households' bid rent functions and to subsequently embed these into the Herbert–Stevens model in order to simulate locational equilibrium. More recently, there have been renewed attempts to estimate households' bid rent functions using hedonic price estimation techniques from econometrics. Examples are the works by Wheaton (1972), Anas (1975), Wheaton (1977a), and Galster (1977).

In recent years, the use of bid rent analysis has been extended from static long run models of urban land use, such as the original Alonso model and its followers, to dynamic and quasidynamic models. A shared assumption of all these dynamic models is that they do not relax the implicit time nature of the bidding–auctioneering process but view nonstationary urban development as a sequence of bidding–auctioneering processes, each of which quickly converges on a short run (temporary) equilibrium. For example, Fujita's dynamic land use model (1976) assumes perfect foresight about the future on the part of land developers, whereas the dynamic model of Anas (1978a) assumes lack of knowledge about the future and myopic land developer and housing supplier behavior. Both authors assume a myopic but perfectly mobile population of households. Despite these differences, both analyses are based on the concept of bid rent and bid price, and trace out urban growth paths as sequences of temporary equilibria, a result made possible through the repeated resolution of implicit bidding–auctioneering processes.

In this chapter, the standard model in urban economics is reviewed in five sections. First, we review the basic behavior of the consumer of housing (the household) and the supplier of housing services (the landlord or land developer) in a stationary urban economy. Second, we formulate the traditional long run bid rent model that derives an equilibrium configuration for the residential land market in a stationary state. We also examine the notion of bid rent in short run equilibrium models that deal with the allocation of households among existing dwellings. In Section 3, we review the application of linear programming as a tool of locational equilibrium analysis. In Section 4, we review and critically evaluate the methodology for empirically estimating bid rent functions. Finally, in Section 5, we present an overview of the fundamental assumptions of bid rent models and a criticism of their theoretical and empirical underpinnings.

1. BEHAVIOR IN A STATIONARY RESIDENTIAL STATE

Following the traditional Alonso model, we assume that all employment in a hypothetical circular city is concentrated in the Central Business District (CBD). The CBD exists because of agglomeration and other transportation related factors that enable industries to outbid land uses near the center. Each household has one working member employed in the CBD, and this member commutes there daily from the household's residential location. All households in the city are assumed to be identical in both income and utility functions (preferences). Land in the residential part of the city is owned by absentee landowners who have the option of allocating their land to residential or agricultural use. The agricultural bid per unit of land is assumed to be the same regardless of location. For simplicity, we will assume that all housing units that will be constructed in the city have identical and infinitely durable structural features and differ only in the size of their lots. Thus a landowner who owns some of the land at a particular location must decide the profit-maximizing partitioning of his land into individual lots. A household choosing a residential location in the city must decide where to locate and what size lot to require at that location so as to achieve the highest possible level of utility. Out of the household's decision process, there arises a set of bid rents for various locations representing what the household would be willing to pay for those locations. Out of the landowner's decision process arises a set of asking rents for each location in the city. At equilibrium, one of the conditions that must hold is that the bid rent must equal the asking rent. Another equilibrium condition is that each land parcel is allocated to the highest bidder. A third equilibrium condition requires that households be indifferent among the different locations and thus uninterested in relocating. A fourth equilibrium condition assures that both residential and agricultural bid rents equal the asking rent of the landlord who owns land at the edge of the city. This assures that the city border between housing and farming is stable and, with residential use overbidding the farming use closer to the CBD, that all of the land between the CBD and the edge of the city is in residential use. A fifth equilibrium condition must assure that each household finds a location in the city. In what follows, we will separately examine the behavior of a typical household and a typical landowner. Before we do this, we must state the assumptions of stationarity. It is assumed that all exogenous economic variables affecting the city's residential sector are unchanging with time. The annual income of a household, its tastes, the costs of transportation, the price of agricultural land, and the total household population all remain fixed. Households and landowners know this and thus have no expectations of a changing world. Because of stationarity, all incomes, prices, and costs can be either in terms of annual values or in terms of the present value of a uniform stream of annual values. Thus suppose that the annual rents of a housing unit is a stream $R(t)$; then its market value at time $t = 0$ will be

$$V_0 = \int_0^\infty e^{-it} R(t)\, dt, \tag{1.1}$$

where i is the market rate of discount. If $R(t) = R$ is a uniform stream, then (1.1) reduces to

$$V_0 = R \int_0^\infty e^{-it}\, dt = \frac{R}{i}. \tag{1.2}$$

In discrete time notation,

$$V_0 = \sum_{t=0}^\infty \frac{R_t}{(1 + i)^t}, \tag{1.3}$$

which, upon assuming $R_t = R$, reduces to

$$V_0 = R\left(\sum_{t=1}^\infty \frac{1}{(1 + i)^t}\right) = R/i. \tag{1.4}$$

Thus, since the value of i is known, V_0 and R are proportional through a constant, and any analysis can be cast in terms of annual rents R or present values V_0.

1.1 Household Choice and Utility Maximization

Each household's utility in the housing market is measured as

$$U = U(Z, Q), \quad \text{with} \quad \partial U/\partial Z,\ \partial U/\partial Q > 0, \tag{1.5}$$

where Q is the dwelling's lot size and Z the household's money income allocated to all expenditures other than transportation and housing. Since in general, households at different locations may consume different amounts of

Z and Q, a more precise statement of (1.5) is

$$U(x) = U[Z(x), Q(x)], \tag{1.6}$$

where Z, Q, and thus U are made to depend on radial distance x from the CBD. It is assumed that the household faces a budget constraint that is

$$Y - Z(x) - R(x)Q(x) - T(x) = 0, \tag{1.7}$$

where Y is the household's income, $T(x)$ the commuting costs to and from the CBD, and $R(x)$ the rent the household pays per unit of land.

In the land market, each household must take the land rent at a particular location as given. In addition to this, each household's income and transportation costs are also fixed. Thus the household's consumer choice problem can be stated as

$$\max_{x} \left[\max_{Z,Q} U(Z, Q | x) \quad \text{subject to} \quad Y - Z - R(x)Q - T(x) = 0 \right]. \tag{1.8}$$

Each inner maximization is a standard problem in nonspatial micro-economics: given that a household has decided on a location x, it should decide how much land and "other goods" it should consume there. The choice of location determines the transport cost $T(x)$ and thus the household's net income at x, $Y - T(x)$. The choice of location also means that the household must take the land rent at that location as given. To solve this, we form the Lagrangian for x,

$$\mathcal{L}_x = U(Z, Q) + \lambda[Y - Z - R(x)Q - T(x)], \tag{1.9}$$

where λ is the Lagrange multiplier (the marginal utility of income). The first-order conditions are

$$\partial \mathcal{L}_x / \partial Z = \partial U / \partial Z - \lambda = 0, \tag{1.10}$$

$$\partial \mathcal{L}_x / \partial Q = \partial U / \partial Q - \lambda R(x) = 0, \tag{1.11}$$

and the budget constraint (1.7). Conditions (1.10), (1.11) imply that

$$R(x) = (\partial U / \partial Q)/(\partial U / \partial Z). \tag{1.12}$$

This states the familiar result that given a location, the household should consume Z and Q in such amounts that the marginal rate of substitution equals the land rent at that location. This maximization is illustrated in Fig. 1.1, where AA' is the household's budget constraint, the slope of which is the land rent $R(x)$, and BB' is the highest indifference level the household can achieve (by consuming Z^* and Q^*). Repeating this solution for each location x, we obtain a Z^* and Q^* for each location given $T(x)$, $R(x)$. These are two

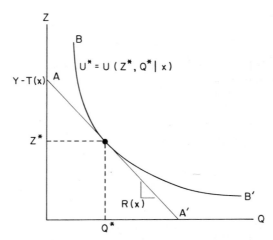

Fig. 1.1. Household's utility maximization given a location at distance x and given the land rent $R(x)$ and transportation cost $T(x)$ at that location.

demand functions for Z and Q, which can be written as

$$Z^*(x) = Z[Y - T(x), R(x)], \tag{1.13}$$

$$Q^*(x) = Q[Y - T(x), R(x)]. \tag{1.14}$$

These are obtained by solving (1.7), (1.10), and (1.11) for Z, Q, and λ at each x.

The household's outer maximization problem can now be viewed as a choice among alternative locations, at each of which the optimal consumption levels Z^*, Q^* have been selected. This can now be written as

$$\max_{x} \ U[Z^*(x), Q^*(x)]. \tag{1.15}$$

The solution is illustrated in Fig. 1.2, which depicts the most preferred location x^*.

In the above discussion, a household's decisions are always conditional on a given land rent gradient $R(x)$ that the household cannot influence directly. We may think of $R(x)$ as the asking rent set by the landowner at x. An implication of the above analysis is that since all households are identical in incomes and tastes, all will have the same preferred location x^*. This cannot be an equilibrium since asking rents at other locations will be lowered to make these as attractive as x^*, and attract some of the households to those locations.

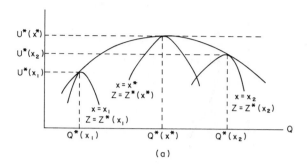

(a)

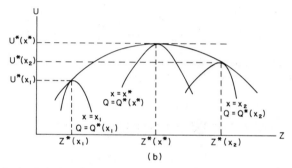

(b)

Fig. 1.2. (a) Optimal choice of location given optimal choice of Z at each location; and (b) optimal choice of location given optimal choice of Q at each location. Both (a) and (b) are conditional on a given land rent structure $R(x)$.

1.2. Landowner's Land Rent Maximization

Each landowner seeks to partition land into optimal size lots that maximize the land rent per unit of land. The landowner must set an asking rent $\bar{R}(x)$ per unit of land at x. The landowner can approach this problem by anticipating the utility level $\hat{U}(x)$ that will be achieved by the households choosing location x. Once such an anticipated utility level is determined, the landowner's problem becomes

$$\max_{Q} \bar{R}(x, Q) = \{Y - T(x) - Z[\hat{U}(x), Q]\}/Q, \qquad (1.16)$$

where $Z[\hat{U}(x), Q]$ is obtained by inverting $\hat{U}(x) = U(Z, Q)$, and $\hat{U}(x)$ is the utility level anticipated by the landlord for location x. The landowner's decision, shown in Fig. 1.3, consists of maximizing the rent the household will pay per unit of land (making as steep as possible the slope of the household's budget constraint) but still allowing the household to afford locating

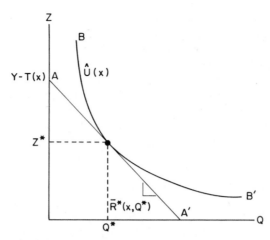

Fig. 1.3. A landowner's asking rent maximization at location x.

at x given the utility level $\hat{U}(x)$. The outcome of this decision is a "supply function" that expresses the size of the lots to be supplied at x given the anticipated utility level $\hat{U}(x)$ and the household's net income $Y - T(x)$. This supply function can be written as

$$Q^*(x) = \hat{Q}[\hat{U}(x), Y - T(x)]. \tag{1.17}$$

Note that since each supplier is assumed to act as a rent-maximizing monopolist, the above supply function is not expressed as a direct function of the market rent $R(x)$. It follows from Fig. 1.3 that the supply function must obey

$$\partial \hat{Q}^*(x)/\partial[Y - T(x)] < 0 \tag{1.18}$$

and can be assumed to obey

$$\partial \hat{Q}^*(x)/\partial \hat{U}(x) > 0. \tag{1.19}$$

2. EQUILIBRIUM ANALYSIS

2.1. Long Run Equilibrium

We must now reconcile the decisions of the households with those of the suppliers in order to obtain a market equilibrium configuration for the city. A crucial step for achieving this in a long run context is that there be free mobility of both housing capital and households. It is not necessary, however, that such mobility take place rapidly. If we allow a sufficient length of time in a stationary state, all households should be able to make their chosen moves and impose an eventual situation in which no household desires to relocate. In a similar way, any misallocations in the parcelization of land can be eventually corrected. As more households move into a location, land rents are increased because the utility level anticipated by the landowner is reduced; as more households choose a specific location, the landowner correctly assumes that each is willing to settle for a lower utility level and thus raises the asking rent. As rents increase in certain locations, fewer households choose that location, and rents stabilize there. This process continues until all utility levels are equalized over space

$$\hat{U}(x) = U^*(x) = U^*, \tag{1.20}$$

where U^* is the equilibrium utility level that prevails at each x. Thus $\hat{U}(x)$ in Fig. 1.3 is the same as $U^*(x)$ in Fig. 1.1, and therefore $\hat{Q}^*(x) = Q^*(x)$, i.e., the supplier's optimal lot size is equal to the household's preferred land consumption level. It also follows from the coincidence of Figs. 1.1 and 1.3 at equilibrium that $\bar{R}^*(x) = R(x)$, i.e., the supplier's maximum asking rent equals the market rent faced by the consumer. Using (1.12) and Fig. 1.3, this also means that

$$R(x) = \left.\frac{\partial U/\partial Q}{\partial U/\partial Z}\right|_{Z^*, Q^*} = \left.\frac{dZ(\hat{U}, Q)}{dQ}\right|_{\hat{U}=U^*}. \tag{1.21}$$

The requirement of a uniform utility level means that Fig. 1.2 should be modified to obtain Fig. 1.4.

To obtain the spatial variation in land rent at long run equilibrium, we can totally differentiate the household's utility function and budget constraint. Since, at equilibrium, utility and income are both constant and assumed to be the same for all locations, we must determine $dU = 0$ and $dY = 0$. These two conditions are

$$dU = 0 = (\partial U/\partial Z)\, dZ + (\partial U/\partial Q)\, dQ \tag{1.22}$$

and

$$dY = 0 = dZ + R(x)\, dQ + Q\, dR(x) + dT(x) = 0. \tag{1.23}$$

Solving (1.22) for dZ and recalling (1.21), we find $dZ = -R(x)\, dQ$. Substituting this into (1.23), we find

$$Q\, dR(x) + dT(x) = 0. \tag{1.24}$$

This implies the differential equation

$$dR(x)/dx = -[dT(x)/dx]/Q, \tag{1.25}$$

indicating that an equilibrium land rent gradient must decline with distance. Solution of this differential equation for $R(x)$ will yield a market land rent

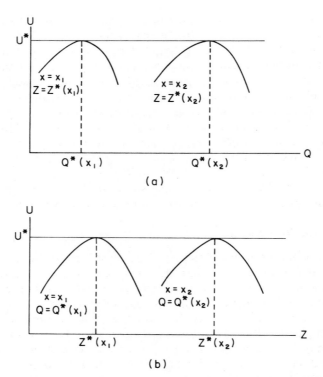

Fig. 1.4. (a) Household's choice of lot size given optimal choice of Z; and (b) choice of Z given optimal choice of Q at equilibrium.

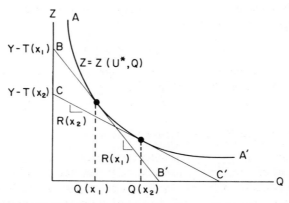

Fig. 1.5. Land rent and residential density as a function of distance at equilibrium.

gradient that is unique up to a constant of integration and that keeps utility invariant over locations ($dU = 0$). To obtain the correct solution, we must solve (1.25) evaluated at $Q = Q^*(x) = Q[R(x), Y - T(x)]$. The uniform equilibrium utility level can then be obtained by evaluating the utility function at any x, using the optimal consumption levels $Z^*(x)$ and $Q^*(x)$ for that x. The result that equilibrium land rent must decline with distance has a simple graphical proof shown in Fig. 1.5. For two locations x_1, x_2, if $x_2 > x_1$ then $T(x_2) > T(x_1)$ and therefore $Y - T(x_1) > Y - T(x_2)$. This sets the two points A and B, which are the intercepts of the budget constraints at x_1 and x_2. The equilibrium utility level sets the indifference curve AA', and the slopes of the budget constraints BB' and CC' set the result $R(x_2) < R(x_1)$ for any $x_2 > x_1$. The same figure also shows that $Q(x_2) > Q(x_1)$, or that equilibrium residential density must decline with distance from the center.

2.2. The Bid Rent Approach

Our discussion up to this point serves to illustrate the consistency of the supplier's and consumer's maximization problems. A simpler formal statement of the model emerges once we recognize that each household must adjust to the equilibrium utility level and must offer such bids for all locations as to achieve equilibrium utility. If a household's bid is too low (its utility level too high), it will be outbid by some other household because of competition. If its bid is too high, it will enjoy an unnecessarily low utility level. The household's bid rent function is defined as the locus of rents the household will offer for various locations in order to maintain a particular utility level $\overline{U}$. The bid rent function is an indifference curve between rent and location. In this model, the household's bid rent function is

$$\hat{R}(x) = [Y - T(x) - Z(\overline{U}, Q)]/Q, \tag{1.26}$$

where the caret (ˆ) denotes a bid rent. At equilibrium, the bid rent function is obtained by letting $\overline{U} = U^*$:

$$\hat{R}(x) = [Y - T(x) - Z(U^*, Q)]/Q. \tag{1.27}$$

Equation (1.27) can be entered into the supplier's maximization problem (1.16) in order to obtain the optimal (equilibrium) lot size $\hat{Q}^*(x)$ and the market rent $R(x) = R^*(x) = \max_Q \hat{R}(x, Q)$.

2.3. Aggregate Long Run Equilibrium Conditions

It was mentioned that the rent gradient obtained by solving (1.25) is unique up to a constant of integration encountered in the solution of the differential equation. Equivalently, the rent gradient obtained from (1.27) is unique up to an equilibrium utility level U^*. In order to determine the rent gradient, two aggregate equilibrium conditions must be specified. One of these is that all households must be accommodated within a circle of radius $\bar{x}$ miles from the city center. The other is that at the city border $\bar{x}$, the price of land should equal the agricultural land rent. These two conditions are expressed as

$$N = 2\pi \int_0^{\bar{x}} \hat{Q}[Y - T(u), U^*]^{-1} u \, du \tag{1.28}$$

and

$$R(\bar{x}) = R_A, \tag{1.29}$$

where N is the number of households, R_A the uniform price of agricultural land, and $\hat{Q}[\cdot, \cdot]^{-1}$ the equilibrium residential density at a location u from the center. Suppose that all CBD land uses occupy a negligible circular area. Then the inner integration limit is zero. Equations (1.28) and (1.29) can be solved simultaneously for U^* and $\bar{x}$, completing the solution.

2.4. Long Run Equilibrium with Several Household Classes

We now consider a more general model in which the population is divided into n classes of households with N_i members in each class. Suppose that all households regardless of class have the same utility function, but that their incomes increase with class so that $Y_1 < Y_2 < \cdots < Y_n$. Consider a special case of this model with two classes ($n = 2$). Since members of different classes have different incomes, they cannot all attain the same utility level. Thus there should be two locational equilibrium conditions assuring that identical households will be indifferent among the locations available to them. Thus let the unknown utility levels for the two classes be U_1^* and U_2^*. The equilibrium bid rent functions for the two classes are

$$\hat{R}(x, Q)_i = [Y_i - T(x) - Z(U_i^*, Q)]/Q, \qquad i = 1, 2. \tag{1.30}$$

The supplier's rent maximization problem is now stated as

$$R(x) = \max_i \left[\max_Q \hat{R}(x, Q)_i, i = 1, 2 \right], \tag{1.31}$$

where each inner maximization yields

$$\hat{Q}^*(x)_i = \hat{Q}[Y_i - T(x), U_i^*], \qquad i = 1, 2. \tag{1.32}$$

Since each land parcel goes to a member of the class bidding the most for that location, if the two bid rent functions $\hat{R}[x, \hat{Q}^*(x)_1]$ and $\hat{R}[x, \hat{Q}^*(x)_2]$ intersect only once, the city will be divided into two annular areas, one occupied by members of one class and the other occupied by members of the other class.

Consider the budget constraint faced by a household from each class at location $x = x_1$, which is the outermost radius of the inner annulus. Since at equilibrium this location may be occupied by both household types

$[\hat{R}(x_1)_1 = \hat{R}(x_1)_2]$, both will face the same market rent $R(x_1)$. This implies two parallel budget constraints, but with $Y_2 - T(x_1) > Y_1 - T(x_1)$, the intercept of the richer household's budget constraint lies above that of the poorer. At this point, we are reminded of the reasonable assumption that *land is a normal good*, namely, other things being constant, the amount of land consumed should increase as a function of income. Thus the richer household located at x_1 will require more land than the poorer, meaning that the indifference curves should be shaped in such a way as to allow $Q^*(x_1)_2 > Q^*(x_1)_1$, as shown in Fig. 1.6. Using the uniform utility equilibrium condition for each class, we establish that

$$-\left[\frac{dT(x)}{dx}\Big|_{x_1}\right] \Big/ Q^*(x_1)_2 > -\left[\frac{dT(x)}{dx}\Big|_{x_1}\right] \Big/ Q^*(x_1)_1, \qquad (1.33)$$

which implies that

$$\frac{dR[x, Q^*(x)]_1}{dx}\Big|_{x_1} < \frac{dR[x, Q^*(x)]_2}{dx}\Big|_{x_1}. \qquad (1.34)$$

This result implies that the bid rent function of the poorer class is steeper than that of the richer class and, as a result, the poor outbid the rich in the inner annulus of radius x_1.

The above result generalizes to the case of n income classes: if the households of a city are divided into n groups of identical tastes but different incomes, the residential land use pattern will consist of n rings, each occupied by the members of a different income class and with income increasing from the centermost ring to the most decentralized ring. The aggregate equilibrium

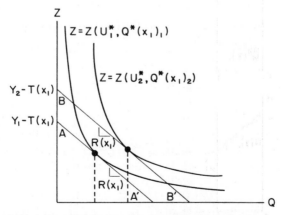

Fig. 1.6. Household choice of lot size as a function of income under the assumption that land is a normal good.

conditions are specified as

$$N_i = \int_{\bar{x}_{i-1}}^{\bar{x}_i} \hat{Q}[Y_i - T(u), U_i^*]^{-1} u \, du, \qquad i = 1, \ldots, n, \qquad (1.35)$$

where $\bar{x}_n = \bar{x}$ and $\bar{x}_0 = 0$,

$$R(\bar{x}_{i-1})_i = R(\bar{x}_{i-1})_{i-1}, \qquad i = 2, \ldots, n, \qquad (1.36)$$

and

$$R(\bar{x}_n)_n = R_A. \qquad (1.37)$$

Conditions (1.35)–(1.37) are $2n$ equations in the $2n$ unknowns $U_1^*, \ldots, U_n^*$ and $\bar{x}_1, \ldots, \bar{x}_n$, where each $\bar{x}_i$ is the border between the ith income class and

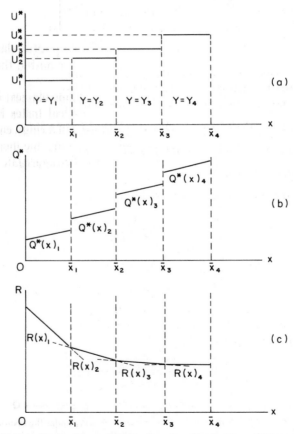

Fig. 1.7. (a) Utility; (b) lot size; and (c) land rent profiles in the multiclass city with homogeneous preferences.

the next $(i + 1)$th income class, with $\bar{x}_n$ the border between the city and farming. The general properties of this result are illustrated in Fig. 1.7.

If preferences as well as incomes change across income classes, the relative location of household groups by income becomes more complex.

2.5.   The Value of Commuting Time and Location by Income

A more general model may be constructed by assuming that the utility function depends on consumption, lot size, and travel time to the CBD. This is written as

$$U = U(Z, Q, t) \quad \text{with} \quad \partial U/\partial t < 0, \tag{1.38}$$

where t is the consumer's travel time. In addition to the constraint on income, the consumer now faces a constraint on time as well. This can be expressed as

$$H = t + L, \tag{1.39}$$

where H is a fixed time budget after fixed allocations for work and other activities, L the household's leisure time, and t the household's travel time. Equilibrium requires that $dU = 0$, $dY = 0$, and $dH = 0$. These yield

$$dU = 0 = (\partial U/\partial Z)\, dZ + (\partial U/\partial Q)\, dQ + (\partial U/\partial t)\, dt, \tag{1.40}$$

$$dY = 0 = dZ + R\, dQ + Q\, dR + dT, \tag{1.41}$$

$$dH = 0 = dt + dL. \tag{1.42}$$

Substituting these into each other, we obtain

$$Q\,\frac{dR}{dx} + \frac{dT}{dx} - \left(\frac{\partial U/\partial t}{\partial U/\partial Z}\right)\frac{dt}{dx} = 0 \tag{1.43}$$

or

$$\frac{dR}{dx} = -\left[\frac{dT}{dx} - \left(\frac{\partial U/\partial t}{\partial U/\partial Z}\right)\frac{dt}{dx}\right]\bigg/ Q^{-1} < 0. \tag{1.44}$$

Equation (1.44) can be used to determine the slope of the bid rent function of each income class. If we assume that poor and rich have the same utility function, then this implies that

$$\left(\frac{\partial U/\partial t}{\partial U/\partial Z}\right)_1\bigg|_x = \left(\frac{\partial U/\partial t}{\partial U/\partial Z}\right)_2\bigg|_x. \tag{1.45}$$

With land a normal good, $Q^*(x)_2 > Q^*(x)_1$, it follows that $(dR/dx)_2 > (dR/dx)_1$, which implies a centralized location for the poor. If, on the other hand, we recognize that the two classes will have different utility functions as well as different incomes, the reasonable assumption is that the higher income class will have a higher marginal rate of substitution for travel time (or higher value of time), and thus

$$-\left(\frac{\partial U/\partial t}{\partial U/\partial Z}\right)_2 > -\left(\frac{\partial U/\partial t}{\partial U/\partial Z}\right)_1.$$

(1.46)

With $Q^*(x)_2 > Q^*(x)_1$, which is still a reasonable assumption, the bid rent function of the rich may still be less steep than that of the poor, but only if the increase in the preference for land consumption (lot size) by income is sufficiently stronger than the increase in the disutility for commuting time by income. If this occurs, the richer classes will locate further away from the center.

2.6. Short Run Equilibrium

While our discussion so far deals with the allocation of land among households in the long run when perfect adjustments in housing stock and land are possible, many housing market problems are more realistically posed as the allocation of households among spatially distributed dwellings, the characteristics and supplies of which are fixed in the short run. In this context, urban history is viewed as a sequence of discrete time intervals $t = 1$, $2, \ldots, \infty$. The housing stock at the beginning of time t may be adjusted from that of $t - 1$ according to landlords' and suppliers' expectations of the future, or it may be assumed that these agents are myopic and only the present time period may be considered in making adjustments to the housing stock. It is further assumed that the market attains a short run (temporary) equilibrium during every time period by the efficient reallocation of households among dwellings. If households can move sufficiently rapidly, the market will achieve an allocation in which each dwelling goes to the highest bidder and in which identical households are indifferent among the dwellings they occupy. As economic conditions (income, population growth, travel costs, etc.) change from one time period to the next, a new reallocation must result to establish a new temporary equilibrium. In the short run, the suppliers' decisions may be to achieve the highest rent by performing marginal changes in the density or parcelization of existing dwellings or by retaining existing dwellings as they are and building new dwellings in vacant areas. It is also possible that some dwellings would be abandoned or left vacant temporarily. In short run equilibrium, households should be indifferent among the dwellings available to them and, through competition and rapid mobility, this requires that the prices of dwellings adjust appropriately to establish such indifference.

If the market consists of $j = 1, \ldots, J$ households for a particular time period t, then the occupant and market rent of a specific dwelling k will be determined by

$$R_k = \max_j \left[0, R_{jk}(U_j^*); j = 1, \ldots, J\right], \tag{1.47}$$

where $R_{jk}(U_j^*)$ is the bid rent of household j for dwelling k given household j's equilibrium utility level U_j^*. If all bid rents are zero or negative, the house remains unoccupied for the duration of this short run equilibrium.

The household's utility function may be defined as

$$U_j = U_j(Z, Q, S, t), \tag{1.48}$$

where Z, Q, and t are other consumption, lot size, and commuting time, and S represents a vector of housing characteristics such as age, floor space, condition, etc. From (1.48), the household's bid rents at equilibrium would be computed as

$$R_{jk} = Y_j - T_k - Z_j(U_j^*, Q_k, S_k, t_k). \tag{1.49}$$

To be assured of a dwelling, a household must lower its utility level until it becomes the highest bidder for at least one dwelling. If, in the short run, the number of dwellings exceeds the number of households, then a number of dwellings equal to the excess will receive a rent equal to zero. The relationship between rent in the short run and rent in the long run is illustrated in Fig. 1.8, which shows the indifference curve for Z and Q, holding constant other attributes of the utility function. In the long run, it is possible to provide lot size Q^* that maximizes the rent per unit of land R_L (budget constraint AA' with tangency at M), whereas in the short run, lot size could be fixed at $\bar{Q}'$,

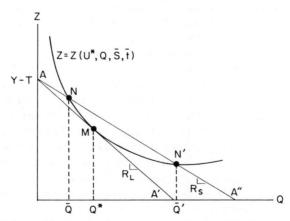

Fig. 1.8. The relationship between long run rent R_L and short run rent R_S given the same equilibrium utility level and fixed S and t.

which, given the equilibrium utility level U^*, implies a rent $R_S < R_L$ (budget constraint AA''). The same short run rent would result if the lot size were fixed at $\bar{Q}$.

2.7   The Rent Gradient in Short Run Equilibrium

The above concept of short run equilibrium can be used in developing a dynamic model of urban spatial expansion. Assume that a city's population as a function of time is given as $N_1, N_2, N_3, \ldots$ with $N_{t-1} < N_t$, where the subscripts denote the time period. In time period $t = 2$, $N_2 - N_1$ households would be located in a ring around the original city, and these households would use land optimally at this fringe, where new housing would be built, while the remaining N_1 households would be allocated among the N_1 housing units occupying the inner ring. Possibly some of these inner ring houses would be left vacant in time period $t = 2$, with the result that more than $N_2 - N_1$ households would be located in the second ring. A model of this kind has been analyzed by Anas (1978a). A crucial assumption in such a model is that of myopic behavior on the part of both households and suppliers. They are assumed not to anticipate the changing variables such as population, income, and transportation costs. Thus the city develops as a series of compact concentric rings, and no land is reserved for future use. If perfect or imperfect anticipations of future trends are introduced, a model emerges in which some of the urban land is possibly reserved for future use. Fujita (1976) has examined the case of perfect knowledge of the future and perfect speculation in land development.

Since at any time period, short run equilibrium requires $dU = 0$ and $dY = 0$, the budget constraint and a utility function such as $U = U(Z, Q)$ can be differentiated to obtain

$$\frac{dR}{dx} = -\left\{ \frac{dT}{dx} - \left[\frac{\partial U/\partial Q}{\partial U/\partial Z} - R(x) \right] \frac{dQ}{dx} \right\} Q^{-1}(x), \qquad (1.50)$$

which holds at each short run equilibrium. Now $Q(x)$ is an exogenous historically determined function that describes the variation in lot size as a function of distance from the center. In the long run equilibrium model, we were able to use $R(x) = (\partial U/\partial Q)/(\partial U/\partial Z)$ to reduce (1.50) to (1.25). It was shown in Fig. 1.8 that this condition does not hold in the short run. The land rent gradient can be an upward sloping function of distance in some parts of the city in order to maintain equilibrium. This occurs because dwellings built in the past and centrally located in the current city are too small or too large (or too old) compared to what would be built there now. Thus rent must adjust to compensate for these vintage effects. It is also possible to find that a portion of the bid rent gradient is negative (zero market rent) in those locations where housing remains vacant. These and other results are discussed in Anas (1978a) and provide analytical evidence that the short run structure of cities can be very different from that predicted by long run equilibrium models.

3. LINEAR PROGRAMMING

We now examine an operational framework designed to simulate housing market equilibrium. The model to be presented here stems from the linear programming formulation of Herbert and Stevens (1960) but is generalized for the case of short run equilibrium, where part of the household population is allocated to existing dwellings while the remaining part is distributed among newly constructed dwellings.

We assume that the household population is divided into $h = 1, \ldots, H$ segments, the members of each segment having identical incomes, workplace, and preferences. The urban area is divided into $i = 1, \ldots, I$ zones, which are relatively small and contiguous spatial areas. There are $k = 1, \ldots, K$ housing types that either exist or can be built on currently vacant land. Each type k dwelling takes up q_k acres of land and costs an annualized amount of c_{ik} dollars to construct in zone i. A type h household bids R_{ikh} for a type k dwelling in zone i. If both suppliers and households are myopic, they will expect the future to remain identical to the present. This means that each supplier of an existing dwelling must maximize R_{ikh}, whereas each supplier of a new dwelling must maximize $R_{ikh} - c_{ik}$. To simplify the presentation, we assume that existing dwellings are not converted during the simulation period. A more general version of this model where such conversions are allowed has been discussed in Anas (1978b).

The primal linear programming problem under the above-mentioned assumptions is formulated as

$$\max \sum_h \sum_i \sum_k \left[(R_{ikh} - c_{ik})\, {}_1X_{ikh} + R_{ikh}\, {}_2X_{ikh} \right] + \sum_i R_{oi} Y_i \qquad (1.51)$$

subject to

$$\sum_h \sum_k q_k\, {}_1X_{ikh} + Y_i \leq L_i, \qquad i = 1, \ldots, I, \qquad (1.52)$$

$$\sum_h {}_2X_{ikh} \leq S_{ik}, \qquad i = 1, \ldots, I, \quad k = 1, \ldots, K, \qquad (1.53)$$

$$\sum_i \sum_k {}_1X_{ikh} + {}_2X_{ikh} \leq N_h, \qquad h = 1, \ldots, H, \qquad (1.54)$$

$${}_1X_{ikh} \geq 0, \qquad {}_2X_{ikh} \geq 0, \qquad Y_i \geq 0. \qquad (1.55)$$

The bid rents must be computed by assuming that the equilibrium utility levels $(\overline{U}_h, h = 1, \ldots, H)$ are known. The bid rents are

$$R_{ikh} = Y_h - T_{ih} - Z_h(\overline{U}_h, q_k, x_{ik}), \tag{1.56}$$

where q_k is lot size and x_{ik} a vector of location and housing attributes. The primal variables $_1X_{ikh}$ are the number of households of type h allocated to new dwellings of type k in zone i, and $_2X_{ikh}$ are the number of households allocated to existing dwellings of type k in zone i. The primal variables Y_i are the acres of land allocated to agriculture or some other opportunity use of land, and R_{oi} is the bid of this opportunity use per acre of land in zone i. The N_h in (1.54) is the maximum number of type h households that must be allocated to dwellings in the simulation period. Constraints (1.52) and (1.53) state that the households allocated to land and dwellings should not exceed the available acreage and dwelling stock in each zone.

For a nontrivial solution, several additional conditions must hold. First, it must be true that there is a sufficient amount of urban land so that all households can be accommodated. Second, the opportunity bids for land must not be so high that no household's bid can match them, since this would result in no development. Finally, note that the formulation corresponds to an open city: the utility levels are fixed, and there are maximum limits on the number of households of each type.

The dual of the above linear program is as follows:

$$\min \sum_i R_i L_i + \sum_i \sum_k R_{ik} S_{ik} + \sum_k W_h N_n \tag{1.57}$$

subject to

$$q_k R_i + W_h \geq R_{ikh} - c_{ik}, \qquad \text{all} \quad (i, k, h), \tag{1.58}$$

$$R_{ik} + W_h \geq R_{ikh}, \qquad \text{all} \quad (i, k, h), \tag{1.59}$$

$$R_i \geq R_0, \qquad \text{all} \quad i, \tag{1.60}$$

$$R_i \geq 0, \qquad R_{ik} \geq 0, \qquad W_h \geq 0. \tag{1.61}$$

The dual variables R_i, R_{ik}, and W_h represent the imputed resource prices (to the developers) of vacant land, existing housing, and population of each type. The dual minimizes the total resource valuation, whereas the primal maximizes total net revenues. Since $R_{io} \geq 0$ in each i, the nonnegativity condition ($R_i \geq 0$) is redundant in view of (1.60), which states that the land rent R_i cannot fall below the opportunity rent for land. Since the primal is a maximization problem and the amount of land that can be allocated to the opportunity use can be as high as L_i in each zone, constraint (1.52) will hold as an equality at the optimal solution.

The duality theorem applied to the above formulation reveals the properties of the optimal solution. First, we have the result that the two objective functions evaluated at the optimal solutions (denoted with an asterisk) must be equal. Doing this yields

$$\sum_h \sum_i \sum_k [(R_{ikh} - c_{ik})\, _1X^*_{ikh} + R_{ikh}\, _2X^*_{ikh}] + \sum_i R_{io} Y^*_i$$
$$= \sum_i R^*_i L_i + \sum_i \sum_k R^*_{ik} S_{ik} + \sum_h W^*_h N_h, \tag{1.62}$$

which states that the total development costs must be matched by total development revenues.

The complementary slackness conditions yield further information. First, we examine the condition

$$(\sum_h \sum_k q_k X^*_{ikh} + Y^*_i - L_i) R^*_i = 0. \tag{1.63}$$

Since the term in parentheses will be zero, we are left with $R^*_i \geqq 0$, which is dominated by the dual constraint $R^*_i \geqq R_{io}$. Another duality condition is

$$(R^*_i - R_{io}) Y^*_i = 0, \tag{1.64}$$

which implies that when $R^*_i > R_{io}$, $Y^*_i = 0$, but when $R^*_i = R_{io}$, $Y^*_i \geqq 0$. This means that when some vacant land remains in a zone, the land price of that zone will be anchored at its opportunity value. Next, from

$$\sum_h (_2X^*_{ikh} - S_{ik}) R^*_{ik} = 0 \tag{1.65}$$

we know that if some dwellings in (i, k) are left vacant $(\sum_h {}_2X^*_{ikh} \leqq S_{ik})$, $R^*_{ik} = 0$, whereas if all dwellings are occupied, $R^*_{ik} \geqq 0$. From

$$(\sum_i \sum_k {}_1X^*_{ikh} + {}_2X^*_{ikh} - N_h) W^*_h = 0, \tag{1.66}$$

we get the result that if all type h households are accommodated, $W^*_h \geqq 0$, whereas if some cannot be accommodated. $W^*_h = 0$. The remaining complementary slackness conditions tell us which housing units will be occupied and which vacant parcels will be developed. These conditions are

$$[q_k R^*_i + W^*_h - (R_{ikh} - c_{ik})]_1 X^*_{ikh} = 0 \tag{1.67}$$

and

$$(R^*_{ik} + W^*_h - R_{ikh})_2 X^*_{ikh} = 0. \tag{1.68}$$

From (1.67), when $q_k R^*_i + W^*_h = R_{ikh} - c_{ik}$, then $_1X^*_{ikh} \geqq 0$, and new construction of type k dwellings in zone i to be occupied by type h households is possible. When $q_k R^*_i + W^*_h > R_{ikh} - c_{ik}$, development costs exceed net revenues and new construction is not possible. From (1.68), when $R_{ik}^* + W_h^* = R_{ikh}$, $_2X_{ikh}^* \geq 0$ and existing type k dwellings in zone i can be occupied by type h households, but when $R_{ik}^* + W_h^* > R_{ikh}$, costs exceed bids, and occupancy by type h households is not possible. Note that when $R_{ik}^* + W_h^* > \max_h \{R_{ikh}\}$, no household can occupy type k housing in zone i.

The dual problem demonstrates that the efficient allocation of households can be decentralized through an appropriate determination of the imputed prices R_i^*, R_{ik}^*, and W_h^*. While R_i^* and R_{ik}^* are land and housing rents, respectively, W_h^* is a head tax a developer must pay for each type h household accommodated. Note, however, that if the N_h are chosen arbitrarily large, (1.65) implies that all $W_h^* = 0$, and the linear program will produce an open city allocation of households to dwellings and land without any head taxes. The number of type h households located in the city can then be computed as

$$N_h^* \equiv \sum_i \sum_k (_1X_{ikh}^* + {}_2X_{i\ kh}^*). \tag{1.69}$$

Simulation of a closed city equilibrium requires an endogenous determination of the utility levels as U_h^*, $h = 1, \ldots, H$. If these are treated as variables in the above formulation, the problem becomes a nonlinear program. It has been suggested by Harris *et al.* (1966) and Wheaton (1974) that an iterative solution of a linear programming problem would determine a set of equilibrium utility levels that would be consistent with the accommodation of all households and with all head taxes being equal to zero. This may be accomplished by adjusting utility levels and allowing lot size to be varied continuously until such a set of utility levels is found that constraints (1.54) become barely binding and thus the associated dual variables become zero. To express the equilibrium conditions without any head taxes, we may restate the complementary slackness expressions without the W_h's. These conditions imply that market rents are the outer envelope of bid rents. More precisely,

$$R_i^* = \max[R_{io}; (R_{ikh} - c_{ik})/q_k, h = 1, \ldots, H] \tag{1.70}$$

and

$$R_{ik}^* = \max[0; R_{ikh}, h = 1, \ldots, H]. \tag{1.71}$$

Substituting for bid rents R_{ikh} from (1.56),

$$R_i^* = \max\{R_{io}; [Y_h - T_{ih} - Z_h(U_h^*, q_k, x_{ik}) - c_{ik}]/q_k, h = 1, \ldots, H\} \tag{1.72}$$

and

$$R_{ik}^* = \max[0; Y_h - T_{ih} - Z_h(U_h^*, q_k, x_{ik}), h = 1, \ldots, H]. \tag{1.73}$$

Although the modified version of the Herbert–Stevens model discussed here provides an algorithmic method for computing locational equilibria, it has been empirically applied in only two instances. One is the study by

Harris *et al.* (1966) that used a linear programming algorithm, similar to the one discussed here, to evaluate various sketch plans based on the transport network for the proposed new town of Flummox, England. The other is an application to sketch plan analysis in the Penn–Jersey transportation study (see Reif, 1973; Harris, 1968). Unfortunately, both applications are rather poorly documented and do not provide reliable evidence of the model's empirical performance. In order to evaluate the practical usefulness of this approach for urban planning, one must consider three important features. First, the application of the method requires the econometric estimation of bid rent functions for various household segments. Thus the statistical reliability and explanatory power of these estimations must be considered. Second, the computational limitations of linear programming for large scale urban simulation may set a potential limit to the widespread and large scale application of this technique. Last, but not least, the bid rent approach has several theoretical shortcomings that will become clear in the context of the next chapter and the remaining part of this chapter.

4. ECONOMETRIC ESTIMATION OF BID RENTS

The major problem with implementing the bid rent models of locational and housing market equilibrium is the reliability of estimated bid rent functions and the difficulty of using such estimated functions to validate the assumption of homogeneous preferences and behavior within each population segment. We develop an empirically based critique by drawing on the author's analyses reported here and the published results by Anas (1975), Wheaton (1977a), and Galster (1977).

4.1. How to Estimate Utility Functions

The first issue that arises in bid rent models is the estimation of utility functions that can be used to predict bid rents. To engage in such estimation, the analyst must meet several requirements. First, it must be assumed that the market is in equilibrium. Second, the market household population must be divided into $h = 1, \ldots, H$ socioeconomic segments, and it must be assumed that preferences are homogeneous within each segment. Third, the analyst must be able to observe the characteristics of a random sample of households and their dwelling choices. Each of these households can then be used as observations in the statistical estimation of utility functions for the H population segments. Each segment is defined on the basis of socioeconomic household characteristics such as income, family size, age of household head, and race. The above procedure can be accomplished in a manner first suggested and implemented by Harris *et al.* (1966) using linear or nonlinear regression techniques. To illustrate the method, suppose that the utility function is of Cobb–Douglas form and given as

$$U_h = Z_j^{a_{0h}} \prod_{n=1}^{N} {}_nX_j^{a_{nh}}\epsilon_j, \tag{1.74}$$

where U_h is the utility level achieved by members of the hth segment; $Z_j = Y_j - R_j - T_j$, as before, measures the amount of annual income left over for consumption not related to housing and travel for the jth household in the observed sample; and ${}_nX_j$, $n = 1, \ldots, N$, are N observed location–housing attributes for the jth household. Finally, ϵ_j is a multiplicative error term representing the effect of location–housing attributes not observed by the analyst. The econometric problem is to estimate the utility coefficients $a_{0h}, a_{1h}, \ldots, a_{nh}$. Since the utility level cannot be observed, Harris has suggested that $\log Z$ be made the dependent variable after linearizing (1.74) by taking the natural logarithm of both sides. This strategy means that the coefficient a_{0h} cannot be estimated. This loss of information can be made explicit by setting $a_{0h} = 1$ in (1.74). Then the estimated equation has the form

$$\log(Y - R - T) = \log U_h + \sum_{n=1}^{N} (-a_{nh}) \log_n X + \log \epsilon, \tag{1.75}$$

where the subscript j has been suppressed. The regression random error term is $\log \epsilon$, and one would assume that it is normally distributed with zero mean and has constant variance σ^2. More precisely, using $E(\cdot)$ to denote expected values,

$$E(\log \epsilon_j |_n X_j, n = 1, \ldots, N) = 0 \qquad \text{for each } j, \tag{1.76}$$

and

$$E[(\log \epsilon_j)^2 |_n X_j, n = 1, \ldots, N] = \sigma^2 \qquad \text{for each } j, \tag{1.77}$$

$$E[(\log \epsilon_j)(\log \epsilon_i) |_n X_j, {}_n X_i, n = 1, \ldots, N] = 0, \qquad \text{all } i \neq j. \tag{1.78}$$

The utility coefficients a_{nh} are estimated from $-a_{nh}$ (the regression coefficients), and the utility level $\log U_h$ is estimated as the regression constant. Once the regression is estimated, it can be transformed to predict the bid rent, denoted as $\hat{R}_j$, of each household j in the sample:

$$\hat{R}_j = Y_j - T_j - U_h \prod_{n=1}^{N} {}_nX_j^{-a_{nh}}\epsilon_j. \tag{1.79}$$

For these predictions of bid rents to be *unbiased*, we must show that

$$E(\hat{R}|_n X, n = 1, \ldots, N) = E(Y - T|_n X, n = 1, \ldots, N) - U_h \prod_{n=1}^{N} {}_nX^{-a_{nh}}. \tag{1.80}$$

For (1.80) to be true, it must be true that $E(\epsilon_j|_nX_j, n = 1, \ldots, N) = 1$; but this requirement contradicts the estimation assumption (1.76). Thus because of the log transformation of the dependent variable, the estimated regression will produce unbiased predictions of $\log(Y - R - T)$ but seriously biased predictions of bid rents $\hat{R}$, because the distributional assumptions required for estimation contradict the assumptions needed for prediction [if $E(\log \epsilon) = 0$ then $E(\epsilon) \neq 1$]. The predictions $\hat{R}$ can be corrected for the bias by the equation

$$E(\hat{R}|_nX, n = 1, \ldots, N)$$

$$= E(Y - T|_nX, n = 1, \ldots, N) - U_h \prod_{n=1}^{N} {}_nX^{-a_{nh}} E(\epsilon), \quad (1.81)$$

where the correction term can be estimated as $E(\epsilon) = e^{\sigma^2/2}$. This correction requires that we know σ^2 and that we assume it remains constant over the time necessary for prediction. This problem of prediction bias and the correction for it remains unmentioned in the work of Harris *et al.* (1966), Wheaton (1977a), and Galster (1977). It should be noted, however, that if the utility function does not involve a logarithmic transformation of the dependent variable, the above problem does not arise. If, for example, one were to specify a generalized constant elasticity of substitution (C.E.S.) utility function of the form

$$U_h = Z^{C_{oh}} + \sum_{n=1}^{N} b_{nh} \, {}_nX^{C_{nh}} + \epsilon, \quad (1.82)$$

one must estimate

$$Z = (U_h - \sum_{n=1}^{N} b_{nh} \, {}_nX^{C_{nh}} + \epsilon)^{1/C_{oh}}, \quad (1.83)$$

which is an awkward specification because the error term is not additive in (1.83). Wheaton circumvents this problem by assuming

$$U_h = (Z + \epsilon)^{C_{oh}} + \sum_{n=1}^{N} b_{nh} \, {}_nX^{C_{nh}}, \quad (1.84)$$

which is estimated as

$$Z = (U_h + \sum_{n=1}^{N} (-b_{nh})_n X^{C_{nh}})^{1/C_{oh}} + (-\epsilon), \quad (1.85)$$

which has an additive error term but is unsatisfactory because all of the error is assumed to occur in the dependent variable Z and cannot be due to missing independent variables. An appealing fact about (1.85) is that the assumption

$E(\epsilon) = 0$ assures unbiased estimation and unbiased predictions of bid rents since Z is untransformed; but this is true only if (1.84) is the correct specification.

Another problem encountered in empirical applications is that no matter how carefully households may be stratified into segments, there would still be some variation in their utility levels because of within-segment variations in income and other socioeconomic characteristics. Wheaton, for example, deals with a segmentation of households by occupation (white-collar), work-place (downtown San Francisco), income, family size, age of household head, and race of head (white). Despite this relatively detailed stratification, there is significant utility level variation within his population segments. To reduce this variation, he suggests the equation

$$\log U_h = b_{0h} + b_{1h} \log Y_h, \tag{1.86}$$

which, if substituted into (1.75), yields two more coefficients, b_{0h} and b_{1h}, to be estimated together with $a_{1h}, \ldots, a_{nh}$. The introduction of income reduces variations in the utility level attributable to income only. These correspond to within-segment shifts in indifference curves but not to changes in preference coefficients. Galster (1977) suggests a similar approach that explains the utility level as a function of several socioeconomic variables including income. Proceeding in this way, both Wheaton and Galster estimate Cobb–Douglas, C.E.S., or other nonlinear utility functions that explain more than 75% of the variance in the dependent variable $\log Z$ (or Z). In these applications, each household is an observation in the estimation, and the samples are small in size, ranging from 45 or so up to 200 households per segment. An overwhelming part of the explanation in variance, however, is almost solely due to the high correlation between $\log(Y - R - T)$, the dependent variable, and $\log Y$, one of the independent variables. The contribution to R^2 by the other variables is extremely small. This fact remains extremely underemphasized in the published results by both Wheaton and Galster.

Another frequently recurring phenomenon noticed by Galster (1977) and this author is the result that the utility coefficient for travel time (one of the independent variables) is often of the wrong sign (positive) and persists in remaining that way despite efforts to correct for the effect of public services, with which travel time is presumably strongly correlated.

4.2. The Quality of Bid Rents Predicted from Estimated Utility Functions

Neither Wheaton nor Galster discuss the quality of their estimated bid rents in a satisfactory manner. There is a need to investigate directly how well the bid rents derived from the estimated utility functions predict the actual rents and housing expenditures of the households in the sample used to estimate the utility functions. The typical finding of such an analysis will be shown below with the use of an empirical but purely illustrative example.

A loglinear utility function was estimated from 62 white, white-collar households employed in downtown San Francisco or Oakland in 1965, with incomes in the \$15,000–\$25,000 range, age of head in the 31–55 year range, and one or two family members. The estimation yielded

$$\bar{U} = e^{-0.64}Y^{1.053} = Zt^{-0.023}S^{0.121}e^{0.070L}A^{-0.025}e^{0.014D}. \quad (1.87)$$

In this utility function, t is the household's travel time, S the number of rooms, L the lot size of the dwelling (0 for most multifamily units), A the age of the dwelling, and D a 0,1 dummy variable denoting travel mode with $D = 1$ transit and $D = 0$ auto. Each independent variable was found to be significant, with the least significant being travel time, at the 17% level of significance. The R^2 of the regression with log Z the dependent variable was 79.3%, but with 75.0% due to the independent variable log Y; but how well is the variation explained when actual rents are compared with predicted rents? To find out, we first predict bid rents by transforming the utility function

$$\hat{R} = Y - T - e^{-0.64}Y^{1.053}t^{0.023}S^{-0.121}e^{-0.070L}A^{0.025}e^{-0.014D}. \quad (1.88)$$

The above does not include the bias correction adjustment of Eq. (1.81). The predicted bid rents $\hat{R}$ are regressed against the observed rents R (which were used to compute $Z = Y - R - T$). This regression yielded

$$R = -558 + 0.890\hat{R} \quad (1.89)$$

with an R^2 of 31.4% compared to the R^2 of 79.3% of the utility function. Significance tests showed that the constant term -558 is not significantly different from zero, while 0.890 (the slope) is not significantly different from one. Examination of residuals shows large overprediction for small R and large underprediction for large R. The R^2 is much too low to allow reliable predictions of actual bid rents to be used in an equilibrium simulation model such as that of Herbert and Stevens. Ideally, for the utility estimates to be acceptable for equilibrium simulation, it would be necessary to obtain a slope coefficient not different from one, a constant term not different from zero, and an R^2 for Eq. (1.85) that would be quite high. Table 1.1 presents my findings for seven population segments. In obtaining these results I used the same data source employed by Wheaton but a smaller number of independent variables. The utility functions are made to depend on travel time, housing age, rooms, lot size, and travel mode but do not include any measure of public services or proxies for these. In addition to the utility estimates, the predictive power of bid rents is also examined by reporting the results for Eq. (1.89).

TABLE 1.1

*Cobb–Douglas Utility Coefficients for Seven Population Segments
with log Z the Dependent Variable*

Group number	1	2	3	4	5	6	7
Group income	$5,000– $10,000	$5,000– $10,000	$5,000– $10,000	$5,000– $10,000	$10,000– $15,000	$15,000– $25,000	$10,000– $15,000
Family size	1, 2 persons	3, 4 persons	1, 2 persons	3, 4 persons	3, 4 persons	1, 2 persons	1, 2 persons
Age of head	30 yr or less	30 yr or less	31–55 yr	31–55 yr	31–55 yr	31–55 yr	56+ yr

			Results of regression with log Z the dependent variable[a]				
Constant	−2.68	−1.62	−2.80	−2.36	−2.74	−0.64	−3.99
	(0.283)	(0.51)	(0.50)	(0.58)	(0.55)	(0.76)	(1.56)
Y	1.28	1.17	1.31	1.26	1.27	1.053	1.38
	(0.033)	(0.056)	(0.06)	(0.06)	(0.06)	(0.077)	(0.17)
t	0.020	0.050	0.034	0.032	0.010	−0.023	−0.061
	(0.008)	(0.016)	(0.015)	(0.017)	(0.009)	(0.017)	(0.025)
S	0.079	0.092	0.167	0.184	0.228	0.121	0.170
	(0.020)	(0.045)	(0.027)	(0.057)	(0.030)	(0.04)	(0.07)
L	0.399	0.563	0.338	0.187	0.057	0.070	0.501
	(0.166)	(0.135)	(0.089)	(0.075)	(0.040)	(0.04)	(0.15)
A	−0.022	−0.029	−0.025	−0.018	−0.034	−0.025	−0.089
	(0.008)	(0.013)	(0.016)	(0.017)	(0.090)	(0.014)	(0.025)
D	−0.028	−0.043	−0.039	−0.045	−0.004	0.014	0.067
	(0.013)	(0.026)	(0.024)	(0.029)	(0.017)	(0.026)	(0.047)
R^2 (%)	95.13	87.70	79.60	72.60	74.90	79.30	65.70
Sample size	90	87	160	162	195	62	60

			Results of regression between observed and predicted bid rents[b]				
Constant	334	−89	236	216	164	−558	−366
	(11.9%)	(72%)	(13.7%)	(57%)	(57%)	(39%)	(44%)
Slope	0.578	0.795	0.785	0.762	0.810	0.890	0.920
	(2%)	(8%)	(2%)	(20%)	(6%)	(100%)	(100%)
R^2 (%)	21.27	38.6	37.7	15.8	28.3	31.4	45.5

[a] Note that for t, S, L, and D, reported utility coefficients $= (-1) \times$ regression coefficient. Standard errors in parentheses.

[b] $R = a + b\hat{R}$, where a is constant and b is the slope. In parentheses under "Constant" is the level of significance at which the constant is not different from zero. In parentheses under "Slope" is the level of significance at which the slope is not different from one.

Wheaton and Galster do not report on the predictive power of the bid rent approach by a direct application of (1.89) or by taking into account correction (1.81). For this reason, I am unable to compare my findings with theirs. One would expect that the inclusion of public service proxy variables would increase the quality of predicted bid rents. Wheaton, for example, uses the income distribution within a household's zone of residence as a proxy for public services. His published results are ambiguous as to the effect of these variables, but in his correspondence with me (1978), he has claimed that these variables, when included in the regression, correct the sign of the travel time coefficient.

4.3. The Quality of Population Segmentation

Another shortcoming of the bid rent approach is the lack of an ability to successfully distinguish among the behaviors of different population segments. From the results of Table 1.1 as well as the conclusions by Wheaton (1977b), we may conclude that often the bid rent functions estimated for various segments are not significantly different from each other. In his above-mentioned article, Wheaton has noted that small perturbations in the utility function coefficients of various population segments differentiated by income lead to small changes in the slope and curvatures of their bid rent functions. Because of the similarity among the estimated coefficients for the various segments, these small changes are enough to lead to drastic reversals in the equilibrium locational patterns of the various segments, at least when one considers (as does Wheaton) the coefficients of travel time and lot size alone. More detailed analysis of the results in Table 1.1 suggests that consideration of other variables is not likely to change this conclusion by a great deal.

Two lessons can be drawn from these findings. First, to be able to successfully simulate realistic equilibrium location patterns of population segments, we must specify more complex utility functions by introducing public service variables that serve to sharply distinguish the preference variations among segments. This claim, implicitly advanced by Wheaton (1977b), appears to be a productive area for future research. Second, the robustness of the predicted locational patterns can be increased by estimating models that view the intrasegment variation in preferences explicitly and that explain the dispersion of choices resulting from intrasegment inhomogeneities in preferences. Predictions based on the bid rent approach ignore intrasegment variations in bid rents. A model that explicitly explains these variations would predict dispersed but more stable locational patterns. Small changes in the coefficients of such models would lead to subtle changes in the spatial distribution of the households of each population segment, whereas much larger changes would be needed to create significant disturbances of locational patterns. In sum, the explicit modeling of intrasegment inhomogeneities appears to be an essential step for achieving improved representation of actual market patterns.

4.4. The Realism of Equilibrium Location Patterns

Finally, we ought to discuss some of the shortcomings of the equilibrium location patterns that emerge from bid rent models and related market equilibrium algorithms such as that described in the previous section. One property is that all identical dwellings within the same zone will be occupied by the same (highest bidding) population segment, unless there are not enough households in that segment to occupy all of that zone. Each household in the same segment will be assumed to bid the same amount for each dwelling, and the intrasegment variation in bid rents can only be captured by dividing that segment into more segments or by explicitly modeling the dispersion of bid rents around the mean predicted bid rent.

In a long run equilibrium solution based on the bid rent approach, each population segment is located within a contiguous ring or subarea, and there is no ring or subarea that is shared by more than one population segment. In more realistic applications of bid rent models that admit a durable and predetermined dwelling stock, short run equilibria will yield similar results. Mixing of segments within a small geographical area will occur only if the zones contained within this area are differentiated from each other in housing. In summary, bid rent models lead to equilibrium patterns with "no cross-hauling" or "dispersion" in location and travel patterns because of the strong assumption that it is possible to empirically identify segments of households that are internally homogeneous in every respect and thus behave identically.

Scholars of urban and regional analysis have long been aware of the no cross hauling implications of bid rent models. This is part of the reason why models able to predict dispersion or cross hauling have been more popular among geographers and urban planners. Models such as those of Lowry (1964) and Wilson (1967) have been recognized as empirically more realistic when compared to bid rent models, but also as less behavioral since they do not base their results on postulates about the behavior of households but rather on the "behavior" of aggregate population groups. One of the aims of this book is to develop a theoretical framework and mathematical models that provide a microbehavioral foundation for Lowry and Wilson type models, while at the same time providing the urban economist with a more flexible analytical and simulation tool suitable for policy testing.

5. SUMMARY CRITIQUE OF THE BID RENT APPROACH

In concluding this chapter, we develop a summary critique of selected theoretical and empirical shortcomings of the bid rent approach. This critique serves as a starting point for developments reported in the remainder of this book.

5.1. Theoretical Shortcomings

(1)   The bid rent approach assumes that each housing supplier (or seller) has perfect knowledge of the bids offered by each household. In turn, each household has perfect knowledge of each dwelling alternative and the bids offered by competing households. This situation of perfect information is assumed to be achieved through a perfect bidding–auctioneering (or perfect arbitrage) process that allocates each dwelling to the highest bidder. A more realistic theory may assume that each housing supplier has knowledge of the choices or demand structure for housing but not of the bid or preferences of each household. Under these assumptions, households can be treated as price takers, and the result of arbitrage need not imply results identical with those of the bid rent models.

(2)   The bid rent approach assumes that the population of households is divided into segments, with each segment treated as homogeneous in preferences. Intrasegment variations are not allowed. A more realistic theory would assume the existence of systematic variations (nonhomogeneities) in incomes, tastes, and other socioeconomic characteristics within each segment and would attempt to explicitly model these variations instead of assuming them away.

(3)   The bid rent approach assumes perfect and costless household mobility. These two assumptions are crucial in assuring the efficient functioning of the perfect arbitrage or bidding–auctioneering process. This shortcoming is not as critical as the previous two because its nature is in large part one of a simplifying assumption. It can be removed by the development of improved dynamic models that take into account mobility costs. These improved models would still rely on the previous two assumptions of bid rent analysis, changing only the real time interpretation (time span) required for a modified perfect arbitrage market outcome.

(4)   Bid rent models can produce rent distributions within homogeneous submarkets or zones of housing only by subdividing the housing stock into a larger number of zones or submarkets.

5.2. Empirical Shortcomings

(1)   To estimate utility functions for household segments, it is necessary to use one of the attributes in the utility function as the dependent variable and then apply linear or nonlinear regression analysis. There are problems with doing so. First, one of the attributes must be selected as the dependent variable, but there are no absolute criteria for making a proper selection. In the studies by Anas (1975), Wheaton (1977a), and Galster (1977), the household's income allocated to all other expenditures is taken as the dependent variable, but since regression analysis is conditional analysis, the choice of another attribute as dependent variable would yield different utility coefficients. Second, the choice of a utility attribute as a dependent variable implies loss of information on at least one empirical coefficient. Third, when a transformation of the dependent variable must be used (such as the log transformation in the case of a Cobb–Douglas function), predictions of bid rents obtained from estimated utility functions are necessarily biased and require unsatisfactory bias correction procedures.

(2)   A problem noticed by both Anas (1975) and Galster (1977) and also hinted at in the results by Wheaton (1977a) is that it is difficult to obtain the right sign for the coefficient of travel time. The working hypothesis for this phenomenon is that other attributes and, in particular, public services and neighborhood quality that are strongly correlated with travel time may be missing from the specification of the utility function. In their absence, their effect on the dependent variable is proxied by travel time, which exhibits the wrong sign.

(3)   The assumption that population segments are internally homogeneous creates a difficulty in empirical estimation. If population segments are large in size, this assumption would lead to great loss of information by ignoring the real internal variations among households and by assuming that all households behave like the "average household." It may be proposed that the first difficulty may be bypassed by defining a large number of population segments in order to maximize the degree of internal homogeneity within each segment; but this remedy leads to another difficulty: with a large number of population segments, the simulation of equilibrium becomes expensive to the point of impracticality. In addition to this, once the number of segments is increased it would become necessary to increase the number of zones and housing types as well in order to assure a realism in locational patterns commensurate with the realism of population segmentation. The linear programming algorithms discussed in Section 3 of this chapter are such that an increase in the number of segments, zones, and housing types would greatly increase their cost.

CHAPTER 2

A PROBABILISTIC DISCRETE CHOICE
THEORY OF RENTAL
HOUSING DEMAND

In this chapter, we depart from the bid rent approach and develop formulations of the demand for rental housing as a probabilistic discrete choice process. Instead of being viewed explicitly or implicitly as a bidder, the household is modeled as a utility-maximizing price taker choosing among discrete housing alternatives. Random utility theory forms the mathematical foundation of the analysis. The use of probabilistic concepts allows us to consider explicitly the preference and socioeconomic inhomogeneities within each population segment as well as the inhomogeneities in the attributes of a group of closely substitutable dwellings.

The purpose of this chapter is to show how aggregate housing demand functions consistent with the underlying microbehavior of households can be developed from various assumptions about systematic variations in preferences and dwelling attributes. We consider the most general and least tractable formulations and successively simplify these until the simplest models emerge. The simplest model derived in this way is the multinomial logit model and several econometric elaborations of it.

The multinomial logit model has been extensively applied to travel demand analysis and particularly to the choice among travel modes (Warner, 1962; Charles River Associates, 1967; Domencich and McFadden, 1975). Several empirical applications of logit analysis to residential location and housing choice have also appeared (Anas, 1975; Quigley, 1976; Lerman, 1977).

Theoretical discussions of multinomial logit and other random utility models of travel and locational choice can be found in Domencich and McFadden (1975), Williams (1977), and McFadden (1978). Major results of these articles are reviewed in this chapter. In addition to synthesizing these findings, this chapter attempts to take a thorough look into the interpretation of random utility theory and its implications for modeling aggregate demand. Particular emphasis is placed on the relationship between deterministic and stochastic aggregate demand functions based on random utility theory.

The developments starting with the next chapter, which are based on the demand functions derived in this chapter, examine the pricing, market clearing, and competitive equilibrium properties of spatial housing markets. While some of the results in the following chapters are quite general in nature, many of the specific results derived apply only to the multinomial logit model. The simulation, empirical, and policy-analytic results presented in the second part of this book are based entirely on the multinomial logit model, and they utilize some of the specific developments of the first part of this book.

1. ASSUMPTIONS

The discrete choice theory to be developed in this chapter is based on several fundamental assumptions, which are briefly stated below.

1.1. Fundamental Assumptions

(1) Each dwelling is a multiattribute commodity comprised of housing, locational, and neighborhood attributes. Following Lancaster's consumer theory (1966), it is assumed that each household's preferences depend directly on these attributes. Thus, implicitly, the demand for housing is derived from the demands for the underlying dwelling attributes. Since each dwelling is an indivisible package of attributes, consumers can substitute various levels of the attributes only by changing their choice of dwelling and location or through maintenance and home improvement activity.

(2) The housing stock of an urban area is divided into *submarkets*. Each dwelling belongs to only one submarket. Each submarket is a group of dwellings with similar attributes. Dwellings belonging to the same submarket are identical in only some of their attributes. For example, the housing stock of a surburban municipality may consist of two submarkets: single family and multiple family housing. Alternatively, more detail may be used defining submarkets as apartments, condominiums, town houses, single family detached dwellings, two-story single family dwellings, etc. The number of rooms, housing age, neighborhood characteristics, and locational contiguity of dwellings can be used as criteria for defining submarkets.

(3)   The population of households is assumed to consist of a number of *population segments*. Each household belongs to only one population segment. Each population segment is a group of households with similar socioeconomic characteristics. Households belonging to a specific population segment need not be identical in all of their characteristics but only in some of them. For example, population segments can be defined on the basis of the number of persons in the household. More detailed definitions can be based on cross classifications of family size, income range, age of household head, workplace of head, etc. No matter how a segment is defined, there will be some variation among the households grouped into the same segment.

(4)   Each household is assumed to select one dwelling that is the utility-maximizing choice for that household. In making this choice, the household can consider all dwellings in the market or restrict consideration to a subset of the dwellings in the market. This subset is called the *choice set* of that household.

1.2.   Simplifying Assumptions

Additional assumptions will be made in order to simplify the nature of the housing market analysis. These are briefly stated:

(1)   Households participating in the housing market are assumed to be *myopic*. This means that households consider only the currently available information in deciding which dwelling to choose.

(2)   The behavior of renters and owners of housing is assumed to be identical, and arbitrage is assumed to exist across tenure categories as well as across submarkets. For homeowners, the sum of mortgage, maintenance, and tax payments is considered a rent equivalent and represents the annual price homeowners pay for housing. Revenues from either rental or owned housing are assumed to accrue to absentee suppliers and to dissipate from the housing market. Capital gains from the sale of homes are not considered explicitly in households' choice of housing. Other complications such as down payments, interest rates, and alternative mortgage plans are also suppressed. The result is that the entire housing market is represented as essentially a rental market. In this respect, there is no departure from the standard bid rent analysis of Chapter 1.

(3)   It is assumed that households are costlessly and perfectly mobile in the market. This implies frequent turnover and efficient arbitrage. It also implies that a household's decision to rent in a specific submarket is independent of that household's current housing situation.

(4)   All households and landlords participating in the market perceive the same submarket and population segmentation structure and have the same choice set structure. This means that households and landlords agree about

submarket definitions and boundaries so that the same definitions apply to all market agents. In an empirical application, this assumption may require that submarket definitions are appropriately chosen to correspond to neighborhood boundaries or specific municipalities. Such an approach may increase the realism of the empirical analysis. The assumption of a common choice set implies that all market alternatives are included in the choice set of each household.

Each of the above assumptions can be relaxed in order to derive a specific discrete choice model of demand. It is possible to develop discrete choice models of demand in which mobility is not perfect or models in which the effect of down payments, interest rates, and mortgage plans is explicitly considered. It is also possible to relax the assumption of myopic behavior or to assume that each household has a personal definition of choice sets or of the urban area's submarket structure. These relaxed assumptions contribute to more realistic but less tractable models. The essence of discrete choice theoretic models becomes abundantly clear without relaxing the above simplifying assumptions. Therefore, the main analysis of this book will adhere to these assumptions.

1.3. Submarkets and Population Segments

We assume that the urban area consists of $j = 1, \ldots, J$ submarkets. Each submarket contains $k = 1, \ldots, S_j$ dwellings. To fix ideas, we may suppose that each submarket is a spatially contiguous set of dwellings forming a community within the urban area. Dwellings within the urban area are distinguished by rent (or housing price), location, accessibility to schools, shopping, public facilities, age of dwelling, condition, number of rooms, lot size, type of appliances, structural type, and many other attributes. Each attribute has a distribution within each submarket. Typically, a submarket may be defined as a set of dwellings that are identical in some attributes but that vary in others. For example, the number of rooms and structural type of dwellings may, by definition, have no variance within a submarket, whereas units in that submarket may differ in age, location, accessibility, and other attributes.

The population of urban households consists of $h = 1, \ldots, H$ population segments. Each segment contains $i = 1, \ldots, N_h$ households. These are differentiated by income, work location, family size, race of family head, age of head, and many other socioeconomic characteristics. Each of these characteristics has a distribution within each population segment. Typically, a population segment may be defined as a set of households identical in some characteristics but different in others. For example, all married households with one child under six years of age, income in the $20,000–$25,000 range, and the husband employed in the city center may be one segment. House-holds within this segment will differ in exact income, workplace of wife (if any), race, age of the household members, etc. The preferences of households belonging to the same segment are assumed to be essentially similar and to vary within the segment according to a known distribution.

2. RANDOM UTILITY FUNCTIONS

The preferences of a household i that belongs to population segment h ($i \in h$) are represented through a utility function of the form

$$U_{jk}^{hi} = U^h(X_{jk}, W_{hi}, \epsilon_{jk}^{hi}), \qquad (2.1)$$

where $U^h(\cdot)$ is the utility function for the hth segment; X_{jk}, the vector of the $n = 1, \ldots, N$ attributes for the kth dwelling in submarket j ($k \in j$); and W_{hi}, the vector of the $m = 1, \ldots, M$ socioeconomic characteristics of the ith household in segment h. The term ϵ_{jk}^{hi} represents the random part of utility for dwelling k in j and varies from household to household i within the hth population segment. The random part of utility is an unknown function of the M socioeconomic and N submarket attributes as well as of other unob-served attributes of the dwelling and the household. Thus U_{jk}^{hi} denotes the total utility household i (which is a member of segment h) derives from a dwelling unit k in submarket j.

An assumption that can be made at this point is that the random and systematic parts of utility are separable. This allows us to write (2.1) as

$$U_{jk}^{hi} = U^h(X_{jk}, W_{hi}) + \epsilon_{jk}^{hi} \qquad (2.2)$$

or

$$U_{jk}^{hi} = U^h(X_{jk}, W_{hi})\epsilon_{jk}^{hi}, \qquad (2.3)$$

where (2.3) implies the log transformation

$$\log U_{jk}^{hi} = \log U^h(X_{jk}, W_{hi}) + \log \epsilon_{jk}^{hi}. \qquad (2.4)$$

In general, the random terms may be expressed as an unknown function of the form

$$\epsilon_{jk}^{hi} = G_{jk}^{hi}(X_{jk}, W_{hi}, \ldots), \qquad (2.5)$$

where "..." represent unknown dwelling and household attributes. In random utility models, the household specific variations of (2.5) cannot be measured, and they are treated like random variables ϵ_{jk}^h that are distributed over the population of households. Thus the analyst does not know the value ϵ_{jk}^{hi} for household i but knows or assumes the probability distribution over the population of households.

2.1. Average Submarket Utility

To provide a specific example of a random utility function of the form (2.2), suppose that utility is linear in all its attributes X_{jk} and W_{hi}. Then

$$U_{jk}^{hi} = \alpha^h X_{jk} + \beta^h W_{hi} + \epsilon_{jk}^{hi}, \tag{2.6}$$

where α^h and β^h are appropriate vectors containing the utility parameters. This specification assumes that we can precisely observe the M socioeconomic and N submarket attributes for each household and dwelling. Suppose, however, that this cannot be done and that we only observe the means of the attributes. We can then rewrite (2.6) by substituting

$$W_{hi} = \overline{W}_h + \delta_{hi} \tag{2.7}$$

and

$$X_{jk} = \overline{X}_j + \gamma_{jk}, \tag{2.8}$$

where $\overline{W}_h$ and $\overline{X}_j$ are the segment and submarket mean vectors, and δ_{hi} and γ_{jk} are the household and dwelling specific deviations from the mean vectors. With these substitutions, we can rewrite (2.6) as

$$U_{jk}^{hi} = \alpha^h \overline{X}_j + \beta^h \overline{W}_h + \alpha^h \gamma_{jk} + \beta^h \delta_{hi} + \epsilon_{jk}^{hi}, \tag{2.9}$$

which can also be written as

$$U_{jk}^{hi} = U_j^h + \xi_{jk}^{hi}, \tag{2.10}$$

where

$$U_j^h = \alpha^h \overline{X}_j + \beta^h \overline{W}_h \tag{2.11}$$

represents the average utility for submarket j, whereas

$$\xi_{jk}^{hi} = \alpha^h \gamma_{jk} + \beta^h \delta_{hi} + \epsilon_{jk}^{hi} \tag{2.12}$$

represents the unobserved part of utility. It should be noted that the ξ's in (2.12) consist of two parts: the ϵ's are assumed to be random over the households i for each (j, k) and segment h, whereas the first two terms in (2.12) are fixed and unobserved for each i and k, but they can be viewed as random over the k's and i's for each j. This observation would allow us to write

$$\xi_{jk}^h = \zeta_j^h + \epsilon_{jk}^h, \tag{2.13}$$

where

$$\zeta_j^h \equiv \alpha^h \gamma_j + \beta^h \delta_h, \tag{2.14}$$

with γ_j and δ_h treated as random terms over k and i, respectively. Separate probability distribution can be assumed for the ζ_j^h and the ϵ_{jk}^h. The ζ_j^h represent the random part of the submarket utility and the ϵ_{jk}^h represent the random part of the dwelling utility over the population of households.

Another example is obtained by expressing the attributes as

$$X_{jkn} = \overline{X}_{jn} \, \gamma_{jkn}, \qquad n = 1, \ldots, N \qquad (2.15)$$

and

$$W_{him} = \overline{W}_{hm} \, \delta_{him}, \qquad m = 1, \ldots, M, \qquad (2.16)$$

where γ and δ now measure multiplicative deviations from the mean attributes. In this case, if the utility function is loglinear in form it can be expressed as

$$\log U_{jk}^{hi} = \sum_{n=1}^{N} \alpha_n^h \log \overline{X}_{jn} + \sum_{m=1}^{M} \beta_m^h \log \overline{W}_{hm} + \sum_{n=1}^{N} \alpha_n^h \log \gamma_{jkn}$$

$$+ \sum_{m=1}^{M} \beta_m^h \log \delta_{him} + \epsilon_{jk}^{hi}. \qquad (2.17)$$

The considerations of (2.10)–(2.14) apply to (2.17) as well with appropriate definitions of the ξ's and ζ's. The dispersion of total utility can be studied further only by specifying probability density distributions for the random terms ζ_j^h and ϵ_{jk}^h. For example, $F^h(\cdot)$ can be the joint probability density function for the ζ's such that

$$\int_{\zeta_1^h = -\infty}^{+\infty} \cdots \int_{\zeta_J^h = -\infty}^{+\infty} F^h(\zeta_1^h, \ldots, \zeta_J^h) \, d\zeta_1^h \cdots d\zeta_J^h = 1. \qquad (2.18)$$

The attributes $\overline{X}_j$ and $\overline{W}_h$ need not be the submarket or segment means. These can be nonmean measures of the underlying attributes. Clearly, if these are not means, the definitions of the deviation measures γ and δ and the assumptions as to their distribution over the population need to be altered accordingly.

In the remainder of this book, the part of utility that is nonrandom will be called *strict utility* (other names for it are *identified, systematic, measurable,* or *common* utility).

2.2. Random Utility as Deterministic Variation

One interpretation of random utility is that it represents variations from household to household within the same segment. According to this interpretation, all households have completely deterministic preferences but these cannot be fully observed, either because the attributes X and W are imperfectly measured by the observer or because there are other unknown but deterministic idiosyncrasies that differentiate otherwise similar households. If preferences are deterministic, households that face the same condition repeatedly will make the same utility-maximizing decisions over and over again. The analyst of such a population of households cannot predict the decision of each household since the analyst does not have full knowledge of each household's underlying utility function. The analyst can only hope to predict the distribution of decisions over the population of households.

2.3. Random Utility as Stochastic Instability

A second interpretation of the random utility term is that it represents a stochastic instability in the utility function of a specific household. According to this interpretation, the household is not deterministic: if faced with the same conditions repeatedly, the household will make a different decision every time because of random (unexplained) changes in the utility function. This is equivalent to assuming that the analyst cannot perfectly observe or replicate the "conditions" surrounding a decision and that some random disturbance in these conditions (including psychological states of the household) will always remain. Under these assumptions, the observer can only hope to predict the probability that a specific household will make a certain decision.

The major difference between the two interpretations can be summarized by saying that the first interpretation uses random utility to explain inter-household variations in utility, whereas the second uses random utility to explain intrahousehold variations in utility. In reality, interhousehold and intrahousehold variations coexist, and the question of whether tastes are deterministic or stochastic may not be answerable via a scientific experiment since it is practically impossible to replicate identical choice contexts for the same household in order to determine the presence of intrahousehold utility variations.

One source of variations in intrahousehold tastes may be the fact that a household's utility function is an "aggregation" or combination of the utility functions of each household member. If the changing relationships among household members are not observed (as they are not in common studies of the housing market), the behavior of each household over a period of time may appear to be partly stochastic even though the underlying behavior of each of the household members may be deterministic.

2.4. Random Utility as Ex Ante Perception

Both of the above interpretations assume that the household making decisions is a perfectly informed economic agent. Another interpretation of random utility allows us to take into account the possible change between the *ex ante* and *ex post* utility of a situation. According to this interpretation, households must make decisions on the basis of an ex ante perceived utility level; but since households do not fully know the attributes facing them, their actual utility after a choice is made (and consumption begins) will differ from their ex ante perceived utility. Thus in (2.2), for example, $U^h(\cdot)$ can measure the ex post utility with the random term representing an additive adjustment so that $U^h(\cdot) + \epsilon$ is the ex ante preceived utility. Households make their decisions on the basis of ex ante utility, but the ex post utility is the correct measure of their actual satisfaction. It is not necessary that the ϵ's entirely vanish ex post, and part of the random terms can still remain to form part of ex post utility. An implication of this third interpretation is that households will be in an ex ante perceived equilibrium with respect to the options facing them but may quickly fall into an ex post disequilibrium after their choices are made. The relevance of this interpretation for housing markets is important: dwellings are complex and unique commodities with many facets. Full inspection and anticipation of the utility that can be derived from a dwelling is not as simple a matter as in the case of other commodities. As a result, some ex ante–ex post discrepancies are unavoidable for the typical household making a dwelling choice.

This third interpretation is not inconsistent with the previous two since one source of the stochastic part of utility may very well be the perceptions of the utilities of various alternatives. Finally, it should be emphasized that the perceived utility components can represent interhousehold or intrahousehold variations in perceptions. This makes the third interpretation fully compatible with the previous two.

2.5. Summary

To summarize, the random terms of the utility function can represent many types of theoretical or econometric uncertainty in microeconomic decision making. Some of these are (a) deterministic variations in tastes due to unobserved interhousehold socioeconomic differences; (b) similar variations due to unobserved attributes; (c) stochastic variations in a household's utility due to unobserved changes in mental states, intrahousehold behavior, and economic conditions; (d) unobserved attributes of location, dwelling, and other objects of choice, and resultant measurement errors; (e) variations in the perceptions of attributes or the utility arising from these attributes; (f) imperfect information about attributes; (g) unobserved constraints that condition households' choices; and (h) irrational behavior.

The key to understanding random utility theory is that to the observer of the behavior of a population of households, the above and other sources of nonhomogeneous or inconsistent behavior are often indistinguishable from each other. The implication is that the dispersion of choices in the population can only be explained by assuming the existence of random terms and by attempting to statistically measure their distribution over the population.

3. PROBABILISTIC CHOICE MODELS

We now discuss the derivation of probabilistic choice models from random utility functions.

3.1. Choice Relative Frequency Functions for a Population Segment

If the random components of utility denote deterministic interhousehold variations in preferences, then the relative frequency or proportion of segment h households choosing an alternative (j, k) is given by P_{jk}^h, where

$$P_{jk}^h = \text{Freq}\left[U_{jk}^h > U_{lm}^h \text{ for all } (l, m) \neq (j, k)\right], \tag{2.19}$$

where U_{jk}^h is the total utility (including strict and random utility) of a randomly selected member of segment h for dwelling k in submarket j, and $\text{Freq}[\cdot]$ means the "relative frequency" or proportion of households that will find (j, k) more attractive than all other (l, m). The precise choice and utility of each household remains unknown. Since there is no truly stochastic element in a household's utility function, each household makes a deterministic choice. Thus, given a large number of households of type h, P_{jk}^h is the proportion of these that will prefer alternative (j, k) to all other alternatives.

3.2. Choice Probability Functions for a Household

If the random components of utility represent stochastic intrahousehold instabilities in preferences, each household's choices can be predicted only up to a probability distribution. The probability that a specific household i that is a member of h will choose (j, k) is then given as

$$P_{jk}^{hi} = \text{Prob}\left[U_{jk}^{hi} > U_{lm}^{hi} \text{ for all } (l, m) \neq (j, k)\right], \tag{2.20}$$

where U_{jk}^{hi} is the total utility (strict and random parts of utility) of household i for dwelling k in submarket j, and $\text{Prob}[\cdot]$ denotes the probability that household i will prefer (j, k) to all other (l, m). We may think of household i as having to repeatedly choose among all alternatives under the same observable conditions. Then, P_{jk}^{hi} is the expected proportion of times the household will choose alternative (j, k) in a large number of repeated choices under the same observable conditions. Since under this interpretation household choices are stochastic, aggregate demand will also be stochastic. Thus the expected proportion of households who will choose (j, k) is computed as

$$\hat{P}_{jk}^h = \left(\sum_{i=1}^{N_h} P_{jk}^{hi}\right)/N_h, \tag{2.21}$$

where the caret (ˆ) stands for "expected." An interesting question is how the $\hat{P}^{hi}_{jk}$ obtained from (2.21) compares with the P^{hi}_{jk} of (2.19). If the same assumptions apply to the interhousehold distribution of utilities as to the intrahousehold distribution of utilities, then clearly $P^h_{jk} = \hat{P}^h_{jk}$. The more realistic problem, of course, is that stochastic intrahousehold utility terms cannot be distinguished from deterministic interhousehold utility by observing the diversity of revealed choices within a population at a given point in time. Thus the issue of whether choices are stochastic or deterministic can be treated by assumption only.

3.3. Some General Properties of Choice Functions

Suppose that the market consists of $j = 1, \ldots, J$ and mutually exclusive "alternatives" available for choice. Then the expected choice frequency for alternative j by members of a population segment h can be denoted as

$$P^h_j = F^h_j(U^h_j, j = 1, \ldots, J; \Sigma^h), \qquad (2.22)$$

where $F^h_j(\cdot)$ is the choice probability function; U^h_j, the strict utility of alternative j common to all households of segment h, and Σ^h, the variance–covariance matrix of the joint distribution of the random utility over the members of the population segment h. In the special case where the random utility terms are independently distributed for each alternative, namely, the off-diagonal covariance terms in the matrix Σ^h are zero, Eq. (2.22) becomes

$$P^h_j = F^h_j(U^h_j, \sigma^h_j, j = 1, \ldots, J), \qquad (2.23)$$

where σ^h_j is the standard deviation of the random utility terms for the jth alternative. In general, we would expect that function (2.22) or its special case (2.23) will obey certain reasonable properties. For example, it may be expected or assumed that

$$\partial F^h_j / \partial U^h_j > 0, \qquad \partial F^h_j / \partial U^h_i < 0, \qquad i \neq j. \qquad (2.24)$$

This states that if the variance–covariance structure is held constant while the strict utility of a distribution for one alternative is increased, the proportion of households choosing that alternative will increase while the proportion choosing a competing alternative will decrease. This argument presupposes that shifts in the strict utilities can be accomplished without disturbing the variance–covariance structure of the distributions or that the distributions are independent of each other. Another result that follows intuitively is that

$$\lim_{\substack{(\sigma^h_j \to 0 \text{ each } j) \\ (U^h_m > U^h_j \text{ each } j \neq m)}} F^h_m = 1. \qquad (2.25)$$

This states the familiar notion that as the variance due to the random utilities vanishes for each alternative, the alternative with the highest strict utility will be selected by the entire population. Next, it can be assumed that

$$\lim_{U_j^h \to -\infty} F_j^h = 0, \tag{2.26}$$

$$\lim_{\substack{U_i^h \to -\infty \\ \forall i \neq j}} F_j^h = 1. \tag{2.27}$$

It is not as straightforward to specify similar properties regarding the variance terms. For example, the partial derivatives $\partial F_j^h / \partial \sigma_j^h$ and $\partial F_j^h / \partial \sigma_i^h$, $i \neq j$, are ambiguous in sign. In general, changing the variance of a distribution may be accompanied with changes in its skewness and other higher moment distributional properties, and all of these changes would potentially affect the above partial derivatives in a different way.

Another set of limiting properties is useful for the case where each of the $j = 1, \ldots, J$ alternatives represents a submarket with $k = 1, \ldots, S_j$ dwellings. If the dwellings belonging to the same submarket are identical in their unobserved attributes and perceived to be so by all households in a segment h, the dwelling with the highest strict utility will be strictly preferred to all other dwellings in the same submarket. Thus choice among submarkets reduces to choice among the most preferred dwelling in each submarket. Thus, letting U_j^h denote the utility $U_j^h = \max_k (U_{jk}^h, \ k = 1, \ldots, S_j)$, at the limit it should be true that

$$\lim_{\text{var}(U_i^h, \forall i) \to 0} P_j^h = \frac{1}{J}. \tag{2.28}$$

If dwellings within the same submarket are identical in strict as well as random utility, it will then be true that

$$\lim_{\text{var}(U_i^h, \forall i) \to 0} P_{jk}^h = \frac{1}{JS_j} \tag{2.29}$$

for any dwelling k that is an element of submarket j.

3.4. Additive Random Utility and Independently and Identically Distributed Choice Models: Multinomial Probit and Logit

First consider that total utility can be assumed to be additively separable into strict and random utility. This can be written as in (2.2), or more simply, by assuming that strict utility does not depend on personal attributes, it can be written as

$$U_{jk}^h = U^h(X_{jk}) + \epsilon_{jk}^h, \tag{2.30}$$

where the function $U^h(\cdot)$ measures the dependence of strict utility on dwelling and submarket attributes, and ϵ_{jk}^h is random utility. Let $\bar{\epsilon}^h$ denote the vector $[\epsilon_{11}^h, \ldots, \epsilon_{1S_1}^h, \ldots, \epsilon_{J1}^h, \ldots, \epsilon_{JS_J}^h]$ and let $\bar{F}(\bar{\epsilon}^h)$ denote the cumulative distribution function of $\bar{\epsilon}^h$. Then the choice probabilities can be computed by rewriting (2.19) as

$$P_{jk}^h = \int_{\epsilon_{jk}^h = -\infty}^{+\infty} (\partial \bar{F}(\bar{\epsilon}^h)/\partial \epsilon_{jk}^h)\, d\epsilon_{jk}^h \tag{2.31}$$

by integrating over the derivative of $\bar{F}$ with respect to its (j, k) argument. This derivative is a distribution function such that

$$\partial \bar{F}(\bar{\epsilon}^h)/\partial \epsilon_{jk}^h = \bar{F}_{jk}\{[U^h(X_{jk}) - U^h(X_{lm}) + \epsilon_{jk}^h]\}, \tag{2.32}$$

where $[\cdot]$ denotes a vector with its (l, m) component shown in the brackets. The integration in (2.31) will yield

$$P_{jk}^h = F_{jk}^h[U^h(X_{jk}) - U^h(X_{lm}), \text{ all } (l, m)], \tag{2.33}$$

where $F_{jk}^h(\cdot)$ is the choice probability function for alternative (j, k). This condition states that the choice probability for alternative (j, k) is a function of the differences of the utility of that alternative and the utility of all other alternatives. This result stems from the assumption of additive random terms. More generally, if the systematic and random terms are nonlinearly related, the choice probabilities can be expressed as

$$P_{jk}^h = F_{jk}^h[U^h(X_{lm}), \text{ all } (l, m)], \tag{2.34}$$

where $F_{jk}^h(\cdot)$ is the choice probability function for alternative (j, k). In both (2.33) and (2.34) the variance–covariance matrix of the random utility terms will influence the form of the choice function, but is suppressed in the notation because it is treated as a constant parameter of the choice functions.

Choice probabilities must sum to one over the range of alternatives since choices must be conserved for each segment h. Thus

$$\sum_j \sum_k P_{jk}^h = 1 \qquad \text{for} \quad h = 1, \ldots, H. \tag{2.35}$$

A specific choice model is *multinomial probit*. It is derived by assuming that the additive random terms are distributed according to the multivariate joint normal distribution. Under these assumptions, the choice probabilities are given by

$$P^h_{jk} = \int_{\epsilon^h_{jk}=-\infty}^{+\infty} \cdots \int_{\epsilon^h_{lm}=-\infty}^{U^h_{jk}-U^h_{lm}+\epsilon^h_{jk}} \cdots \int_{\epsilon_{JS_J}=-\infty}^{U^h_{jk}-U^h_{JS_J}+\epsilon^h_{jk}} n(\bar{\epsilon}^h; 0, \Sigma^h)\,d\bar{\epsilon}^h \quad (2.36)$$

where the number of integrals is equal to the number of alternatives and $n(\bar{\epsilon}^h; 0, \Sigma^h)$ is the multivariate normal density with mean vector 0 and variance–covariance matrix Σ^h.

A special class of tractable choice models is derived by assuming that the random terms are *independently* and *identically* distributed (IID). For example, the IID version of the above probit model is obtained by assuming that the variance–covariance matrix $\Sigma^h = (\sigma^h)^2 I$, where $(\sigma^h)^2$ is the variance of the identical distributions for each alternative (j, k) and I is the identity matrix.

Multinomial probit models including IID probit become intractable when the number of alternatives is large. This intractability stems in part from the need to compute the choice probabilities through numerical integration by relying on various approximation formulas.

The most tractable class of probabilistic choice models are multinomial logit (MNL) models. The derivation of these models is now examined in more detail. The *multinomial logit* model is derived by assuming that the random utility terms for each alternative are independently and identically distributed according to the extreme value (Weibull) distribution, which is given by

$$\text{Prob}[\epsilon^h_{lm} \leq v] = \exp[-\exp(-\lambda^h v)], \qquad \text{each} \quad (l, m), \qquad (2.37)$$

and which has the density function

$$\partial \, \text{Prob}[\cdot]/\partial v = \lambda^h \exp(-\lambda^h v) \exp[-\exp(-\lambda^h v)] \qquad (2.38)$$

with $\lambda^h = (\pi/\sqrt{6})/\sigma^h$, where σ^h is the standard deviation of the distribution for each alternative and the mode of the distribution is equal to zero.

Following (2.19), the choice probabilities can now be expressed as

$$\text{Prob}\{\epsilon^h_{jk} + U^h(X_{jk}) > \underset{(l,m)\neq(j,k)}{\text{Max}} [\epsilon^h_{lm} + U^h(X_{lm})]\}. \qquad (2.39)$$

Next, the assumption that the random terms of each alternative are independently distributed enables us to write

$$\text{Prob}\{\epsilon^h_{jk} + U^h(X_{jk}) > \underset{(l,m)\neq(j,k)}{\text{Max}} [\epsilon^h_{lm} + U^h(X_{lm})]\}$$

$$= \prod_{(l,m)\neq(j,k)} \text{Prob}[\epsilon^h_{lm} < \epsilon^h_{jk} + U^h(X_{jk}) - U^h(X_{lm})].$$

$$(2.40)$$

Recalling (2.37), we see that given a fixed value $\epsilon_{jk}^h = w$, each ϵ_{lm}^h in (2.40) is Weibull distributed with $v \equiv w + U^h(X_{jk}) - U^h(X_{lm})$. Thus, using (2.37), the right side of (2.40) becomes equal to

$$\exp(- \sum_{(l,m) \neq (j,k)} \exp\{-\lambda^h[w + U^h(X_{jk}) - U^h(X_{lm})]\}) \tag{2.41}$$

$$= \exp\{-\exp[-\lambda^h w - \lambda^h U^h(X_{jk})] \sum_{(l,m) \neq (j,k)} \exp[\lambda^h U^h(X_{lm})]\}. \tag{2.42}$$

Since the summation in (2.42) is a constant, it is established from (2.42) and (2.40) that the maximum total utility value is also Weibull distributed, with

$$v \equiv w + U^h(X_{jk}) - \left(\frac{1}{\lambda^h}\right) \log \sum_{(l,m) \neq (j,k)} \exp[\lambda^h U^h(X_{lm})].$$

The choice probabilities can now be computed following (2.39) and evaluating it using a convolution formula:

$$\text{Eq. (2.39)} = \int_{-\infty}^{+\infty} \left[\frac{\partial \, \text{Prob}(\epsilon_{jk}^h \leqq w)}{\partial w}\right]$$

$$\times \{\text{Prob}[\epsilon_*^h \leqq U^h(X_{jk}) - U^h(X_*) + w]\} \, dw, \tag{2.43}$$

where the asterisk ($*$) represents the alternative with maximum total utility over all $(l, m) \neq (j, k)$ for $\epsilon_{jk}^h = w$. Equation (2.43) is evaluated by using the probability density function (2.38) for the first term in the integrand and (2.42) for the second term in the integrand. Integration is straightforward and yields the multinomial logit (MNL) model

$$P_{jk}^h = \exp[\lambda^h U^h(X_{jk})] / \sum_{l=1}^{J} \sum_{m=1}^{S_l} \exp[\lambda^h U^h(X_{lm})], \quad \text{all } (j, k). \tag{2.44}$$

The chief advantage of MNL is that it is highly more tractable econometrically compared to multinomial probit and other probabilistic choice models while being a very close approximation to IID multinomial probit. This stems from the fact that the extreme value (Weibull) distribution is essentially similar but slightly skewed compared to the normal distribution with the same mean and variance.

The logit model as it is known today was proposed by Luce (1959) as a rule of psychological choice behavior to explain the dispersion of an individual's repeated choices under seemingly identical conditions. Luce's model did not rely on a utility-maximizing basis. More recently, McFadden (1973, 1978) examined this model's application within the premises of random utility theory in order to study the dispersion of economic choices within a population.

3.5.   Major Properties of the MNL Model

As with other choice models, multinomial logit choice functions are estimated using econometric techniques. The purpose of these econometric procedures is to find λ^h and the coefficients of the strict utility function $U^h(\cdot)$. One obvious property of MNL models is that the parameter λ^h [which is inversely related to the standard deviation σ^h of the distributions of random utility for each alternative, by $\lambda^h = (\pi/\sqrt{6})/\sigma^h$] is simply a scale factor to systematic utility. Thus λ^h can be absorbed into the definition of strict utility $U^h(\cdot)$ and will hereafter be removed from Eq. (2.44). Suppressing λ^h in this manner is entirely inconsequential when the strict utility function is linear in its attributes (or known transformations of its attributes). In such a case, the MNL model in (2.44) becomes

$$P_{jk}^h = \exp(\lambda^h \sum_{n=1}^{N} \bar{\alpha}_n^h X_{jkn})/ \sum_{l=1}^{J} \sum_{m=1}^{S_l} \exp(\lambda^h \sum_{n=1}^{N} \bar{\alpha}_n^h X_{lmn}) \qquad (2.45)$$

and is identical to dropping λ^h from (2.44) and defining the linear utility coefficients as $\alpha_n^h \equiv \lambda^h \bar{\alpha}_n^h$. In estimating (2.45), λ^h is clearly unidentified, and obtaining estimates of $\bar{\alpha}_n^h$ yields no information on the standard deviation σ^h of the random terms. If, on the other hand, strict utility is specified as appropriately nonlinear, the utility coefficients λ^h and the coefficients of strict utility can be separately estimated. Hereafter we follow the practice of suppressing λ^h.

Another important property of the MNL model is that the relative odds for the choice of any two alternatives are independent of the attributes or even the availability (existence) of any other alternative. This follows directly from the form of the model and is expressed as

$$P_{jk}^h/P_{lm}^h = \exp[U^h(X_{jk}) - U^h(X_{lm})] \qquad \text{for any two } (j, k) \text{ and } (l, m). \quad (2.46)$$

This property, termed *independence from irrelevant alternatives* (IIA), is useful in simplifying the econometric estimation of the MNL model as discussed by McFadden (1977). This property is a direct consequence of the assumption of independently distributed random terms and is not a reasonable assumption when correlations among the random utility components are known to exist. If the MNL model is the true model governing choice behavior, the IIA property is valid and becomes particularly useful in econometric estimation as we will discuss in Section 4 of this chapter, where this property is more fully explored.

A third property of MNL models is that socioeconomic characteristics of the population can be included in the utility function but not in a linear additive way. Since these have common values for each alternative (j, k), they would cancel from the choice function and would have no effect on the choice probabilities. Thus the specification of a utility function such as (2.6), where the W_{ih} enter linearly, is ruled out in an MNL context.

3.6. Additively Separable Strict Utility and Sequential Choice Versions of the MNL Model

It is often possible and useful to express the strict utility function $U^h(\cdot)$ in the additively separable form

$$U^h(\cdot) = {}_1U^h(X_j) + {}_2U^h(X_{jk}), \tag{2.47}$$

where X_j is a vector of attributes that vary by submarket only and X_{jk} is a second vector of attributes that vary by both submarket j and dwelling k. For example, X_j may include accessibility, air quality, quality and proximity of public facilities, dwelling type, and other such attributes that are uniform within a submarket, whereas X_{jk} may include exact location, dwelling price, dwelling characteristics, etc. To abbreviate notation, let $\overline{V}_{jk}^h \equiv U^h(\cdot)$ and $V_j^h \equiv {}_1U^h(X_j)$, $V_{jk}^h \equiv {}_2U^h(X_{jk})$. We can now verify by substituting (2.47) into (2.44) with $\lambda^h = 1$ that the choice of dwelling, given the choice of submarket, can be expressed as a conditional probability, whereas the choice of submarket is a marginal probability. These are given as

$$P_{k|j}^h = e^{\overline{V}_{jk}^h} / \sum_{m=1}^{S_j} e^{\overline{V}_{jm}^h} = e^{V_{jk}^h} / \sum_{m=1}^{S_j} e^{V_{jm}^h}, \tag{2.48}$$

which is the conditional probability of choosing dwelling k given that submarket i is chosen and

$$P_j^h = \sum_{k=1}^{S_j} e^{V_{jk}^h} / \sum_{l=1}^{J} \sum_{m=1}^{S_l} e^{\overline{V}_{lm}^h} \tag{2.49}$$

$$= e^{V_j^h} \left(\sum_{k=1}^{S_j} e^{\overline{V}_{jk}^h} \right) / \sum_{l=1}^{J} e^{V_l^h} \left(\sum_{m=1}^{S_l} e^{V_{lm}^h} \right). \tag{2.50}$$

By defining an *inclusive value*,

$$I_j^h \equiv \log\left(\sum_{k=1}^{S_j} e^{V_{jk}^h} \right), \tag{2.51}$$

we can rewrite (2.48) and (2.50) in a condensed way as

$$P_{k|j}^h = \exp(V_{jk}^h) / \exp(I_j^h), \tag{2.52}$$

$$P_j^h = \exp(V_j^h + I_j^h) / \sum_{l=1}^{J} \exp(V_l^h + I_l^h), \tag{2.53}$$

with the joint choice probability given by

$$P_{jk}^h = P_j^h P_{k\,|\,j}^h. \tag{2.54}$$

The sequential formulation allows us to think of the household's choice process as if it is a hierarchical one based on the concept of the utility tree (Strotz, 1957): first a submarket is chosen, and this is done on the basis of the strict utility for that submarket and a measure of the submarket's dwelling content (the inclusive value), and next a dwelling is chosen, given the choice of submarket.

A special case of the above MNL model (2.51)–(2.53) arises when all dwellings within the same submarket are identical in the attributes of the strict utility function, but independent in the unobserved attributes as assumed above. This implies that $V_{jk}^h = V_{jl}^h$ for any k and $l \in j$. Thus the dwelling specific part of utility could be absorbed into V_j^h, allowing us to set $V_{jk}^h = 0$ for all $k \in j$. This reduces the inclusive value (2.51) to $I_j^h = \log S_j$, and the submarket choice probability (2.52) becomes

$$P_j^h = S_j e^{V_j^h} / \sum_{l=1}^{J} S_l e^{V_l^h}. \tag{2.55}$$

The conditional probability of dwelling choice for this special case is

$$P_{k\,|\,j}^h = 1/S_j. \tag{2.56}$$

3.7. Nested Logit and the Generalized Extreme Value (GEV) Models

McFadden (1978) has suggested an empirical generalization of the MNL model (2.51)-(2.53) by allowing the inclusive value I_j^h to have a coefficient other than one. Thus, Eq. (2.53) can be replaced by

$$P_j^h = \exp[V_j^h + (1 - \delta^h)I_j^h] / \sum_{l=1}^{J} \exp[V_l^h + (1 - \delta^h)I_l^h], \tag{2.57}$$

where $(1 - \delta^h)$ is a coefficient to be estimated econometrically ($0 \leqq \delta^h < 1$) together with the coefficients of the strict utility functions V_j^h and V_{jk}^h. Equation (2.57) together with (2.51) and (2.52) is called the *nested multinomial logit* model. If we estimate $\delta^h = 0$, then the nested model reduces to the joint choice model represented by (2.51)–(2.53). Finding $\delta^h = 0$ confirms that dwellings within the same submarket are viewed as distinct alternatives with uncorrelated (independent) unobserved attributes. At the other extreme, when $\delta^h = 1$, (2.57) reduces to

$$P_j^h = e^{V_j^h} / \sum_{l=1}^{J} e^{V_l^h}, \tag{2.58}$$

which implies that submarkets are viewed as distinct alternatives regardless of their size and the distribution of the utility of dwellings within the submarkets. This will follow from utility maximization when the dwelling specific random utility obtains precisely the same value for each dwelling within the same submarket (i.e., it is not random within the submarket). If this is the case and dwellings within the same submarket are also identical in observed dwelling attributes ($V_{jk}^h = V_{jl}^h$ for any $k, l \in j$), the choice problem reduces simply to one of choice among entirely homogeneous submarkets, and the choice model is given by (2.58). If, on the other hand, dwellings within the same submarket are identical in the random utility terms but not identical in strict utility, the choice model (2.58) should be rewritten with $V_j^h = \max_k \{V_{jk}^h, k = 1, \ldots, S_j\}$ for each j since all households will only choose among the best dwellings in each zone. Should ties exist (i.e., $V_{jk}^h = V_{jm}^h$ for any k and $m \in j$), the probability of dwelling choice given the submarket is restricted to the number of tied dwellings and is equal to one divided by the number of such ties within that submarket.

While the estimation of nested logit models has been explored by Domencich and McFadden (1975) and Ben-Akiva (1973), a theoretical derivation of such nested logit models developed by McFadden (1978) shows that these models are a special case of the *generalized extreme value* (GEV) model.

To derive the GEV model, McFadden assumed that the random terms are jointly distributed according to the *multivariate extreme value* distribution given by

$$\bar{F}(\bar{\epsilon}^h) = \exp\left[-G(e^{-\epsilon_{11}^h}, \ldots, e^{-\epsilon_{1S_1}^h}, \ldots, e^{-\epsilon_{j1}^h}, \ldots, e^{-\epsilon_{jS_j}^h})\right], \quad (2.59)$$

where $G(y_1, \ldots, y_N)$ is a nonnegative, homogeneous-of-degree-one function of $(y_1, \ldots, y_N) \geq 0$ and satisfies $\lim_{y_i \to +\infty} G(y_1, \ldots, y_N) = +\infty$ for $i = 1, \ldots, N$. Suppose for any distinct $(i_1, \ldots, i_k)$ from $\{1, \ldots, N\}$, $\partial^k G/\partial y_{i_1}, \ldots, \partial y_{i_k}$ is nonnegative if k is even and nonpositive if k is odd. Then, according to McFadden, the model that is consistent with utility maximization under the distributional assumption (2.59) is

$$P_{jk}^h = e^{U^h(X_{jk})} G_{jk}[e^{U^h(X_{lm})}, \text{all } (l, m)]/G[e^{U^h(X_{lm})}, \text{all } (l, m)], \quad (2.60)$$

where $G_{jk}(\cdot)$ denotes the derivative of G with respect to its (j, k) argument. A particular $G(\cdot)$ function suggested by McFadden (1978) is

$$G^h(\cdot) = \sum_{j=1}^{J} a_j^h \left[\sum_{k=1}^{S_j} \exp \frac{U^h(X_{jk})}{1 - \delta_j^h}\right]^{1 - \delta_j^h}, \quad (2.61)$$

with $a_j^h > 0$ and $0 \leq \delta_j^h < 1$ for each j. The MNL model is obtained in the special case when all $a_j^h = 1$ and all $\delta_j^h = 0$. This reduces (2.61) to

$$G^h(\cdot) = \sum_{j=1}^{J} \sum_{k=1}^{S_j} \exp[U^h(X_{jk})]. \quad (2.62)$$

The coefficient δ_j^h is an index of the similarity (correlation) of the random utility of the dwellings belonging to submarket j for population segment h. As in the nested logit model, when $\delta_j^h = 0$ the dwellings within submarket j are uncorrelated in their unobserved attributes. At the other extreme, when δ_j^h is approximately one, dwellings within submarket j are identical in unobserved attributes.

The GEV model (2.61) collapses to the nested logit model (2.57) when we impose $\delta_1^h = \delta_2^h = \cdots = \delta_j^h = \delta^h$ and we set all $a_j^h = 1$. Clearly other econometric parametrizations of the GEV model are possible. It could be assumed, for example, that groups of "similar" submarkets have the same a_j^h and δ_j^h. This strategy reduces the number of coefficients to be estimated when the number of submarkets is large.

4. ESTIMATION OF PROBABILISTIC CHOICE MODELS

We now consider the state-of-the-art knowledge in the estimation of probabilistic choice models and the relevance of this knowledge to the estimation of housing choice models.

4.1. General Strategies

In principle, the theoretically most appealing approach for estimating probabilistic choice models is through observation of the repeated choices of the same household, assuming that the preferences of the household have not changed over the period of observation. If this assumption is valid, the parameters of the strict utility function can be estimated, yielding the utility function for each household. The random utility terms can be interpreted as stochastic variations in the household's preferences due to unobserved internal decisions or unobserved elements in the household's environment of attributes. By repeating this estimation procedure for a large number of households, one can begin to quantify the variation in the parameters of the strict utility function over the population. Clearly, this approach, while extremely appealing, is extremely cumbersome. Repeated observations of the same household are both costly and—in the context of housing choice—unworkable in terms of the time that normally elapses between consecutive choices. This means that important and systematic changes in a household's socioeconomic status, information, and even preferences may occur during the time that elapses between two consecutive choices, invalidating the assumption of a stable strict utility function. Thus if data were to be used in this longitudinal manner, the statistical results would not necessarily reflect a strict utility function that correctly represents a household's preferences at any given point in time. Furthermore, in the context of housing choice, the cost of obtaining sufficient data would be prohibitive.

An empirically tractable approach to estimation is based on the use of cross-sectional data: the analyst observes the choices of households in a population at roughly the same point in time and determines the parameters of the strict utility function from the dispersion of these choices. As we have discussed, the dispersion reflects the confounded effect of both deterministic and stochastic variations in the unobserved part of the utility function. This estimation technique is unable to distinguish between interhousehold and intrahousehold variations in tastes.

4.2. Choice Sets

Up to this point, we assumed that all dwellings enter the choice set of each household. This is an assumption of convenience that can be relaxed to allow for the possibility that choice sets vary over the population. By relaxing this assumption, we recognize that a household's behavior is subject to many external constraints that act to exclude certain choice alternatives from that household's consideration. These constraints include the availability of information, knowledge of an alternative's existence, and unobserved cost, time, or social constraints restricting or prohibiting the consideration of certain alternatives. One way to reconcile the nonuniformity of choice sets over the population is by defining the utility function in such a way that certain choice alternatives yield a utility level of minus infinity when their attributes interact with certain attributes of the choice-making household. This approach is extremely intractable in practice because it requires complex utility function specifications and a large number of interactive variables in the utility function. A second approach to dealing with the choice set problem resembles the above, but is more general because it proposes to take into account choice set formation as a utility-maximizing process explicitly. In this process, households can be modeled to first decide whether the alternatives in a superchoice set should be included in a smaller choice set among which a utility-maximizing selection will be made. At the first stage, the household must balance the costs of obtaining information about an alternative, the existence of which is known, with the uncertain expectation that the alternative will ultimately be the most preferred. This approach is also intractable and only partially satisfactory for contexts involving many alternatives. A third approach is to group households into population segments on the basis of choice set variations. If this can be done, each household in segment h will have the same choice set, and the problem of choice set variations will not exist within each segment. This approach is somewhat intractable, particularly because of the potential difficulties in identifying population segments without any choice set variation and because of the difficulties of observing choice set variations.

The existence of household specific choice sets raises several difficult issues in econometric estimation. Often, these are resolved by assumption. For example, in Quigley's estimation (1976) the Pittsburgh rental housing market is divided into 18 housing types (nonspatial submarkets), and it is assumed that each household in the observed sample has all 18 submarkets in the choice set. Quigley assumes a hierarchial choice process. Each household first chooses that spatial zone which contains the dwellings of a submarket and is closest to the household's workplace in terms of a generalized transportation cost measure. Thus 18 distinct spatial zones each representing a submarket are selected in a deterministic manner and entered into the choice set of each household. In Lerman's study (1977) of Washington, D.C., choice sets are constructed using information on a household's income, availability of driving license, and automobile ownership. In another study, Anas (1975) assumes that all 30 subzones of the San Francisco region enter all choice sets.

4.3. Attribute Variation and Predicted Choice Probabilities

In observing the choices of a population of households, it may be necessary to take into account both household characteristics and choice set variations. Because of this, predicted choice probabilities can be expressed as

$$P^{hi}_{jk \in A_i} = F^{hi}_{jk} \big[U^h(W_{hi}, X_{lm}, \alpha_h), \text{all } (l, m) \in A_i \big], \tag{2.63}$$

where F^{hi}_{jk} is the conditional choice probability function that alternative (j, k) will be selected by household i of population segment h, given that (j, k) is in the choice set A_i of household i and given the strict utility function $U^h(\cdot)$, the household attributes W_{hi}, the estimated vector of utility parameters α_h, and the variance–covariance structure of random utility. The predicted probability that household i $(i \in h)$ will choose (j, k) can now be expressed as

$$P^{hi}_{jk} = \big\{ P^{hi} \big[(j, k) \in A_i \big] \big\} F^{hi}_{jk}. \tag{2.64}$$

The first term, $P^{hi}[\cdot]$, is the probability that alternative (j, k) is included in the choice set of household i, and the second term, F^{hi}_{jk}, is (2.63), the conditional probability that (j, k) is selected. Mathematical construction of specific models $P^{hi}(\cdot)$ has not been attempted, but presumably the underlying decision-making process is one of utility maximization, whereby the household trades off the costs of obtaining information about alternatives against the a priori prospects that the most preferred (best) alternatives will be included in the choice set. The MNL choice probability given in (2.44) may be modified to include only the alternatives that are elements of the choice set.

For example, it can be rewritten as

$$P^{hi}_{jk\in A_i} = \exp[\lambda^h U^h(X_{jk}, W_{hi})] / \sum_{(l,m)\in A_i} \exp[\lambda^h U^h(X_{lm}, W_{hi})]. \quad (2.65)$$

If the strict utility function does not depend on household attributes and the choice set does not vary over the population of segment h, (2.65) becomes

$$P^h_{jk\in A^h} = \exp[\lambda^h U^h(X_{jk})] / \sum_{(l,m)\in A^h} \exp[\lambda^h U^h(X_{lm})], \quad (2.66)$$

where A^h is the choice set of segment h households.

4.4. Maximum Likelihood Estimation

Two workable approaches can be used to obtain econometric estimates of the utility parameters of probabilistic choice models. One approach is to use disaggregate data by observing the choices and choice sets of a sample of households and using these as observations in the statistical analysis. Another approach, often dictated by the unavailability of disaggregate data, is to use aggregations of choices by observing the proportion of households in a market segment choosing various submarkets. Maximum likelihood is the established method of estimation for both approaches.

If the choices and choice sets of a sample of households of segment h are known, one maximizes the likelihood function for each population segment h,

$$\mathscr{L}(\beta_h) = \prod_{i=1}^{N^s_h} \prod_{(l,m)\in A_i} [P^{hi}_{lm\in A_i}(\beta_h)]^{\delta^i_{lm}}, \quad (2.67)$$

where β_h is the vector of all parameters such as strict utility coefficients, variance–covariance terms, and inclusive value coefficients to be estimated, and $\delta^i_{lm} = 0$ if (l, m) is not the alternative selected by household i, and $\delta^i_{lm} = 1$ if (l, m) is the alternative selected by household i. Finally, N^s_h is the number of households (cases) in the randomly drawn observation sample.

If the analyst must work with aggregate data and only the proportion of households of each segment choosing each submarket is known, then the likelihood function becomes

$$\mathscr{L}(\beta_h) = \frac{N_h!}{n^h_1! n^h_2! \cdots n^h_{J_h}!} \prod_{j=1}^{J_h} [P^h_j(\beta_h)]^{n^h_j}, \quad (2.68)$$

where n^h_j is the number of households of segment h observed to choose submarket j and P^h_j is the probability (expected proportion) of households choosing alternative j, assuming that all alternatives enter the choice sets of all households. In this case, there are J_h alternatives and N_h households. If the choice set varies among the N_h households, there is no reason why the likelihood function (2.67) cannot be used. The chief advantage of aggregate estimation via (2.68) becomes apparent when the attributes of alternatives (submarkets) are observed as submarket averages, but the distribution of dwelling attributes within the submarket and the attributes of the exact choice (dwelling) remain unknown to the analyst. In such cases, it is well known that estimated coefficients will be substantially biased, reflecting aggregation error. The larger are the submarket sizes, the larger is the uncertainty about the exact dwelling choice and the larger is the aggregation bias in the estimated parameters. McFadden and Reid (1974) outlined complex statistical procedures whereby the true utility coefficients can be recovered by adjusting the parameters found from aggregate estimation. These procedures depend on knowledge of the variance–covariance structure of the attributes of the strict utility function, and they are cumbersome computationally.

A major advantage of multinomial logit models is that statistically consistent estimates of the coefficients of the utility function can be obtained without observing the full choice set but by observing a random sample of alternatives from the full choice set. Approximately consistent estimates can be obtained by observing any random subset of the full choice set. Thus, suppose that the full choice set for segment h is denoted as A_h and that it does not vary over the households in that segment (this assumption is inessential and can be easily generalized). If the true choice probabilities satisfy the independence from irrelevant alternatives (IIA) property, then

$$j \in D \subseteq A_h \Rightarrow P(j|A_h, \beta^h) = P(j|D, \beta^h) \sum_{k \in D} P(k|A_h), \qquad (2.69)$$

which is a feature of the MNL model. In (2.69), D is a subset of the full choice set A_h to be used in estimating the MNL choice model $P(j|D, \beta^h)$, which is the probability that a randomly drawn household will select alternative j given the choice set D. McFadden (1977) has shown that as long as D is drawn from A_h according to a probability distribution over the number of households in the sample given by $\pi(D|j)$, where j is an observed choice for a particular household, and if (1) D is a fixed subset of A_h independent of the observed choice j, (2) D is a random subset of A_h independent of the observed choice, or (3) D consists of the observed choice and one or more alternatives selected randomly, then consistent estimates of β_h can be obtained by maximization of the likelihood functions discussed above. Furthermore, if the choice set D does not conform to one of the three cases above, then consistent estimates can be obtained by maximizing a weighted likelihood function or by maximizing the unweighted likelihood function but introducing a full set of alternative-specific zero–one dummy variables into the utility function. In this case, consistent estimates of all coefficients except the alternative specific dummies are obtained.

The above-mentioned properties for sampling the choice set make the estimation of MNL models extremely tractable and set these apart from other probabilistic choice models. It should be clear, however, that at least in theory, serious estimation errors may occur if the observer includes in the choice set alternatives that in reality are known not to be in the choice set. This problem of choice set specification is not, of course, limited to MNL models but extends itself to any discrete choice analysis.

5. AGGREGATE DEMAND

The aggregate demand for a dwelling or submarket is obtained by summing each household's choice probability for that dwelling or submarket. If the choice model is interpreted as a choice frequency model (see Section 3.1), the underlying assumption is that each household's utility function is deterministic and that the choice frequency function measures the proportion of a large number of households in a particular segment choosing a particular alternative. In this case, aggregate demand is treated as deterministic and, given a large number of households relative to the number of alternatives (submarkets), the demand for each submarket can be computed precisely. If, on the other hand, the choice model is interpreted to predict the probability with which a specific household will choose an alternative, the utility function is treated as stochastic (see Section 3.2), and aggregate demand for a dwelling or submarket is also treated as stochastic. These two interpretations of aggregate demand and the attendant aggregation procedures will now be discussed.

5.1. Deterministic Demand

Let the household population consist of $h = 1, \ldots, H$ segments with N_h households in segment h. Suppose that the urban area is divided into $j = 1, \ldots, J$ submarkets and that the size of each segment, N_h, is large relative to the number of submarkets J. If P_j^h denotes the deterministic proportion of type h households that will prefer submarket j, the number of type h households choosing submarket j (demand) can be expressed as

$$D_j^h = N_h P_j^h \tag{2.70}$$

or, more precisely, by rounding D_j^h to the nearest integer, a small error if N_h is large relative to J. The total demand summed over all segments is

$$D_j = \sum_{h=1}^{H} N_h P_j^h. \tag{2.71}$$

Note that if N_h is not large relative to J, the above formulations are not accurate measures of actual demand. In such cases, if the P_j^h are interpreted as deterministic proportions, these would be accurate proportions only if the population N_h were to be copied n times (n arbitrarily large and integer) to yield nN_h large relative to J; then total demand would be given by

$$\bar{D}_j = n \sum_{h=1}^{H} N_h P_j^h, \tag{2.72}$$

where $\bar{D}_j$ is the exact (to the nearest integer) number of households choosing j in the expanded population $nN_1, nN_2, \ldots, nN_H$.

It will be recalled that submarket choice frequencies are functions of the strict utilities of various alternatives. Thus

$$P_j^h = F_j^h(V_l^h, l = 1, \ldots, J), \tag{2.73}$$

where

$$V_l^h = U^h(X_{ln}, n = 1, \ldots, N), \tag{2.74}$$

and X_{ln} is the value of the nth attribute for submarket l. Suppose that attribute $X_{l1} \equiv R_l$ is the rent of dwellings in submarket l; then (2.73) can be written as

$$V_l^h = U^h(R_l, X_{l2}, \ldots, X_{lN}). \tag{2.75}$$

It is assumed that

$$\partial U^h / \partial R_l < 0. \tag{2.76}$$

In examining the structure of a traditional demand function, we must keep all attributes except rents constant. Thus (2.73) may be rewritten as

$$P_j^h = F_j^h(R_1, R_2, \ldots, R_J), \qquad j = 1, \ldots, J, \tag{2.77}$$

where all other attributes have been suppressed. From (2.73) and (2.76) it can be shown for any reasonable specific choice model of form (2.77) that

$$\partial D_j^h / \partial R_j = (\partial F_j^h / \partial V_j^h)(\partial U^h / \partial R_j) \leqq 0 \qquad \text{for each } j \tag{2.78}$$

and

$$\partial D_j^h / \partial R_i = (\partial F_j^h / \partial V_i^h)(\partial U^h / \partial R_i) \geqq 0 \qquad \text{for } i \neq j. \tag{2.79}$$

Taken together, these conditions simply state that alternatives $j = 1, \ldots, J$ are *gross substitutes*: the demand functions have the usual downward sloping form.

The aggregate demand function (2.71) can also be written as

$$D_j(R_1, R_2, \ldots, R_J) = \sum_{h=1}^{H} N_h F_j^h(R_1, R_2, \ldots, R_J), \tag{2.80}$$

which has the properties

$$\frac{\partial D_j}{\partial R_j} = \sum_{h=1}^{H} N_h \frac{\partial F_j^h}{\partial R_j} \leq 0 \tag{2.81}$$

and

$$\frac{\partial D_j}{\partial R_i} = \sum_{h=1}^{H} N_h \frac{\partial F_j^h}{\partial R_i} \geq 0 \qquad \text{for} \quad i \neq j. \tag{2.82}$$

These follow from (2.78) and (2.79). Again the demand functions are downward sloping, and considering the entire population, submarkets are *gross substitutes*.

If we now impose the additional conditions that for each h,

$$\partial F_j^h / \partial R_j = 0 \qquad \text{only for} \quad R_j \geq R_{j \ \text{max}} \tag{2.83}$$

and

$$\partial F_j^h / \partial R_i = 0 \qquad \text{only for} \quad R_i \geq R_{i \ \text{max}}, \tag{2.84}$$

then (2.81) and (2.82) imply that given a range $0 \leq R_j \leq R_{j \ \text{max}}$ for each j, alternative submarkets are *strict gross substitutes* in the allowable rent ranges.

5.2. Stochastic Demand

Let the choice model be given as P_j^h, which is the probability that any household that is a member of segment h will select submarket j. In this case, let x_j^h denote the number of type h households choosing j. Then the expected number of households choosing j is

$$E(x_j^h) = \sum_{n=0}^{N_h} n \, \text{Prob}(x_j^h = n), \tag{2.85}$$

where $\text{Prob}(x_j^h = n)$ is the probability that the number of type h households choosing submarket j equals n. Since each household's utility maximizing choice is viewed as an independent action (independent of the choices of others), the actual demand for submarket j must be generated from a binomial process: each household of segment h will select j with a probability P_j^h. Thus the probability that n out of N_h households will select j is

$$\text{Prob}(x_j^h = n) = \frac{N_h!}{n!(N_h - n)!}(1 - P_j^h)^{N_h - n}(P_j^h)^n. \tag{2.86}$$

The mean of the binomial distribution is the probability P_j^h times the number of observations (households N_h). Thus letting $E[\cdot]$ denote the expected value operator,

$$E(x_j^h) = N_h P_j^h \equiv D_j^h, \tag{2.87}$$

and since

$$E(\sum_{h=1}^{H} x_j^h) = \sum_{h=1}^{H} [E(x_j^h)], \tag{2.88}$$

we obtain

$$E(\sum_{h=1}^{H} x_j^h) = \sum_{h=1}^{H} N_h P_j^h \equiv D_j. \tag{2.89}$$

The variance of the binomial distribution implies

$$\text{Var}(x_j^h) = N_h P_j^h(1 - P_j^h), \tag{2.90}$$

and since each x_j^h, $h = 1, \ldots, H$, is an independently distributed random variable, we can state that

$$\text{Var}(\sum_{h=1}^{H} x_j^h) = \sum_{h=1}^{H} N_h P_j^h(1 - P_j^h). \tag{2.91}$$

It also follows from the binomial distribution that

$$E(x_j^h/N_h) = P_j^h \tag{2.92}$$

and

$$\text{Var}(x_j^h/N_h) = P_j^h(1 - P_j^h)/N_h, \tag{2.93}$$

where x_j^h/N_h is the proportion of type h households choosing submarket j. We note from (2.92) and (2.93) that as N_h becomes large, the variance of the proportion goes to zero, and that the choice probability P_j^h predicted by the model is the expected (mean) frequency. From (2.87) and (2.89), the demand predicted by the deterministic choice model is the expected value of the aggregate stochastic demand. From this reasoning and from (2.93), we conclude that if the number of households of each type is large, the deterministic demand functions (2.71) and (2.80) are not only unbiased but also accurate measures of the expected demand obtained according to the stochastic procedure. It follows that *the expectation of demand given by (2.87) and (2.89) satisfies the gross substitutability properties embodied in (2.78), (2.79) and (2.81), (2.82).* Actual demand x_j does not necessarily satisfy these conditions.

In the above, it was assumed that all households belonging to the same segment have the same choice probability structure. If the choice probabilities vary by household characteristics, each household's choice probability must be predicted separately, and the expected frequency is obtained by summing the household choice probabilities for each household and dividing by the number of households N_h, as shown in (2.21).

5.3. Properties of Aggregate Demand Based on the MNL Model

The properties of aggregate demand functions (deterministic demand or the expected value of stochastic demand) will depend on the specific form of the utility function and the specific form of the choice model. The multinomial logit models discussed in this chapter have straightforward elasticity properties, which are now considered.

Consider the following possible specifications of submarket specific strict utility:

$$V_j^h = \alpha_1^h R_j + \sum_{n=2}^N \alpha_n^h X_{jn}, \qquad\qquad \alpha_1^h < 0, \qquad (2.94)$$

$$V_j^h = \beta_1^h \log R_j + \sum_{n=2}^N \beta_n^h X_{jn}, \qquad\qquad \beta_1^h < 0, \qquad (2.95)$$

$$V_j^h = \gamma_1^h \log[\bar{R}_j^h - R_j] + \sum_{n=2}^N \gamma_n^h \log X_{jn}, \qquad \gamma_1^h > 0, \qquad (2.96)$$

where the utility coefficients are denoted as α^h, β^h, or γ^h, and the attributes consist of rent R_j and $N - 1$ other attributes X_{jn}. In (2.96), $\bar{R}_j^h$ is a maximum rent for households of segment h in submarket j. Note that

$$\lim_{R_j \to \bar{R}_j^h} V_j^h = -\infty. \qquad (2.97)$$

The MNL model $[(2.55), (2.57), \text{ or } (2.58)]$ of submarket choice (or, more generally, with J alternatives) has the properties

$$\partial P_j^h / \partial V_j^h = P_j^h(1 - P_j^h) > 0 \qquad (2.98)$$

and

$$\partial P_j^h / \partial V_i^h = -P_j^h P_i^h < 0 \qquad \text{for} \quad i \neq j, \qquad (2.99)$$

which are specific forms of (2.24). We also note that for any attribute X_{jn}, we can state

$$\partial P_j^h / \partial X_{jn} = P_j^h(1 - P_j^h) \partial V_j^h / \partial X_{jn}, \qquad n = 1, \ldots, N \qquad (2.100)$$

and

$$\partial P_j^h / \partial X_{in} = -P_j^h P_i^h \partial V_i^h / \partial X_{in}, \qquad n = 1, \ldots, N. \qquad (2.101)$$

Evaluating (2.100) for (2.94)–(2.96), we find

$$\partial P_j^h / \partial X_{jn} = \alpha_n^h P_j^h(1 - P_j^h) \qquad\qquad \text{for (2.94)}, \ n = 1, \ldots, N \qquad (2.102)$$

$$= (\beta_n^h / X_{jn}) P_j^h(1 - P_j^h) \qquad\qquad \text{for (2.95)}, \ n = 1, \ldots, N \qquad (2.103)$$

$$= -[\gamma_1^h / (\bar{R}_j^h - R_j)] P_j^h(1 - P_j^h) \qquad \text{for (2.96)}, \ n = 1, \qquad (2.104)$$

and as in (2.103) for $n = 2, \ldots, N$.

Similarly, for $i \neq j$,

$$\partial P_j^h / \partial X_{in} = -\alpha_n^h P_j^h P_i^h \qquad \text{for (2.94)}, \quad n = 1, \ldots, N \quad (2.105)$$

$$= -(\beta_n^h / X_{in}) P_j^h P_i^h \qquad \text{for (2.95)}, \quad n = 1, \ldots, N \quad (2.106)$$

$$= -[\gamma_1^h / (\bar{R}_i^h - R_i)] P_j^h P_i^h \qquad \text{for (2.96)}, \quad n = 1, \qquad (2.107)$$

and as in (2.106) for $n = 2, \ldots, N$.

The own and cross elasticities (ϵ_o and ϵ_c) of the choice frequency P_j^h with respect to an attribute X can now be derived by recalling that

$$\epsilon_o \equiv (\partial P_j^h / \partial X_{jn}) / (P_j^h / X_{jn}) \qquad \text{for} \quad n = 1, \ldots, N \quad (2.108)$$

and

$$\epsilon_c \equiv (\partial P_j^h / \partial X_{in}) / (P_j^h / X_{in}) \qquad \text{for} \quad n = 1, \ldots, N. \quad (2.109)$$

Evaluating (2.108) and (2.109) for (2.94)–(2.96), we find

$$\epsilon_o = \alpha_n^h X_{jn} (1 - P_j^h) \qquad \text{for (2.94)}, \quad n = 1, \ldots, N \quad (2.110)$$

$$= -\beta_n^h (1 - P_j^h) \qquad \text{for (2.95)}, \quad n = 1, \ldots, N \quad (2.111)$$

$$= -[\gamma_1^h / (\bar{R}_j^h - R_j)] R_j (1 - P_j^h) \qquad \text{for (2.96)}, \quad n = 1, \qquad (2.112)$$

and as in (2.111) for $n = 2, \ldots, N$.

$$\epsilon_c = -\alpha_n^h X_{in} P_i^h \qquad \text{for (2.94)}, \quad n = 1, \ldots, N \quad (2.113)$$

$$= -\beta_n^h P_i^h \qquad \text{for (2.95)}, \quad n = 1, \ldots, N \quad (2.114)$$

$$= -[\gamma_1^h / (\bar{R}_i^h - R_i)] R_i P_i^h, \qquad n = 1, \qquad (2.115)$$

and as in (2.114) for $n = 2, \ldots, N$.

6. SUMMARY

This chapter elaborated the theory of utility maximizing discrete choice behavior in the context of the demand for rental housing. The probabilistic discrete choice approach provides an alternative to the bid rent approach reviewed in Chapter 1. Bid rent models do not explain the dispersion of choices within the members of a market segment in a theoretically satisfactory manner. In the bid rent approach, the dispersion of choices among the members of a market segment can be described only by subdividing that population into additional subsegments and then estimating separate bid rent functions for each subsegment. This procedure is both costly and potentially inaccurate. The major source of inaccuracy arises from the fact that no matter how extensive the detail of segmentation, substantial heterogeneity in preferences within a segment still exists. Given the usual segmentation criteria available from common data sources or even from extensive survey information, it may not be possible to define population segments with negligible intrasegment heterogeneity. Theoretical and empirical shortcomings of the bid rent approach were discussed in more detail in Chapter 1 and are summarized in Section 1.5.

The probabilistic discrete choice approach resolves difficulties associated with the bid rent approach by explicitly modeling the dispersion of preferences and choices within population segments. Such dispersion can be attributed to various sources of uncertainty. Some of this uncertainty is econometric in nature and reflects the observer's inability to identify all sources of variation in preferences. Another part of the uncertainty is due to inherent instabilities in household behavior. These two sources of uncertainty cannot be separated via common econometric techniques and associated statistical experiments. The end result is that the choices of households can only be predicted up to a probability distribution that explicitly incorporates the dispersion of choices. In accordance with this view, we have shown in this chapter that expected demand can be measured through a discrete choice approach and that the variance of expected submarket choice frequencies approaches zero, as each population segment contains a large number of households relative to the number of housing submarkets that serve as choice alternatives.

In addition to reviewing the general reasoning behind random utility theory, this chapter briefly summarized the major developments related to the specification, estimation, and aggregation of multinomial logit and associated probabilistic choice models applicable in the housing market residential choice contexts.

CHAPTER 3

WALRASIAN EQUILIBRIUM ANALYSIS

In this chapter we examine equilibrium rent determination in a system of interdependent dwellings and housing submarkets, the demand for which is characterized as a probabilistic discrete choice process. Two kinds of markets are distinguished and discussed. The first kind is an *open* market. In an open market, it is assumed that each household either succeeds in occupying its most preferred (utility-maximizing) dwelling or else it exists the market. The second kind of market is a *closed* market. In a closed market, households cannot exit, and thus if they cannot occupy their most preferred dwelling, they remain in the market, selecting again from the remaining unoccupied dwellings untill they eventually succeed in occupying some dwelling. Funda-mental results of uniqueness and stability are demonstrated for the general case, and the special case of logistic demand structures is fully examined. First, the properties of equilibrium are examined for a multisubmarket housing market with a single segment of households competing for housing. Special cases of this general problem are analyzed fully for several formula-tions of the strict utility function, allowing for simultaneous as well as sequen-tial representations of the choice probabilities and the structure of demand. Results are obtained for the differential mean submarket rent structure at equilibrium, but also for the distribution of rents within submarkets at equilibrium. The analysis is then repeated for the more complex case of several household segments, each with a distinct strict utility function.

All analysis in this chapter is for the case of fixed submarket sizes and dwelling attributes in the short run under the assumption that the total number of households equals the total number of dwellings and that the housing market is in an expectational steady state with a frequent turnover of renters assured by free and rapid mobility. The equilibrium conditions derived under these assumptions are those of a short run temporary Walrasian equilibrium. An exogenous disturbance in such an equilibrium can arise from changes in the supply and attributes of housing or from changes in the socioeconomic characteristics and composition of households. Given any exogenous disturbance, the housing market will rapidly converge on a new temporary equilibrium as long as the above-mentioned assumptions about mobility and the assumption that renters have static myopic expectations are valid. It is a purpose of this chapter to show that the equilibrium rent structure under these assumptions is readily computable for single-segment markets regardless of the complexity and detail in dwelling attributes and submarket definitions. Similar computations are shown to be more difficult for the case of multisegmented markets with a high level of complexity in dwelling attributes and submarket definitions, and to require iterative numerical solution techniques. Regardless of computability, however, standard theorems on the uniqueness and stability of multimarket Walrasian systems are applicable and are used to demonstrate the uniqueness and stability of equilibrium rent determination. In Section 7 of this chapter, deterministic utility-maximizing models such as those of Chapter 1 are shown to be special limiting cases of multinomial logit models based on stochastic utility maximization.

The concepts of open and closed markets are defined in Section 1. Section 2 provides definitions of stochastic Walrasian equilibria and contrasts these with the traditional definitions for deterministic equilibria. Properties of Walrasian equilibria for open and closed markets are examined in Sections 3–6. Section 7 demonstrates that traditional deterministic equilibrium analyses can be viewed as special cases of the stochastic equilibrium analyses of this chapter. Finally, Section 8 is a brief digression into the probability of market clearing at stochastic equilibrium.

1. OPEN AND CLOSED MARKET CLEARING

1.1. Equilibrium Clearing of Open Markets

Definition 1. A rental housing market is an *open* market if those households which cannot achieve their utility-maximizing choice (occupy their utility-maximizing dwelling) at a certain point in time exit the market at that point in time and each household remaining in the market succeeds in occupying its utility-maximizing dwelling at that point in time.

Suppose that N_h, $h = 1, \ldots, H$, households wish to locate in the market at a certain point in time. A probabilistic utility-maximizing distribution of these households among the dwellings will generally result in a nonmarket clearing assignment. Some dwellings will be chosen by more than one household, while some others will remain vacant. Only in rare cases will each dwelling be the utility-maximizing choice of only one household. In an open housing market, those households which cannot be located in their utility maximizing dwellings will temporarily exit the market. Thus if a number of households are assigned to the same dwelling, all except one of these must exit the market. The total number exiting the market at time t is thus $\sum_{j \in G} (x_j^t - 1)$, where x_j^t is the number choosing j, and G the set of dwellings for which $x_j^t \geq 1$. This sum is also equal to the number of dwellings left vacant at time t, as long as the total number of households seeking dwellings equals the total number of dwellings.

1.2. Disequilibrium Clearing of Closed Markets

Definition 2. A rental housing market is a *closed* market if households that fail to achieve their utility maximizing dwelling choices cannot exit the market but must choose from remaining unoccupied dwellings in a succession of rounds until all households are located.

Although for open markets it is always possible to guarantee an assignment of households to dwellings such that each allocated household succeeds in maximizing utility (since those who fail to do so exit the market), in a closed market this occurs only in the rare case of an equilibrium clearing where the utility-maximizing choice of each household is a different dwelling. If such clearing comes about, then each household occupies a different utility-maximizing dwelling, and no dwelling is left unoccupied if the total number of households equals the total number of dwellings in the market under the assumptions of this chapter's Walrasian analysis, to be discussed in detail in Section 2. Our concern is to determine how a closed market is cleared when a utility-maximizing clearing does not occur for each household. The basic idea is an exceedingly simple one: since, in a closed market, households cannot exit, if they fail to locate in their first choices they will choose again among the remaining vacant dwellings. Households not located in this second round will choose again among the dwellings left vacant at the end of the second round, and so on until all households are eventually located. This is a disequilibrium market clearing process since in the final outcome not all households will be located in their utility-maximizing dwelling. A more precise description of this market clearing process follows:

(1)   Each of the N_h, $h = 1, \ldots, H$, households chooses among the M dwellings according to the choice probability structure of its segment.

(2)   We collect all except one of the households from each dwelling to which one or more households have been assigned in step 1. If a dwelling has been assigned households of several types, the type that remains there is randomly determined. The collected households are reclassified into their respective segments.

(3)   The collected households are reassigned to the vacant dwellings according to recomputed choice probabilities for each segment, under the assumption that choice sets consist of the dwellings left vacant after the first round of choices.

(4)   The process continues until all households are located.

The final outcome is an extremely complex combinatorial process laden with unpleasant computations. It can be generated numerically with relative ease, and repeated numerical generations of it can be used to sample the space of possible outcomes.

1.3.   Conclusion

The definitions of equilibrium developed in Section 2 and the analysis that follows in Sections 4 and 5 are based on the notion that household allocations are utility maximizing and demands are computed as the aggregation of utility-maximizing first round choices without any consideration of second, third, and subsequent round utility maximizing choices. Thus the analysis is for the case of open markets and applies precisely to this case, while it may apply only approximately to the case of closed markets. The reason the results do not apply exactly to the case of closed markets is because in that case, expected demand consists of the average of first, second, third, and subsequent rounds of utility maximizing choices whereas, in the open market case, demand consists of the average of the first and only round of choices. The case of closed markets is briefly discussed in Section 6, which draws on the results of the open market analysis of Sections 4 and 5.

2.   STOCHASTIC WALRASIAN EQUILIBRIUM

We now review several assumptions and define key concepts.

2.1.   Assumptions

The fundamental assumptions discussed in Section 1.1 of Chapter 2 and the simplifying assumptions discussed in Section 1.2 of Chapter 2 apply to the analysis of this chapter as well, and they are crucial to the definitions that follow.

2.2. Definitions

We now define the concept of a *deterministic equilibrium allocation of households to submarkets*.

Definition 3. A deterministic equilibrium allocation of households to submarkets results when (given fixed submarket sizes, fixed dwelling attributes for all attributes except dwelling rents, fixed household characteristics, and the number of households equal to the total number of dwellings) the dwelling rent for each dwelling is determined such that the (actual) number of households choosing, via utility maximization, any dwelling in each submarket exactly equals the number of dwellings in that submarket.

Next, we define the concept of a *stochastic equilibrium allocation of households to submarkets*.

Definition 4. A stochastic equilibrium allocation of households to submarkets results when (given fixed submarket sizes, fixed dwelling attributes for all attributes except dwelling rents, fixed household characteristics, and the **number of households equal to the total number of dwellings**) the dwelling rent for each dwelling is determined such that given random turnover of renters, the expected number of households choosing, via utility maximization, and dwelling in each submarket exactly equals the number of dwellings in that submarket.

The notion of a stochastic equilibrium becomes useful when aggregate demand cannot be predicted exactly but only up to a probability distribution. If this is the case, the number of households choosing a submarket in stochastic equilibrium will on the average equal the number of dwellings in that submarket. It is clear that a deterministic equilibrium maintained over time satisfies the definition of a stochastic equilibrium, but the converse is not true: a market may be in a state of stochastic equilibrium without at any point in time achieving a deterministic equilibrium. A stochastic equilibrium implies that if a market has random turnover of renters and stochastic equilibrium rents remain fixed over a period of time, the average frequency of households choosing a particular submarket will have a probability limit equal to the expected number of households choosing that submarket.

Next, note that the equilibrium allocation of households to submarkets does not imply an equilibrium allocation of households to dwellings: submarkets may be in equilibrium according to definitions 3 or 4, but the allocation of households to dwellings within each submarket need not conform to an equilibrium.

We now define the concept of a *deterministic equilibrium allocation of households to dwellings*.

Definition 5. A deterministic equilibrium allocation of households to dwellings results when (given fixed attributes for all attributes except dwelling rents, fixed household characteristics, and an equal number of households and dwellings) the dwelling rent for each dwelling is determined such that each dwelling is the utility-maximizing choice of a distinct household and that household has no other dwelling that yields higher utility.

A corresponding concept of a *stochastic equilibrium allocation of households to dwellings* is defined as follows:

Definition 6. A stochastic equilibrium allocation of households to dwellings results when (given fixed dwelling attributes for all attributes except dwelling rents, fixed household characteristics, and an equal number of households and dwellings) the dwelling rent for each dwelling is determined such that given a random turnover of renters, the expected number of households choosing each dwelling equals one.

Clearly, when an allocation of households to dwellings satisfies the above equilibrium definitions then, for any definition of submarkets, the implied allocation of households to submarkets will satisfy the corresponding equilibrium definitions for the allocation of households to submarkets. As noted above the converse is not true.

The practical question of interest is whether deterministic or stochastic equilibrium concepts are more appropriate for purposes of *prediction*. As we have already seen in Chapter 2, the question of whether the underlying behavior is deterministic or stochastic remains empirically unanswerable; but the hard fact at the observer's disposal is that the dispersion of choices in a population can only be predicted through a probability distribution. This calls for the notion of stochastic equilibrium. We note, however, that when the size of each market segment (number of households) is sufficiently large relative to the number of submarkets, then the assumption that the equilibrium allocation of households to submarkets is a deterministic equilibrium (Definition 3) yields a good approximation to the assumption that the equilibrium allocation of households to submarkets is a stochastic equilibrium (Definition 4). On the other hand, if we are considering the allocation of households to dwellings, the size of each market segment (number of households) is smaller than the number of dwellings. Thus the assumption that the equilibrium allocation of households to dwellings is a deterministic equilibrium is not appropriate unless it can be shown that there is no variance in the random utility terms, or equivalently that households belonging to the same segment have identical and fully known utility functions. Since this case is unrealistic and not of interest, the equilibrium allocation of households to dwellings is better viewed as a stochastic equilibrium.

The concepts of equilibrium developed here are based on demand functions derived from utility-maximizing behavior such as the demand functions elaborated in Chapter 2. It should be noted, however, that the concept of stochastic equilibrium has certain real time disequilibrium implications since under the concept of stochastic equilibrium a market is not necessarily cleared at every point in time. Since actual utility maximizing choices at a certain point in time are not market clearing, a queue may develop for each dwelling consisting of those households that find that dwelling to be the most preferred at that point in time. The existence of such queues implies that a closed market may have to be cleared via a disequilibrium rationing process that allocates households to other than their most preferred dwellings at every time period, as discussed in Section 1.2; but as long as all households seek to recontract at every time period, new queues and new reallocations will occur at every time period independently of previous allocations or choices (recall the assumption of costless and frictionless mobility). The length of queues for the same dwelling at different time periods will be independent as long as the costless mobility assumptions hold. It is possible, of course, to develop explicit disequilibrium adjustment models in which rents for one time period would change in response to the length of the queue in the previous time period(s). In such models, stochastic equilibrium rents would not be fixed for all time periods in the stationary state but would fluctuate around a vector of mean stochastic equilibrium rents, the extent of each fluctuation being related to the history of recent queue lengths. The simple notion of stochastic equilibrium defined above is needed to examine the average tendency of such a stochastic disequilibrium rent adjustment process in a stationary state.

2.3. Market Clearing at Stochastic Equilibrium

It is clear from the above definitions that in a market that is in a state of stochastic equilibrium (with random turnover), market clearing may be a rare event. In contrast to this, the definition of a deterministic equilibrium requires that the market is always cleared by stating that the number of households that maximize their utility by choosing a submarket equals the number of dwellings in that submarket (deterministic submarket equilibrium) or that the number of households choosing each dwelling equals one deterministic dwelling equilibrium).

If we let X_j^t denote the actual number of households (nonnegative integer) observed to prefer submarket j at exact time t, then the actual excess demand for submarket j at exact time t is

$$A_j^t = X_j^t - S_j. \tag{3.1}$$

The market is cleared at exact time t if and only if $A_j^t = 0$ for each j at exact time t. Similarly, if x_j^t is the actual number of households (nonnegative integer) choosing dwelling j at exact time t, the actual excess demand for dwelling j at time t is

$$a_j^t = x_j^t - 1, \tag{3.2}$$

and the market is cleared at exact time t if and only if $a_j^t = 0$ for each dwelling j at exact time t.

With a deterministic equilibrium, the above conditions of market clearing are always satisfied, but if the market is in a state of stochastic equilibrium we ought to ask: what is the probability that the market will be cleared and still achieve a utility-maximizing equilibrium at any point in time t under frequent turnover of renters? The probability that there will be market clearing, stochastic equilibrium allocation of households to submarkets at exact time t is expressed as

$$\text{Prob}[(A_1^t = 0) \cap (A_2^t = 0) \cap \cdots \cap (A_J^t = 0)]. \tag{3.3}$$

The probability that a market clearing allocation of households to *dwellings* at time t will occur is

$$\text{Prob}[(a_1^t = 0) \cap (a_2^t = 0) \cap \cdots \cap (a_M^t = 0)], \tag{3.4}$$

where (3.3) and (3.4) embody the fact that in the theory of demand used here, the choices exercised by a household are independent of the choices exercised by others (*given* a set of rents and all the exogenous characteristics).

Now suppose that the market consists of a single population segment with submarket choice probabilities $P_1, \ldots, P_J$; then the probability (3.3) is given by the multinomial distribution and is

$$\text{Prob}[\bigcap_{j=1}^{J} (A_j^t = 0)] = \binom{N}{S_1, \ldots, S_J} \prod_{j=1}^{J} P_j^{S_j}, \tag{3.5}$$

where the leading term in $(\cdot)$ is the multinomial coefficient $N!/\prod_{j=1}^{J} (S_j!)$, where N is the number of households and S_j the number of dwellings in submarket j such that $\sum_j S_j = N$.

Next, suppose that $P_1, \ldots, P_M$ denote the dwelling choice probabilities, then the probability of market clearing (3.4) is also obtained from the multinomial distribution and is

$$\text{Prob}\Big[\bigcap_{j=1}^{M} (a_j^t = 0)\Big] = M! \prod_{j=1}^{M} P_j, \tag{3.6}$$

where $M = N$ is the number of dwellings (households).

If the population of households consists of $h = 1, \ldots, H$ segments of N_h households, each with a distinct strict utility function and thus a distinct probabilistic choice structure, then the computation of the probability of market clearing is somewhat more complex. For this case, let x_j^{ht} denote the nonnegative integer number of households of segment h choosing dwelling j at exact time t, and X_j^{ht} the nonnegative integer number of households of segment h choosing submarket j at exact time t. The excess demand functions can now be written as

$$a_j^t \equiv \sum_{h=1}^{H} x_j^{ht} - 1 \qquad \text{for dwelling } j \tag{3.7}$$

and

$$A_j^t \equiv \sum_{h=1}^{H} X_j^{ht} - S_j \qquad \text{for submarket } j. \tag{3.8}$$

The probability of the event $a_j^t = 0$ is

$$\text{Prob}(a_j^t = 0) = \text{Prob}\Big[\bigcup_{h=1}^{H} \big[(x_j^{ht} = 1) \bigcap_{k \neq h} (x_j^{kt} = 0)\big]\Big\}. \tag{3.9}$$

The probability of each event in parentheses on the right side of (3.9) is given by the binomial distribution. Thus the right side of (3.9) becomes

$$\text{Prob}(a_j^t = 0) = \sum_{h=1}^{H} N_h P_j^h (1 - P_j^h)^{N_h - 1} \prod_{k \neq h} (1 - P_j^k)^{N_k}. \tag{3.10}$$

From this, the market clearing probability is given as

$$\text{Prob}\Big[\bigcap_{j=1}^{M} (a_j^t = 0)\Big] = \prod_{j=1}^{M} \Big[\sum_{h=1}^{H} N_h P_j^h (1 - P_j^h)^{N_h - 1} \prod_{k \neq h} (1 - P_j^k)^{N_k}\Big]. \tag{3.11}$$

The probability of submarket clearing can be found as follows: let S_j^1, $S_j^2, \ldots, S_j^H$ denote a partition of the housing stock in submarket j among the H segments, such that each S_j^h is a nonnegative integer and $\sum_{h=1}^{H} S_j^h = S_j$, $\sum_{j=1}^{J} S_j^h = N_h$ for each such partition. Let the number of all such possible distinct partitions of dwellings be denoted as C and let each such partition be indexed as $c = 1, \ldots, C$. Now let S_j^{hc} denote the number (nonnegative integer) of dwellings reserved for segment h in submarket j under partition c.

Then the probability of market clearing is expressed as

$$\text{Prob}[\bigcap_{j=1}^{J} (A_j^t = 0)] = \text{Prob}(\bigcup_{c=1}^{C} \{\bigcap_{j=1}^{J} [\bigcap_{h=1}^{H} (X_j^{ht} = S_j^{hc})]\})$$

$$= \sum_{c=1}^{C} \left[\prod_{j=1}^{J} \prod_{h=1}^{H} \frac{N_h!}{S_j^{hc}!(N_h - S_j^{hc})!} P_j^{hS_j^{hc}}(1 - P_j^h)^{N_h - S_j^{hc}} \right]. \quad (3.12)$$

3. UNIQUENESS AND STABILITY OF STOCHASTIC WALRASIAN EQUILIBRIA

To reconcile the notion of interdependent housing submarkets with traditional economic concepts, each housing submarket can be viewed as a stock of commodities (dwellings) differentiated from other submarkets by some unique combination of attributes. The dwellings of the various submarkets are thus unique but closely substitutable commodities. Dwellings belonging to the same submarket may have a higher degree of substitutability than dwellings belonging to different submarkets, but with expected demand functions conforming to their usually assumed properties, all dwellings are *strict gross substitutes* in the allowable rent ranges.

Let the number of dwellings in the market be denoted by M and let the number of households be N with $N = M$. Now let the vector of dwelling rents be $\bar{R} = [R_1, R_2, \ldots, R_j, \ldots, R_M]$. Then the system of the M expected excess demand functions is

$$e_i(\bar{R}) \equiv d_i(\bar{R}) - 1, \qquad i = 1, \ldots, M, \quad (3.13)$$

where $d_i(\bar{R})$ is the expected number of households choosing dwelling i if the rent vector is $\bar{R}$. Suppose that the households are divided into $h = 1, \ldots, H$ segments with N_h households in segment h such that $M = N = \sum_h N_h$, and let $d_i^h(\bar{R})$ denote the expected number of households of segment h choosing dwelling i if the dwelling rent vector is $\bar{R}$. Then, letting x_i^h denote the actual number of households of segment h choosing i as their utility-maximizing choice, we note that for an open market,

$$d_i^h(\bar{R}) \equiv \sum_{n=1}^{N_h} n \, \text{Prob}(x_i^h = n | \bar{R}) = N_h P_i^h(\bar{R}), \quad (3.14)$$

and using the binomial process (2.86),

$$d_i(\bar{R}) \equiv \sum_{h=1}^{H} d_i^h(\bar{R}) = \sum_{h=1}^{H} N_h P_i^h(\bar{R}), \quad (3.15)$$

where P_i^h is the probability that a segment h household will choose dwelling i given the dwelling rent structure $\bar{R}$.

Definition 7. The conditions for a stochastic equilibrium allocation of households to dwellings are $e_i(\bar{R}^*) \equiv d_i(\bar{R}^*) - 1 = 0$ for $i = 1, \ldots, M$, and say that the expected excess demand for each dwelling vanishes when the rent vector $\bar{R} = \bar{R}^*$, the equilibrium dwelling rent vector.

Proposition 1. The equilibrium vector $\bar{R}^*$ of definition 7 is unique up to an arbitrary specification of any one of its elements (any dwelling rent) and satisfies local and Hicksian stability conditions if for each i,

$$\frac{\partial e_i(\bar{R})}{\partial R_j} = \frac{\partial d_i(\bar{R})}{\partial R_j} \begin{cases} <0 & \text{for } j = i, \quad R_j \leq R_{j\max} > 0, \\ >0 & \text{for } j \neq i, \quad R_j \leq R_{j\max} > 0, \end{cases} \tag{3.16}$$

and $\lim_{R_j \to R_{j\max}} d_j(\bar{R}) = 0$ for each $j = 1, \ldots, M$; namely, all dwellings are *strict gross substitutes* in the allowable rent ranges ($R_{j\max} = +\infty$ without and loss of generality).

Proof. The proof of the above proposition is a well-known result in multimarket Walrasian analysis and the stability of multimarket equilibrium. In the above theorem, each dwelling is treated as a unique commodity and thus, in effect, a separate "submarket."

For a review of Walrasian multimarket equilibrium see Henderson and Quandt (1958, Chapter 5).

The above results can be repeated for the case of submarket equilibrium. Suppose that the stock of dwellings in each of the J submarkets is fixed and denoted as S_i, $i = 1, \ldots, J$. Let $N = \sum_{h=1}^{H} N_h = \sum_i S_i = M$. A system of J excess demands can be defined as follows:

$$E_i(\bar{R}) \equiv D_i(\bar{R}) - S_i, \qquad i = 1, \ldots, J, \tag{3.17}$$

where $D_i(\bar{R})$ is the expected number of households choosing submarket i given the vector $\bar{R} = [\bar{R}_1, \bar{R}_2, \ldots, \bar{R}_j, \ldots, \bar{R}_J]$ of mean submarket dwelling prices, where $\bar{R}_j$ is the mean rent of the dwellings belonging to the jth submarket. If dwellings within submarket j are identical (perfect substitutes), each of these will have a rent equal to $\bar{R}_j$, but in general dwellings within the same submarket will exhibit a variance in their rents.

Definition 8. The conditions for a stochastic equilibrium allocation of households to dwellings are $E_i(\bar{\bar{R}}^*) \equiv D_i(\bar{\bar{R}}^*) - S_i = 0$ for $i = 1, \ldots, J$, and say that the expected excess demand for each submarket vanishes when the vector of mean submarket rents $\bar{R} = \bar{\bar{R}}^*$, the equilibrium mean rent vector.

Proposition 2. The equilibrium vector $\bar{\bar{R}}^*$ of mean submarket rents of definition 8 is unique up to an arbitrary specification of any one of its elements (any mean submarket rent), and it satisfies local and Hicksian stability conditions if for each i,

$$\frac{\partial E_i(\bar{\bar{R}})}{\partial \bar{R}_j} = \frac{\partial D_i(\bar{\bar{R}})}{\partial \bar{R}_j} \begin{cases} <0 & \text{for} \quad j = i, \quad \bar{R}_j \leq \bar{R}_{j\max} > 0, \\ >0 & \text{for} \quad i = j, \quad \bar{R}_j \leq \bar{R}_{j\max} > 0, \end{cases} \tag{3.18}$$

and $\lim_{\bar{R}_j \to \bar{R}_{j\max}} D_j(\bar{\bar{R}}) = 0$ for each $j = 1, \ldots, J$; namely, all submarkets are *strict gross substitutes* in the allowable rent ranges ($\bar{R}_{j\max} = +\infty$ without any loss of generality).

Proof. Again, the proof is a well-known textbook result in multimarket Walrasian analysis and the stability of multimarket equilibrium. In the above theorem, each submarket is treated as a market of dwellings in a system of such markets, i.e., the dwellings in a submarket are treated as a stock of commodities different from but substitutable with the dwellings of other submarkets.

To determine either a dwelling or a submarket equilibrium allocation, the rent of any one dwelling or the mean rent of any one submarket must be taken as the numeraire and fixed at an arbitrary value within its allowable range. Then the remaining rents can be uniquely determined to form an equilibrium submarket rent vector $\bar{\bar{R}}^*$. Changes in the numeraire will change the elements of this vector without changing the equilibrium. If there are no upper bounds $\bar{R}_{j\max}$ on the rents of the submarkets, then by appropriate adjustments of the numeraire, positive rents can be assured for each submarket.

Note that propositions 1 and 2 are based on Eqs. (3.14) and (3.15), which measure demand under the assumption of an open market, in which households that cannot achieve their utility-maximizing choices exit the market. The demand for a closed market is easy to conceptualize, if much more difficult to compute, and Propositions 1 and 2 will apply to the case of closed markets as well, as long as the expected demand functions $d_j(\bar{R})$ and $D_j(R)$ are appropriately computed for a closed market and are shown to obey the gross substitutability conditions (3.16) and (3.18). As discussed in Section 1.2, the demand for dwellings or submarkets in a closed market is computed by summing the expected demands from each round of choices. Thus let $^m x_j^{ht}$, $m = 1, 2, 3, \ldots$, denote the number of type h households choosing dwelling j in the mth round allocation of time t. Note that if $^m x_j^{ht} > 0$, then $^{m+1} x_j^{ht} = 0$. The expected demand of segment h for dwelling j is now expressed as

$$d_j^h(\bar{R}) = \sum_{m=1}^{T} E(^m x_j^{ht} | \bar{R}), \tag{3.19}$$

where it is assumed that market clearing occurs in T rounds. The submarket demands are similarly computed as

$$D_j^h(\bar{\bar{R}}) = \sum_{m=1}^{T} E(^mX_j^{ht}|\bar{\bar{R}}), \tag{3.20}$$

where $^mX_j^{ht}$ is the number choosing submarket j in the mth round. Total expected demand functions are obtained by summing the expected demand functions for the H segments. If each expected value in the summations (3.19) and (3.20) satisfies the strict gross substitutability assumption, the expected demand functions for closed markets will also satisfy these conditions, obeying the conclusions of propositions 1 and 2. Further examinations of expected demand functions in a closed market context is beyond the scope of this chapter. An approximate investigation of closed markets is postponed until Section 6 of this chapter. It should be noted, however, that when the housing market consists of a number of submarkets, each of which is small relative to the number of households and relatively homogeneous internally, closed and open market formulations of demand will provide approximately the same solution. This is the case that is relevant to the empirical application reported in the second part of this book.

4. EQUILIBRIUM IN SINGLE-SEGMENT OPEN MARKETS

We now examine the properties of stochastic equilibrium for the case of an open market in which the population of households is treated as a single homogeneous segment with a common strict utility function and a logistic demand structure. The number of households is fixed and denoted N. The number of dwellings, M, is equal to N and fixed. The supply of dwellings in each submarket j is denoted S_j and is also fixed.

4.1. Stochastic Dwelling Equilibrium

First, consider the case where the unobserved dwelling attributes are independently distributed in the population of N households. This implies the logit model

$$P_j(\bar{R}) = e^{V_j(R_j)}/\sum_{k=1}^{M} e^{V_k(R_k)}, \qquad j = 1, \ldots, M, \tag{3.21}$$

where $P_j(\cdot)$ is the choice probability for dwelling j, and $V_j(R_j) = V(R_j, X_j)$ is the strict utility function evaluated at the dwelling rent R_j and the dwelling attributes X_j. Since in the short run, dwelling attributes are assumed unalterable, these become parameters of the utility function and are suppressed. To show this, the utility function becomes subscripted with j. The expected demand function for a dwelling j can be expressed as

$$d_j(\bar{R}) = NP_j(\bar{R}), \qquad j = 1, \ldots, M. \tag{3.22}$$

Equilibrium requires

$$NP_j(\bar{R}) = 1, \qquad j = 1, \ldots, M. \tag{3.23}$$

We note that since $\sum_{j=1}^{M} NP_j(\bar{R}) = M$, one of the M equations in (3.23) is redundant. If we let this be the ith equation we can then divide each of the M equations by the ith, obtaining

$$P_j(\bar{R})/P_i(\bar{R}) = 1, \qquad j = 1, \ldots, M, \tag{3.24}$$

with the ith (redundant) equation reducing to $1 = 1$. Each of the equations in (3.24) can be written as

$$\exp[V_j(R_j) - V_i(R_i)] = 1, \qquad j = 1, \ldots, M \tag{3.25}$$

or

$$V_j(R_j) - V_i(R_i) = 0, \qquad j = 1, \ldots, M. \tag{3.26}$$

If we now set R_i equal to an arbitrary numeraire value, say $R_i = \tilde{R}_i$, we can proceed to solve for the elements of the equilibrium vector $\bar{R}^*$ directly from the $M - 1$ equations in (3.26), obtaining

$$R_j^* = V_j^{-1}[V_i(\tilde{R}_i)], \qquad j \neq i. \tag{3.27}$$

It is clear that each of (3.26) has a single root since $\partial V_j(R_j)/\partial R_j < 0$ throughout.

Thus, for the case of distinctly independent dwellings (i.e., independent unobserved attributes), stochastic equilibrium requires the equalization of strict utility for all dwellings.

4.2. Submarket Equilibrium

Next, consider the case where the market is divided into $j = 1, \ldots, J$ submarkets. Each submarket contains $k = 1, \ldots, S_j$ dwellings. Suppose that the submarket choice probabilities are given by the nested logit model,

$$P_j(\bar{R}) = \exp[V_j(\bar{R}_j) + (1 - \delta)I_j^*]/\sum_{k=1}^{J} \exp[V_k(\bar{R}_k) + (1 - \delta)I_k^*],$$

$$j = 1, \ldots, J, \quad (3.28)$$

where $\bar{R}$ is the vector of mean submarket rents; $\bar{R}_j$. the mean rent of submarket j; I_j^*, the inclusive value for submarket j (assumed fixed); and δ, the dwelling similarity coefficient of the nested logit model. At one extreme, when $\delta = 0$ dwellings in the same submarket are independent in their unobserved attributes. At the other extreme, when $\delta = 1$ dwellings in the same submarket are identical (fully dependent) in their unobserved attributes.

The expected number of households choosing submarket j is

$$D_j(\bar{R}) = NP_j(\bar{R}), \qquad j = 1, \ldots, J, \tag{3.29}$$

and equilibrium requires that

$$NP_j(\bar{R}) = S_j, \qquad j = 1, \ldots, J. \tag{3.30}$$

Since on the aggregate

$$N = \sum_j S_j, \tag{3.31}$$

one of the equations in (3.30) is redundant. Dividing each of the J equations by the ith, we obtain

$$P_j(\bar{R})/P_i(\bar{R}) = S_j/S_i, \qquad j = 1, \ldots, J, \tag{3.32}$$

which becomes

$$\exp[V_j(\bar{R}_j) - V_i(\bar{R}_i) + (1 - \delta)(I_j^* - I_i^*)] = S_j/S_i, \qquad j = 1, \ldots, J \tag{3.33}$$

or

$$V_j(\bar{R}_j) - V_i(\bar{R}_i) + (1 - \delta)(I_j^* - I_i^*) - \log(S_j/S_i) = 0, \qquad j = 1, \ldots, J. \tag{3.34}$$

Choosing $\bar{R}_i = \tilde{\bar{R}}_i$ to be the numeraire rent, we obtain the equilibrium submarket rents by solving

$$V_j(\bar{R}_j^*) = V_i(\tilde{\bar{R}}_i) - (1 - \delta)(I_j^* - I_i^*) + \log(S_j/S_i), \qquad j = 1, \ldots, J \tag{3.35}$$

for $\bar{R}_j^*, j \neq i$. These are $J - 1$ single-zeroed functions and yield

$$\bar{R}_j^* = V_j^{-1}[V_i(\tilde{\bar{R}}_i) - (1 - \delta)(I_j^* - I_i^*) + \log(S_j/S_i)], \qquad j \neq i. \tag{3.36}$$

4.3. IIA, The Aggregate Rent Level and Specific Solutions

Dwelling and submarket equilibrium conditions (3.26) and (3.34) are a direct reflection of the "independence from irrelevant alternatives" property of the multinomial logit model: at equilibrium, the "relative" rents of any two choice alternatives (dwellings or submarkets) depend on the attributes of those two alternatives alone.

It follows from (3.27) and (3.36) that increasing the value of the arbitrary numeraire rent will increase the value of all the other rents at equilibrium. This is seen by verifying that

$$dR_j^*/d\tilde{R}_i > 0 \qquad \text{for (3.27)} \tag{3.37}$$

and

$$d\bar{R}_j^*/d\tilde{\bar{R}}_i > 0 \qquad \text{for (3.36).} \tag{3.38}$$

This implies that if an arbitrary numeraire rent value leads to a negative equilibrium rent for any alternative, the value of the numeraire can be arbitrarily increased until all equilibrium rents become nonnegative, as long as the rents for an alternative do not have an upper bound at which demand becomes zero.

Specific equilibrium conditions can be derived by assuming specific strict utility functions. For example, utility functions (2.94), (2.95), and (2.96) can be rewritten in simplified terms as

$$V_i = \alpha R_i + K_i \qquad \text{for (2.94),} \qquad (3.39)$$

$$V_i = \beta \log R_i + K_i \qquad \text{for (2.95),} \qquad (3.40)$$

$$V_i = \gamma \log(R_i^M - R_i) + K_i \qquad \text{for (2.96),} \qquad (3.41)$$

where K_i denotes the part of utility involving all attributes other than rent, and R_i^M is the maximum rent for dwelling i. Applying these to dwelling market equilibrium, we find for any two dwellings (i, j):

$$R_i^* - R_j^* = (1/\alpha)(K_j - K_i) \qquad \text{for (3.39),} \qquad (3.42)$$

$$R_i^*/R_j^* = \exp[(K_j - K_i)/\beta] \qquad \text{for (3.40),} \qquad (3.43)$$

and

$$(R_i^M - R_i^*)/(R_j^M - R_j^*) = \exp[(K_j - K_i)/\gamma] \qquad \text{for (3.41).} \qquad (3.44)$$

Applying (3.39)–(3.41) to submarket equilibrium, we get conditions (3.46)–(3.48), where K_j, K_i are replaced by K_j', K_i', and

$$K_j' = K_j'' + (1 - \delta)I_j^* \qquad \text{for any submarket } j, \qquad (3.45)$$

with K_j'' an abbreviation for the terms in the submarket part of the strict utility function that include attributes other than rent:

$$\bar{R}_i^* - \bar{R}_j^* = (1/\alpha)(K_j' - K_i') + (1/\alpha) \log(S_i/S_j) \qquad \text{for (3.39), (3.46)}$$

$$\bar{R}_i^*/\bar{R}_j^* = (S_i/S_j)^{1/\beta} \exp[(K_j' - K_i')/\beta] \qquad \text{for (3.40), (3.47)}$$

and

$$(R_i^M - \bar{R}_i^*)/(R_j^M - \bar{R}_j^*) = (S_i/S_j)^{1/\gamma} \exp[(K_j' - K_i')/\gamma] \qquad \text{for (3.41). (3.48)}$$

The locus of equilibrium rents $\bar{R}_1^*$ and $\bar{R}_2^*$ for any two submarkets is linear, and a simple graphical illustration for the above special cases is given in Fig. 3.1.

It is also straightforward to demonstrate that the aggregate rent is a linear function of the numeraire submarket rent. Denoting aggregate rent as L, we can compute it as follows for the cases represented by (3.39)–(3.41), respectively:

$$L = \tilde{R}_j S_j + \sum_{i \neq j} S_i \left[\tilde{R}_j + \frac{1}{\alpha}(K'_j - K'_i) + \frac{1}{\alpha} \log\left(\frac{S_i}{S_j}\right) \right], \qquad (3.49)$$

$$L = \tilde{R}_j S_j + \sum_{i \neq j} S_i \left\{ \tilde{R}_j \left(\frac{S_i}{S_j}\right)^{1/\beta} \exp[(K'_j - K'_i)/\beta] \right\}, \qquad (3.50)$$

and

$$L = \tilde{R}_j S_j + \sum_{i \neq j} S_i \{R_i^M - (R_j^M - \tilde{R}_j) \exp[(K'_j - K'_i)/\gamma]\}, \qquad (3.51)$$

where $\tilde{R}_j$ is the numeraire submarket rent.

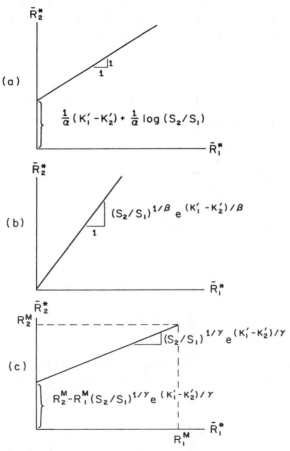

Fig. 3.1. Loci of Walrasian equilibrium rents for two submarkets: cases (3.39)–(3.41) [(a)–(c)].

4.4. Hierarchical Choice Structures and the Equilibrium Distribution of Dwelling Rents within Submarkets

We now examine the case in which housing demand is represented by a sequential choice frequency structure. As we saw in Chapter 2, this occurs when the strict utility function is decomposable into two additive parts, the first expressing the strict utility due to submarket attributes, the second the strict utility due to attributes that vary by dwelling and submarket. This can be expressed as

$$V(R_{jk}, Y_j, X_{jk}) = V_1(Y_j) + V_2(R_{jk}, X_{jk}), \tag{3.52}$$

where R_{jk} is the rent of dwelling k in submarket j; X_{jk}, the vector of attributes that vary by dwelling and submarket; and Y_j, the set of attributes that vary by submarket alone. We will now assume that $V_2(\cdot)$ is given by one of the following:

$$V_2(R_{jk}, X_{jk}) = \alpha R_{jk} + V_3(X_{jk}) \tag{3.53}$$

or

$$V_2(R_{jk}, X_{jk}) = \beta \log R_{jk} + V_3(X_{jk}). \tag{3.54}$$

In the case of (3.53), dwelling rent can be expressed as

$$R_{jk} \equiv \bar{R}_j + r_{jk}, \tag{3.55}$$

where $\bar{R}_j$ is the mean submarket rent and r_{jk} the deviation of dwelling k's rent from the mean. By this definition,

$$\bar{R}_j = (\sum_{k=1}^{S_j} R_{jk})/S_j, \qquad j = 1, \ldots, J, \tag{3.56}$$

which, of course, implies

$$\sum_{k=1}^{S_j} r_{jk} = 0, \qquad j = 1, \ldots, J. \tag{3.57}$$

In the case of (3.54), we express dwelling rent as

$$R_{jk} \equiv \bar{R}_j \rho_{jk}, \tag{3.58}$$

where $\bar{R}_j$ is the mean submarket rent as in (3.56), and ρ_{jk} a multiplicative deviation of dwelling k's rent from the mean rent. It follows by definition of $\bar{R}_j$ that

$$(\sum_{k=1}^{S_j} \rho_{jk})/S_j = 1, \qquad j = 1, \ldots, J. \tag{3.59}$$

These redefinitions allow us to rewrite the utility function (3.52) as follows:

$$V(R_{jk}, Y_j, X_{jk}) = \alpha \bar{R}_j + V_1(Y_j) + \alpha r_{jk} + V_3(X_{jk}) \tag{3.60}$$

or

$$V(R_{jk}, Y_j, X_{jk}) = \beta \log \bar{R}_j + V_1(Y_j) + \beta \log \rho_{jk} + V_3(X_{jk}), \tag{3.61}$$

where the first two terms on the right side represent submarket wide utility, and the last two terms represent dwelling specific utility.

We know from Chapter 2 that the specification of the utility function according to (3.60) or (3.61) will yield the following sequential choice probability structure:

$$P_{jk} = P_j(\bar{R}_j, Y_j, I_j, j = 1, \ldots, J) P_{k|j}[(r_{jk} \text{ or } \rho_{jk}), X_{jk}, \text{ all } k \in j], \tag{3.62}$$

where the I_j's are inclusive values. Suppressing all but the rent specific information and using the definitions $V_j \equiv V_1(Y_j)$ and $V_{jk} \equiv V_3(X_{jk})$, the nested logit version of (3.62) is

$$P_j = \exp[\alpha \bar{R}_j + V_j + (1 - \delta)I_j] / \sum_{i=1}^{J} \exp[\alpha \bar{R}_i + V_i + (1 - \delta)I_i], \tag{3.63}$$

where we have assumed (3.53), and

$$P_{k|j} = \exp(\alpha r_{jk} + V_{jk}) / \exp(I_j), \tag{3.64}$$

$$I_j = \log \sum_{k=1}^{S_j} \exp(\alpha r_{jk} + V_{jk}). \tag{3.65}$$

If we assume (3.54) instead of (3.53), the corresponding choice structure is obtained by replacing $\alpha \bar{R}_j$ in (3.63) with $\beta \log \bar{R}_j$ and αr_{jk} in (3.64)–(3.65) with $\beta \log \rho_{jk}$.

The equilibrium adjustments implied by these sequential choice structures are as follows: average submarket rents must adjust to insure an equilibrium allocation of households to submarkets, and dwelling rents must adjust to insure an equilibrium allocation of households to dwellings within a submarket. The first of these problems, the allocation of households to submarkets, can be approached in a manner identical to the preceding discussions if we recall that the inclusive values must obtain values that are consistent with the allocation of households to dwellings within submarkets. We first solve the intrasubmarket allocation problem, noting that the equilibrium conditions are

$$S_j P_{k|j} = 1, \quad k = 1, \ldots, S_j, \quad j = 1, \ldots, J. \tag{3.66}$$

Dividing each of the S_j equations for submarket j with the equation for the

mth dwelling ($m \in j$), we obtain

$$P_{k|j}/P_{m|j} = 1, \qquad k = 1, \ldots, S_j, \quad j = 1, \ldots, J, \tag{3.67}$$

which yields the equilibrium condition

$$\alpha r_{jk} - \alpha r_{jm} + V_{jk} - V_{jm} = 0, \qquad k = 1, \ldots, S_j, \quad j = 1, \ldots, J \tag{3.68}$$

or

$$\beta \log \rho_{jk} - \beta \log \rho_{jm} + V_{jk} - V_{jm} = 0, \qquad k = 1, \ldots, S_j, \quad j = 1, \ldots, J. \tag{3.69}$$

We now recall that rent deviations within a submarket must be normalized according to (3.57) or (3.59). This allows us to solve each of the S_j equations in (3.68) or (3.69) for r_{jk} or ρ_{jk}, substitute these into (3.57) or (3.59) for market j, and solve the resulting equation for r_{jm} or ρ_{jm}. This yields

$$r_{jm} = \left[(1/\alpha) \sum_{k=1}^{S_j} (V_{jk} - V_{jm})\right]/S_j \tag{3.70}$$

or

$$\rho_{jm} = S_j / \sum_{k=1}^{S_j} \exp[(1/\beta)(V_{jm} - V_{jk})]. \tag{3.71}$$

We can now substitute (3.70) into each of the S_j equations for submarket j in (3.68), which can be solved uniquely for each r_{jk}, $k = 1, \ldots, S_j$, for that j. Equivalently, (3.71) must be substituted into (3.69) to solve for the ρ_{jk}.

We have thus established the following result: when utility satisfies the separability conditions (3.52) and (3.53) or (3.54), the around-the-mean variation of dwelling rents within each submarket can be determined independently for each submarket and independently of the mean submarket rent for that submarket. This hinges on the separable sequential choice structure (3.62), and it will be true for any model of that general form. An additional result established above is that when the conditional dwelling choice model is logistic, the intrasubmarket dwelling rent distribution will also satisfy the IIA property: the "relative" rents of any two dwellings within a submarket depend on the attributes of these two dwellings alone.

The inclusive values that are consistent with intrasubmarket equilibrium can be computed directly from (3.65) or the equivalent expression when rent enters the utility function loglinearly. Denoting these equilibrium inclusive values as I_j^*, we now note that the equilibrium condition for the allocation of households to submarkets is

$$\bar{R}_i^* - \bar{R}_j^* = (1/\alpha)[V_j - V_i + (1 - \delta)(I_j^* - I_i^*)] + (1/\alpha) \log(S_i/S_j), \tag{3.72}$$

which holds for the case of (3.60), and

$$\bar{R}_i^*/R_j^* = (S_i/S_j)^{1/\beta} \exp\{1/\beta[V_j - V_i + (1 - \delta)(I_j^* - I_i^*)]\}, \tag{3.73}$$

which holds for the case of (3.61). These conditions are identical to (3.46) and (3.47). Any mean submarket rent can be selected as the numeraire to uniquely determine all other submarket rents. The rent of each dwelling can then be determined by adjusting the mean submarket rent according to the uniquely determined deviations from the mean given by the intrasubmarket equilibrium allocation. Since each mean submarket rent is an increasing function of the numeraire rent, appropriate adjustment of this numeraire will insure that the rent of each dwelling becomes nonnegative as long as there are no upper bounds on dwelling rents.

It has thus been demonstrated that both intersubmarket and intrasubmarket equilibration are susceptible to Walrasian analysis. The allocation of households to dwellings within a submarket uniquely determines the distribution of dwelling rents within that submarket. The allocation of households among submarkets uniquely determines the distribution of mean submarket rents up to an arbitrary specification of any one mean submarket rent. For the nested multinomial logit model both of these distributions can be determined analytically.

5. EQUILIBRIUM IN MULTIPLE-SEGMENT OPEN MARKETS

5.1. Submarket Equilibrium

We now examine the more general case in which there are $h = 1, \ldots, H$ household segments whose demand behavior is governed by distinctly different strict utility functions. The assumption of no vacancies is now stated as

$$\sum_h N_h = \sum_j S_j, \tag{3.74}$$

where N_h is the fixed number of households in the hth segment. The submarket demand function of each segment is denoted as

$$D_j^h(\bar{\bar{R}}), \quad j = 1, \ldots, J \quad \text{and} \quad h = 1, \ldots, H, \tag{3.75}$$

where each demand function was shown to obey the strict gross substitutability condition

$$\frac{\partial D_j^h}{\partial \bar{R}_i} \begin{cases} <0 & \text{for} \quad i = j, \\ >0 & \text{for} \quad i \neq j, \end{cases} \tag{3.76}$$

where $\bar{R}_i$ is the mean rent of submarket i. It also follows that

$$\sum_{j=1}^{J} D_j^h(\bar{\bar{R}}) = N_h, \quad h = 1, \ldots, H. \tag{3.77}$$

The Walrasian equilibrium of the J submarkets is now expressed as

$$E_j(\bar{\bar{R}}) = \sum_{h=1}^{H} D_j^h(\bar{\bar{R}}) - S_j = 0, \qquad j = 1, \ldots, J. \qquad (3.78)$$

If the choice model is a nested logit model, we can write the following equilibrium condition for each submarket j:

$$\sum_{h=1}^{H} D_j^h(\bar{\bar{R}}) = \sum_{h=1}^{H} N_h P_j^h(\bar{\bar{R}})$$

$$= \sum_{h=1}^{H} \{N_h \exp[V_j^h + (1 - \delta_h)I_j^{h*}] / \sum_{i=1}^{J} \exp[V_i^h + (1 - \delta_h)I_i^{h*}\} = S_j, \qquad (3.79)$$

where the $V_j^h = V^h(\bar{R}_j, X_j)$ are the strict utility functions of type h households with the attributes and rent suppressed; I_j^{h*}, the fixed inclusive values of type h households for submarket j; and δ_h, the dwelling similarity coefficients.

In a multisegment market, households of different segments can locate in the housing stock of the same submarket. The equilibrium problem must determine the rent vector $\bar{R}^*$ as well as the partitioning of a submarket's stock among the H segments. This implies the following J equations:

$$\sum_{h=1}^{H} S_j^h = S_j, \qquad j = 1, \ldots, J, \qquad (3.80)$$

where S_j^h is the number of dwellings in submarket j chosen by households of segment h. The equilibrium allocation can be denoted as S_j^{h*} or, in vector form $S^* = [S_1^{1*} \cdots S_j^{1*} \cdots S_1^{H*} \cdots S_J^{H*}]$. Both $\bar{R}^*$ and S^* are unknown and must be determined by the market equilibration process.

From our analysis of the unsegmented market, we know that the following conditions must hold for each segment h:

$$D_j^h(\bar{R}) - S_j^h = 0, \qquad j = 1, \ldots, J, \quad h = 1, \ldots, H, \qquad (3.81)$$

which can be simplified using the nested logit structure, yielding

$$V_i^h(\bar{R}_i) - V_j^h(\bar{R}_j) + (1 - \delta_h)(I_i^{h*} - I_j^{h*}) - S_i^h/S_j^h = 0,$$

$$j = 1, \ldots, J, \quad h = 1, \ldots, H. \qquad (3.82)$$

To the JH equations of (3.82) we must add the J equations of (3.80), which assure that the dwelling stock of each submarket cannot be exceeded. We must also add the following H equations that assure that all members of each segment h are accounted for:

$$\sum_{j} S_j^h - N_h = 0, \qquad h = 1, \ldots, H. \qquad (3.83)$$

Thus (3.82), (3.80), and (3.83) are a system of $JH + J + H$ equations equivalent to the J Walrasian excess demand conditions of (3.78). These $JH + J + H$ equations have $JH + J$ unknowns, which are the elements of the vectors $\bar{R}^*$ and S^*. We note, however, that each of the jth equations in (3.82) is redundant because it reduces to $1 = 1$. This eliminates H equations, leaving $JH + J$ equations in the $JH + J$ unknowns. In addition to this fact, the sum of the equations (3.83) must equal the sum of (3.80), implying that one of these equations is also redundant. Each of (3.80) can be solved for S_i^h, yielding

$$S_i^h = S_j^h \exp[V_i^h(\bar{R}_i) - V_j^h(\bar{R}_j) + (1 - \delta_h)(I_i^{h*} - I_j^{h*})],$$

$$i = 1, \ldots, J, \quad h = 1, \ldots, H. \quad (3.84)$$

Substituting the above into (3.80) and (3.83), we reduce these equations to

$$\sum_h S_j^h \exp[V_i^h(\bar{R}_i) - V_j^h(\bar{R}_j) + (1 - \delta_h)(I_i^{h*} - I_j^{h*})] - S_i = 0,$$

$$i = 1, \ldots, J \quad (3.85)$$

and

$$\sum_i S_j^h \exp[V_i^h(\bar{R}_i) - V_j^h(\bar{R}_j) + (1 - \delta_h)(I_i^{h*} - I_j^{h*})] - N_h = 0,$$

$$h = 1, \ldots, H, \quad (3.86)$$

any one of which is redundant since the sum of (3.85) equals the sum of (3.86). This implies that one unknown (say, $\bar{R}_j$) must be arbitrarily fixed at, say, $\bar{R}_j = \tilde{\bar{R}}_j$. Then all but one of the above equations must be solved for $\bar{R}_i^*$, $i \neq j$, and S_j^{h*}, $h = 1, \ldots, H$.

While in the single-segment case it was possible to solve for explicit equilibrium conditions that showed the relationship between relative rents at equilibrium, for multisegmented markets such an analytical solution is not possible since (3.85) and (3.86) cannot be simplified further. A numerical procedure is implied by the structure of (3.85), (3.86). First, it is seen that each of (3.85) can be solved for a unique $\bar{R}_i^*$ given $\tilde{\bar{R}}_j$ and an arbitrary partition of the stock at j, $S_j^* = [S_j^{1*} \cdots S_j^{H*}]$. Second, from (3.86) we see that one can obtain a unique S_j^* by solving each of these, given a rent vector $\bar{R}^*$. Thus, iterating from one set of equations to another could be one method for converging on the unique Walrasian $\bar{R}^*$ (and the implied S_j^*) given the numeraire $\tilde{\bar{R}}_j$. The entire solution S^* can then be obtained by substitution into (3.84).

It should be noted that the "independence from irrelevant alternatives" property of logit models does not reflect itself in the equilibrium conditions for multisegmented markets. Because of the presence of several segments, an interactive effect is established whereby the equilibrium rent of each submarket depends on the equilibrium rents of all other submarkets.

5.2. Stochastic Dwelling Equilibrium

The equilibrium of multiple-segment markets can also be examined at the level of dwellings. Again, let M be the number of dwellings, with

$$\sum_{h=1}^{H} N_h = M. \tag{3.87}$$

The expected excess demand function for the jth dwelling is given as

$$e_j(\bar{R}) = d_j(\bar{R}) - 1 = 0, \qquad j = 1, \ldots, M, \tag{3.88}$$

where $\bar{R}$ is the dwelling rent vector, and $d_j(\bar{R})$ the expected demand for the jth dwelling, which can be computed as

$$d_j(\bar{R}) = \sum_{h=1}^{H} N_h P_j^h(\bar{R}), \qquad j = 1, \ldots, M, \tag{3.89}$$

where $P_j^h(\bar{R})$ is the probability or relative frequency with which members of h will choose dwelling j given the dwelling rent vector $\bar{R}$. This relative frequency is given as

$$P_j^h(\bar{R}) = \exp[V_j^h(R_j)] / \sum_{k=1}^{M} \exp[V_k^h(R_k)]. \tag{3.90}$$

The M Walrasian excess demand equations in (3.88) must be solved for the M elements of $\bar{R}$, and because of (3.87), any one dwelling rent is redundant and can be arbitrarily set to be the numeraire.

The assignment of households to dwellings cannot be approximated as deterministic because the number of dwellings (the number of alternatives in the discrete choice market) is larger (possibly much larger) than the number of households in each segment (N_h smaller than M). For any one dwelling, the segment (type) of its occupying household is uncertain.

Let p_j^h denote the expected number of type h households choosing dwelling j. By the definition of stochastic equilibrium, it should be true that at equilibrium,

$$\sum_{h=1}^{H} p_i^h = 1, \qquad i = 1, \ldots, M. \tag{3.91}$$

In fact, the left side of (3.91) measures total expected demand and is the same as (3.89). In addition to (3.91), we can state the following for each segment h:

$$N_h P_i^h(\bar{R}) = p_i^h, \qquad i = 1, \ldots, M, \quad h = 1, \ldots, H, \tag{3.92}$$

which is, in fact, the definition of p_i^h. Dividing each equation in (3.92) by the jth equation for the same h, we obtain

$$P_i^h(\bar{R})/P_j^h(\bar{R}) = p_i^h/p_j^h, \qquad i = 1, \ldots, M, \quad h = 1, \ldots, H. \qquad (3.93)$$

With the choice structure (3.90), the above becomes

$$\exp[V_i^h(R_i) - V_j^h(R_j)] - (p_i^h/p_j^h) = 0, \qquad i = 1, \ldots, M, \quad h = 1, \ldots, H. \quad (3.94)$$

Finally, we should also note that the number of households of each segment is conserved by the equation

$$\sum_{i=1}^{M} p_i^h = N_h. \qquad (3.95)$$

Equations (3.91), (3 94), and (3.95) are $MH + M + H$ equations in the $MH + M$ unknowns that can be solved for the elements of the equilibrium dwelling rent vector $\bar{R}^*$ and the elements of the vector $\bar{p}^* = [p_1^{1*} \cdots p_1^{H*} \cdots p_M^{1*} \cdots p_M^{H*}]$. We note that each of the jth equations in (3.94) reduces to $1 = 1$, and thus H equations can be deleted from the system to obtain an $MH + M$ system in the same number of unknowns. Furthermore, the sum of (3.91) equals the sum of (3.95), which means that R_j can be chosen as the numeraire and set arbitrarily at $\tilde{R}_j$. Solving (3.94) for p_i^h, we obtain

$$p_i^h = p_j^h \exp[V_i^h(R_i) - V_j^h(\tilde{R}_j)], \qquad i = 1, \ldots, M, \quad h = 1, \ldots, H. \quad (3.96)$$

Substituting these into (3.91), we obtain

$$\sum_h p_j^h \exp[V_i^h(R_i) - V_j^h(\tilde{R}_j)] - 1 = 0, \qquad i = 1, \ldots, M. \qquad (3.97)$$

Substituting (3.96) into (3.95), we find

$$\sum_{i=1}^{M} p_j^h \exp[V_i^h(R_i) - V_j^h(\tilde{R}_j)] - N_h = 0, \qquad h = 1, \ldots, H. \qquad (3.98)$$

The problem has been reduced to (3.97) and (3.98), which can be solved simultaneously for $\bar{R}^*$ and $\bar{p}_j^* = [p_j^{1*} \cdots p_j^{H*}]$. Equations (3.97) and (3.98) are analogous to (3.85), (3.86) and have identical mathematical form. Thus all comments following those equations also apply to (3.97), (3.98).

5.3. Hierarchical Choice Structures and the Equilibrium Distribution of Dwelling Rents within Submarkets

The properties of equilibrium in a multiple segment market with a hierarchical choice structure for each household segment can be examined in a manner that follows the reasoning of Sections 4.4, 5.1, and 5.2. As in Section

4.4, we assume that the strict utility function of segment h has the form

$$V^h(R_{jk}, Y_j, X_{jk}) = \alpha^h R_{jk} + V_1^h(Y_j) + V_3^h(X_{jk}) \tag{3.99}$$

or

$$V^h(R_{jk}, Y_j, X_{jk}) = \beta^h \log R_{jk} + V_1^h(Y_j) + V_3^h(X_{jk}), \tag{3.100}$$

where the meaning of symbols is as in Section 4.4. Definitions (3.55) and (3.58) hold with the meaning of r_{jk} and ρ_{jk} as before.

The submarket choice probabilities can now be written as

$$P_j^h = \exp[\alpha^h \bar{R}_j + V_j^h + (1 - \delta_h)I_j^h]/\sum_{i=1}^{J} \exp[\alpha^h \bar{R}_i + V_i^h + (1 - \delta_h)I_i^h], \tag{3.101}$$

where $V_j^h \equiv V_1^h(Y_j)$, and $\bar{R}_j$ is the mean submarket rent. The conditional dwelling choice probabilities are

$$P_{k|j}^h = \exp(\alpha^h r_{jk} + V_{jk}^h)/\exp(I_j^h) \tag{3.102}$$

for a dwelling k in submarket j, and the inclusive values are

$$I_j^h = \log \sum_{k=1}^{S_j} \exp(\alpha r_{jk} + V_{jk}^h). \tag{3.103}$$

If we assume (3.100) instead of (3.99), then the corresponding choice structure is obtained by replacing $\alpha^h \bar{R}_j$ in (3.101) with $\beta^h \log \bar{R}_j$ and $\alpha^h r_{jk}$ in (3.102), (3.103) with $\beta^h \log \rho_{jk}$.

To show how a solution could be obtained, consider the following iterative procedure. Suppose that the allocation of households among submarkets has been solved as in Section 5.1 using the submarket choice structure (3.101) with fixed inclusive values I_j^h. This allocation yields a trial submarket rent vector $\bar{R}$, which is an equilibrium vector *given* the fixed inclusive values. The procedure also yields a trial vector $\bar{S} = [S_1^1 \cdots S_1^H \cdots S_j^1 \cdots S_j^H]$. Given this trial vector $\bar{S}$ of household allocations to submarkets, what is the stochastic equilibrium allocation of households within each submarket? This problem can be solved by following a procedure analogous to that of Section 5.2, keeping in mind that for each submarket j, S_j^h [the (j, h)th element of vector S] assumes the role of N_h, and the conditional choice probabilities $P_{k|j}^h$ assume the role of the dwelling choice probabilities of Section 5.2. Proceeding in this way, one would obtain a unique determination of the rent deviations from the mean r_{jk} and ρ_{jk} by imposing rent normalization conditions (3.57) or (3.59) within each submarket. These will be trial values of the equilibrium r_{jk} or ρ_{jk}. Given these, the inclusive values can be recomputed, treated as fixed, and the allocation of households to submarkets can be readjusted as in Section 5.1, so that new trial values for $\bar{R}$ and $\bar{S}$ are obtained. One can continue in this way until revised estimates of $\bar{R}$ differ only very slightly from the previous estimates. One would thus obtain equilibrium estimates of the mean submarket rent vector $\bar{\bar{R}}^*$ and the equilibrium values of the inclusive values I_j^{h*} and of the dwelling rent deviation measures r_{jk}^* or ρ_{jk}^*. These equilibrium values are unique up to an arbitrary specification of any one mean submarket rent $\tilde{R}_j$ as the numeraire. Adjustments in this numeraire price would assure nonnegative equilibrium rents for all dwellings.

The precise steps of the procedure described above are left as an exercise for the reader, who can formulate these by imitating the reasoning of Sections 4.4, 5.1, and 5.2 and using the hints given above. It should be noted that one can also ignore the presence of a hierarchical choice structure and solve the problem directly as in Section 5.2 by approaching it as a direct allocation of households to dwellings. If this approach is taken, one must use the choice probabilities $P_{jk}^h = P_j^h P_{k|j}^h$ as in Section 5.2. The uniqueness of the solution is apparent from Section 5.2 since the above choice probabilities satisfy the strict gross substitutability conditions for each dwelling.

The presence of multiple population segments introduces a major complexity to the distribution of dwelling rents within each submarket. In Section 4.4 we saw that with only one segment in the market, the intrasubmarket rent distribution was independent of its mean and of the rents of any dwellings outside the submarket. This is not so in markets with multiple segments: the distribution of rents within a submarket depends on the number of households from each segment allocated to that submarket, which, in turn, reflects the distribution of mean submarket rents among submarkets.

6. EQUILIBRIUM IN CLOSED MARKETS

The crucial difference in the computation of expected demand for closed and open markets was discussed at the end of Section 3, and the expected demand functions for closed markets were formulated in Eqs. (3.19), (3.20), where closed market demand was viewed as a summation of recursive demands computed combinatorially by assigning households to unoccupied dwellings. Given the complexity of these computations, an approximate method for appropriately analyzing closed markets is proposed here. Recalling that the open market excess demand functions are a lower bound for the closed market demand functions, one can define parameters θ_j for dwelling j such that $\theta_j > 1$. Then the closed market demand for dwelling j can be expressed as

$$d_j(\bar{R}) \equiv \theta_j E(x_j^t | \bar{R}). \tag{3.104}$$

For submarket demand, one can define similar parameters $\Theta_j > 1$ such that

$$D_j(\bar{R}) \equiv \Theta_j E(X_j^t | \bar{R}). \tag{3.105}$$

We can now rederive the Walrasian equilibrium solution of Sections 3 and 4 using the demand expressions (3.104) and (3.105). This approach will produce equilibrium conditions for differential rents in which the θ_j's or Θ_j's appear as parameters. One can then empirically estimate the values of these parameters in an effort to assess the extent to which the closed market equilibrium conditions differ from the open market conditions. If they do not differ, the deviations between one and the empirically estimated θ_j^*'s or Θ_j^*'s can be explained by reference to random error, choice model specification error, etc. Precise methods for estimating these parameters is a topic left for future work. It suffices to say that at an acceptable level of aggregation of dwellings into submarkets, the closed market and open market formulations should produce small differences because errors due to the probabilistic assignment of households to dwellings will be minimized when the households assigned to submarkets are large relative to the number of submarkets.

7. DETERMINISTIC EQUILIBRIUM AS A SPECIAL CASE OF STOCHASTIC EQUILIBRIUM

Following the discussion in Section 3.5 of Chapter 2, the strict utility function of any logit model can be rescaled by the following rule:

$$U_{jk} = \lambda \tilde{U}_{jk}, \qquad \lambda = (\pi/\sqrt{6})/\sigma, \tag{3.106}$$

where U_{jk} is the strict utility level for alternative (j, k); $\tilde{U}_{jk}$, the rescaled utility level; and λ the factor that includes the common standard deviation σ of the random utility terms for each alternative (j, k). It was noted in Chapter 2 that when the utility function is linear, namely,

$$U_{jk} = \sum_n \alpha_n X_{jkn}, \tag{3.107}$$

the estimated coefficient α_n are equal to $\lambda \bar{\alpha}_n$ such that

$$\tilde{U}_{jk} = \sum_n \bar{\alpha}_n X_{jkn}, \tag{3.108}$$

where $\bar{\alpha}_n$ are rescaled coefficients.

Although in this book we follow the practice of assuming constant σ and thus absorbing λ into the utility function, the implications of varying λ and the effects of this on the Walrasian equilibrium conditions derived in this chapter will now be examined.

First, consider the submarket equilibrium condition (3.34) derived in the single-segment analysis of Section 4.2. When the dwelling similarity coefficient δ equals one, the inclusive values drop out of (3.34), and the equilibrium condition becomes

$$V_j(\bar{R}_j) - V_i(\bar{R}_i) = \log(S_j/S_i) \qquad \text{for any } i, j. \tag{3.109}$$

If we make the substitution $V_j(\bar{R}_j) = \lambda \tilde{V}_j(\bar{R}_j)$ and $V_i(\bar{R}_i) = \lambda \tilde{V}_i(\bar{R}_i)$, we obtain the equivalent equilibrium condition

$$\tilde{V}_j(\bar{R}_j) - \tilde{V}_i(\bar{R}_i) = (1/\lambda) \log(S_j/S_i). \tag{3.110}$$

We now note that as $\sigma \to 0$, $1/\lambda \to 0$, and the households become identical in their preferences since the random portion of their utility function vanishes. Thus as households tend to become homogeneous in their preferences (strict utilities), the submarket equilibrium conditions become (at the limit)

$$\tilde{V}_j(\bar{R}_j) = \tilde{V}_i(\bar{R}_i) \qquad \text{for any } i, j, \tag{3.111}$$

which states that at equilibrium, households will be indifferent as to their submarket choice since total utility (strict utility plus the *zero* random term) is the same for any two alternatives i and j. The limiting condition (3.111) is identical to the equilibrium condition encountered in the deterministic bid rent models reviewed in Chapter 1. Thus working with logit models and setting λ to a very large value (or setting σ approximately equal to zero), we can approximate a market clearing situation in which choice of submarket is deterministic.

For choice of dwelling, the equilibrium conditions (3.24) can also be rescaled to yield (assuming $\lambda \to \infty$)

$$\tilde{V}_j(R_j) - \tilde{V}_i(R_i) = 0, \tag{3.112}$$

where $\tilde{V}_j$ and $\tilde{V}_i$ are the total utility (strict utility plus the *zero* random term) of choosing dwelling j or i. Thus the equilibrium condition is again the equalization of utility for all choice alternatives. This case corresponds to setting $\delta = 0$ in the nested logit model, which reduces the nested model to a direct dwelling choice model.

For nested logit models with the value of δ between zero and one [see (3.63)–(3.65)], the joint probability of dwelling and submarket choice is

$$P_{jk} = P_j \, P_{k|j} = \frac{\exp[\alpha(\bar{R}_j + r_{jk}) + V_j + V_{jk} - \delta I_j]}{\sum_{i=1}^{J} \exp[\alpha \bar{R}_i + V_i + (1 - \delta)I_i]}. \tag{3.113}$$

We can rescale utility; replace V_j, V_i, and V_{jk} with $\lambda \tilde{V}_j$, $\lambda \tilde{V}_i$, and $\lambda \tilde{V}_{jk}$; and replace α with $\lambda\alpha$ throughout Eq. (3.113). Now as $\sigma \to 0$ and $\lambda \to \infty$, the inclusive value given by equation (3.65) becomes

$$I_j = \lambda + \log \sum_{k=1}^{S_j} \exp(\bar{\alpha} r_{jk} + \tilde{V}_{jk}) \qquad \text{for each } j. \qquad (3.114)$$

Substituting (3.114) into (3.113) for each term in the denominator and the term in the numerator, we find that $\exp(-\delta\lambda)$ cancels out of (3.113). Application of the dwelling equilibrium condition to the modified model (3.113) yields the equilibrium conditions

$$\lambda\bar{\alpha}(\bar{R}_j + r_{jk}) + \lambda\tilde{V}_j + \lambda\tilde{V}_{jk} - \delta \log \sum_{k=1}^{S_j} \exp(\bar{\alpha} r_{jk} + \tilde{V}_{jk})$$

$$= \lambda\bar{\alpha}(\bar{R}_i + r_{im}) + \lambda\tilde{V}_i + \lambda\tilde{V}_{im} - \delta \log \sum_{m=1}^{S_i} \exp(\bar{\alpha} r_{im} + \tilde{V}_{im}), \quad (3.115)$$

which can be rearranged as

$$\left[\bar{\alpha}(\bar{R}_j + r_{jk}) + \tilde{V}_j + \tilde{V}_{jk}\right] - \left[\bar{\alpha}(\bar{R}_i + r_{im}) + \tilde{V}_i + \tilde{V}_{im}\right]$$

$$= \left(\frac{\delta}{\lambda}\right) \log \frac{\sum_{k=1}^{S_j} \exp(\bar{\alpha} r_{jk} + \tilde{V}_{jk})}{\sum_{m=1}^{S_i} \exp(\bar{\alpha} r_{im} + \tilde{V}_{im})}. \qquad (3.116)$$

This has a right side approaching zero as $\lambda \rightarrow \infty$ $(\sigma \rightarrow 0)$. The bracketed terms on the left side are the total rescaled utility levels for alternatives (j, k) and (i, m). Abbreviating these as $\tilde{U}_{jk}$ and $\tilde{U}_{im}$, we establish the equilibrium condition

$$\tilde{U}_{jk}(\bar{R}_{jk}) - \tilde{U}_{im}(\bar{R}_{im}) = 0 \qquad \text{for any } (j, k), (i, m), \qquad (3.117)$$

which states the same result as (3.108) for the case of nested logit models with $0 \leq \delta < 1$.

Clearly the above **derivations can** be repeated for each population segment in a market with $h = 1, \ldots, H$ segments. In each case, the implication of letting the variance of the random utility terms approach zero $(\sigma^h \rightarrow 0)$ is to let $\lambda^h \rightarrow \infty$ and thus establish the result of the equalization of total utility for each alternative (dwelling or submarket); but this result is a bit more complex for the case of markets with multiple segments than it is for single segment markets. Consider the stochastic dwelling equilibrium condition (3.94). If utility is rescaled, this can be rewritten as

$$\tilde{V}_i^h(R_i) - \tilde{V}_j^h(R_j) = (1/\lambda^h) \log(p_i^h/p_j^h) \qquad (3.118)$$

for any two dwellings i and j. As λ^h approaches infinity (σ^h approaches zero and random utility vanishes), (3.118) approaches its limiting form, which can be written as

$$\left[\log p_i^h - \log p_j^h\right]^{-1} \left[\tilde{V}_i^h(R_i) - \tilde{V}_j^h(R_j)\right] = 0. \qquad (3.119)$$

Consider the following theorem.

Theorem 1. Let the vector of dwelling rents $\bar{R} = (R_1, R_2, \ldots, R_M)$ be such that the number of the most preferred n dwellings ($1 \leqq n \leqq M$) are tied in strict utility for a household segment h. For that household segment h, as the variance σ^h of the random utility terms for each dwelling approaches zero ($\lambda^h \to \infty$), the dwelling choice probability for each dwelling approaches $1/n$ for the most preferred dwellings and zero for each of the other dwellings.

Proof. First note that if for any two dwellings i and j, $\tilde{V}_i^h(R_i) = \tilde{V}_j^h(R_j)$, the choice probabilities at the limit must be equal and positive, i.e., $P_i^h = P_j^h > 0$. Second, if $\tilde{V}_i^h(R_i) > \tilde{V}_j^h(R_j)$, it is seen from (3.118) that $\lambda^h[\tilde{V}_i^h(R_i) - \tilde{V}_j^h(R_j)]$ approaches $+\infty$ and thus $\log(p_i^h/p_j^h) = \log(P_i^h/P_j^h)$ must also approach $+\infty$; but this can happen only if P_j^h approaches zero and P_i^h approaches a number greater than zero (but, of course, not greater than one). It follows from these demonstrations that several dwellings may be tied in their strict utility levels and this tied strict utility level must be higher than the strict utility level of any other dwelling that is not in the group of tied dwellings. If it was not higher, this would imply that all dwellings must be tied in strict utility. Now let us rewrite the choice probabilities as

$$P_i^h = 1/\{1 + \sum_{k \neq i} \exp \lambda^h[\tilde{V}_k^h(R_k) - \tilde{V}_i^h(R_i)]\}, \qquad i - 1, \ldots, J. \quad (3.120)$$

Note that if n dwellings are tied in strict utility, then as $\lambda^h \to \infty$, $P_j^h \to 1/n$ for any tied dwelling j. We can also verify from (3.120) that as $\lambda^h \to \infty$, $P_j^h \to 0$ for those dwellings j that are not among the tied for first place. Q.E.D.

The implications of this theorem are straightforward. As the variance of the random utility terms vanishes, strict utility becomes total utility and all households agree perfectly about their preference rankings of the dwellings. If only one dwelling has the highest strict utility, each household will behave deterministically and choose that dwelling with a probability approaching one. If n dwellings are tied for first place, each household will be indifferent among these and choose each with a probability of $1/n$.

8. STOCHASTIC EQUILIBRIUM AND THE PROBABILITY OF MARKET CLEARING

In this section we prove that the stochastic equilibrium conditions derived in this chapter are such that a single household segment demand system behaving according to these conditions has the highest probability of clearing the market. To show this, consider first equation (3.6) of Section 3, which gives the probability of market clearing under the assumption that $P_1, \ldots, P_M$ are the choice probabilities for the M dwellings in a market with a single segment. Now suppose we ask the normative question: What should the choice probabilities be so that the probability that the market is cleared is maximized? This can be posed as the following simple nonlinear programming problem:

$$\text{Max} \ \log\{\text{Prob}[\bigcap_{j=1}^{M} (a_j^t = 0)]\} \tag{3.121}$$

subject to

$$\sum_{j=1}^{M} P_j = 1. \tag{3.122}$$

Using (3.6) to rewrite the objective function (3.121), we get

$$\text{Max} \ \mathcal{L} = \log(M!) + \sum_{j=1}^{M} \log P_j + \mu(\sum_{j=1}^{M} P_j - 1), \tag{3.123}$$

where $\mathcal{L}$ is the Lagrangian and μ the Langrangian multiplier of the constraint (3.122). Maximization yields the constraint (3.122) and

$$\partial\mathcal{L}/\partial P_j = 1/P_j - \mu = 0. \tag{3.124}$$

The Lagrange multiplier μ must be chosen so that constraint (3.122) is satisfied. This implies $\mu = N$, the number of households (recall $N = M$ by assumption), which in turn implies

$$NP_j = 1, \qquad j = 1, \ldots, M. \tag{3.125}$$

However, (3.125) are precisely the M Walrasian excess demand equations for stochastic dwelling market equilibrium. The structure of equilibrium rents consistent with these has already been derived. We have thus established that the conditions for a stochastic dwelling market equilibrium maximize the probability that the market will be cleared at any exact time t.

Utilizing the probability of submarket clearing (3.5) instead of (3.6), we can, in a way similar to the above, establish the result that the probability of submarket clearing is maximized when

$$NP_j = S_j, \qquad j = 1, \ldots, J, \tag{3.126}$$

where P_j is now the submarket choice probability, and S_j the number of dwellings in submarket j. Again, (3.126) means that the stochastic submarket equilibrium conditions [which are precisely (3.126)] maximize the probability that the submarkets will be cleared at exact time t. The Walrasian rent structure consistent with (3.126) has already been derived.

The above result does not carry over to markets with several household segments. To see this, consider the simplest example of two dwellings and two households with different strict utility functions. In this simple case, market clearing will occur only when household one chooses one dwelling and household two chooses the other. The probability of this occurring is $P_1^1 P_2^2 + P_1^2 P_2^1$. What should be the four choice probabilities so that the above probability that the market is cleared is maximized? This is posed as

$$\text{Max } P_1^1 P_2^2 + P_1^2 P_2^1 \tag{3.127}$$

subject to

$$P_1^1 + P_2^1 = 1, \qquad P_1^2 + P_2^2 = 1, \tag{3.128}$$

where P_j^h ($h = 1, 2; j = 1, 2$) is the probability that household h will choose dwelling j. Maximization yields the two constraints (3.128) and the following first-order conditions, where μ_1 and μ_2 are the two Lagrange multipliers:

$$\partial \mathscr{L}/\partial P_1^1 = P_2^2 + \mu_1 = 0, \tag{3.129}$$

$$\partial \mathscr{L}/\partial P_2^1 = P_1^2 + \mu_1 = 0, \tag{3.130}$$

$$\partial \mathscr{L}/\partial P_1^2 = P_2^1 + \mu_2 = 0, \tag{3.131}$$

$$\partial \mathscr{L}/\partial P_2^2 = P_1^1 + \mu_2 = 0. \tag{3.132}$$

These conditions, together with (3.128), imply the result $P_1^1 = P_2^1 = P_1^2 = P_2^2 = \frac{1}{2}$. Although these probabilities imply the equilibrium $P_1^1 + P_1^2 = 1$ and $P_2^1 + P_2^2 = 1$, as long as the two strict utility functions are different it is not in general possible to find a rent structure R_1 and R_2 that will yield that all four probabilities equal one-half. This counterexample suffices to demonstrate that in multisegmented markets, the Walrasian equilibrium conditions do not maximize the probability that the market will be cleared.

9. SUMMARY

This chapter defined stochastic Walrasian equilibrium conditions for an open rental housing market in which the demand for housing is based on probabilistic choice models. Properties of such equilibria were fully analyzed for the case of multinomial logit specification of demand for open markets with single and multiple household segments and for the cases of simultaneous as well as sequential specifications of logistic demand. Analysis for markets with a single population segment demonstrated that the problem of equilibrium rent determination is fully tractable at the level of submarkets or dwellings regardless of the complexity of detail in the representation of households and dwellings. The case of open markets with multiple household segments is much less tractable computationally, but workable numerical solution procedures have been suggested by the analysis of this chapter. The key result in a market with a single segment is that the "relative" equilibrium rents for any two dwellings reflect the property of the independence from irrelevant alternatives. This result does not hold when the market is divided into multiple segments. Another result that holds for single-segment markets occurs when the submarket utility is additively separable from dwelling utility. When this is the case, the variance of dwelling rents within a submarket is independent of the rents of any dwellings outside the submarket, while the "relative" mean submarket rents conform to the IIA property. This result does not hold for markets with multiple household segments.

This chapter also established several results regarding the probability of market clearing under conditions of stochastic equilibrium. First, it was shown that as taste differences among households in the same segment diminish and ultimately vanish, the conditions for stochastic market equilibrium converge at the limit to the familiar deterministic equilibrium conditions reviewed in Chapter 1. It was also demonstrated in Section 7 that the stochastic equilibrium conditions in an open market with a single household segment assure that the probability of market clearing is maximized.

This chapter focused solely on Walrasian notions of equilibrium in markets. As such, it was assumed that the number of dwellings in the market equals the number of households and that relative rents can be determined only up to an arbitrarily specified numeraire rent. More general models in which the number of households in the market are less than the number of dwellings have been proposed and analyzed in Anas (1980). In these models landlords maximize an expected rental revenue function that is derived from the probabilistic demand behavior of households. A competitive equilibrium solution of these interdependent revenue maximizations produces not only the rent of each dwelling, but also the probability that a dwelling will remain vacant and the expected proportion of vacant dwellings in each submarket. In such models equilibrium solutions can be nonunique and very difficult to compute for many submarkets, even if uniqueness can be established. A much simpler model that overcomes these difficulties is developed in Section 4 of Chapter 4. In that model each landlord's supply behavior consists of a binary stochastic profit maximizing decision of whether to offer the dwelling for rent or to withhold it from the market. The result is a supply function from which the expected proportion of dwellings that remain vacant in each submarket can be determined. Such a supply-side model lends itself to an empirically and computationally tractable Walrasian equilibrium analysis that generates submarket vacancies and submarket average housing prices. In Chapter 5 this model is applied to policy testing.

PART II

ECONOMETRIC ESTIMATION AND TRANSPORTATION POLICY ANALYSIS

CHAPTER 4

ESTIMATION OF DEMAND-
AND SUPPLY-SIDE CHOICE MODELS
FOR THE CHICAGO SMSA

The purpose of this chapter is to begin the task of empirical application suggested by the critique of Chapter 1 and the theoretical developments of Chapters 2 and 3. More precisely, probabilistic discrete choice models such as those of Chapter 2 will be derived, empirically estimated, and evaluated.

One important difference between the models to be estimated in this chapter and those derived in Chapter 2 is that in that chapter we emphasized the choice of location while suppressing the choice of travel mode: all theoretical models in Chapters 2 and 3 were assumed to be single travel mode models. In this chapter, we pay particular attention to the interaction of commuting mode choice with residential location choice, and we develop multinomial logit and nested multinomial logit models of travel mode–location choice. These models are developed and specified in light of the limitations of the data for the Chicago SMSA, and then estimated with appropriate methodological considerations. The aggregate (relative frequency) form of the data, coupled with the "smallness" of the aggregation units (geographical zones), enables us to obtain estimates that are easily validated and are consistent with the state-of-the-art estimates obtained by others. The models estimated in this way combine the objectives of "travel demand analysis" with those of "location demand analysis" and provide a new tool for urban economic policy testing in a way that is theoretically and empirically superior to the bid rent approach overviewed in Chapter 1.

117

The chapter begins with a review and an evaluation of the various sources of bias to be encountered in the estimation of choice models, and the available strategies for minimizing these biases. Section 2 is a detailed presentation of the 1970 Census based data to be used in the empirical estimation. Section 3 presents the theoretical derivation of the demand-side travel mode–residence location choice models. The impact of aggregation on the model and the compatibility of the model with the data are examined. The supply-side model of landlord behavior is derived in Section 4. The fifth section presents the estimation methods and the model evaluation and goodness-of-fit measures. The models are estimated in Section 6, and the resulting elasticities and aggregate predictions are evaluated in Section 7. Results and conclusions are summarized in Section 8.

1. SOURCES OF BIAS IN THE ESTIMATION
OF CHOICE MODELS

We begin with a qualitative discussion of the various sources of bias encountered in specifying and estimating choice models. These sources of bias exist because the analyst must make specific decisions as to the theoretical specification of the choice model and as to the utilization of the data in the estimation of the model.

The bias with which we are concerned is the bias in the estimated coefficients. Maximum likelihood applied to probabilistic choice models will yield asymptotically consistent coefficients, but the estimated asymptotically consistent coefficients and corresponding choice probabilities will deviate from the "true" coefficients and choice probabilities according to the model specification, aggregation, sampling, segmentation, and other assumptions employed in a particular estimation.

There are *ten* major sources of bias. These are (1) specification of the *choice model type* such as logit, nested logit, generalized extreme value, and probit; (2) specification of the form of the choice model's *objective function* (e.g., *utility* or *profit function*) such as linear, loglinear, and generalized constant elasticity of substitution; (3) specification of the *explanatory variables* or *attributes* to be included in the choice model; (4) a precise definition of the *choice alternatives*; (5) specification of the assumptions or processes by which the *choice set* of each chooser is determined (e.g., the list of the choice alternatives to be entered into the choice set of each chooser); (6) *population segmentation* or grouping of choosers into distinct categories within which a single and distinct choice model or utility function is sufficient to describe the dispersion of preferences and choices; (7) *aggregation* of the choice alternatives into groups (aggregation units) and commensurate aggregation of the attributes (explanatory variables) within each aggregation unit; (8) *sampling* of the choosers within each population segment and sampling of the choice alternatives within each chooser's choice set to form an estimation sample; (9) *measurement method* used in determining the values of the explanatory variables for each choice alternative and each chooser in the data; and (10) *estimation method* applied to obtain estimates of the choice model's coefficients.

Sources of error (1–5) are various forms of model specification bias, while sources of error (6–10) are forms of bias related to the manner in which data are used to estimate a choice model. Most of the above sources of bias are not specific to choice models but will occur in any behavioral econometric modeling. We will now review the type of bias introduced by each source of error and will discuss the state-of-the-art knowledge regarding each of the ten forms of bias. Of particular interest are the ways in which these biases appear in or affect the estimated coefficients of the logit model family and the conditions or assumptions that, if true, rule out a particular form of bias. Each type of bias is separately discussed below.

1.1. Choice Model Type

It was seen in Chapter 2 that a particular probabilistic choice model is derived from specific assumptions as to the joint distribution of the random terms associated with the discrete choice alternatives. If this distribution is multivariate normal with an arbitrary variance–covariance structure, the choice model is a generalized probit. If the random terms are normal but independently and identically distributed (IID) for each alternative, the choice model is IID probit. If the random terms have the generalized extreme value distribution, the choice model is the generalized extreme value model, with nested logit being a special case. Finally, if the random terms are IID and have the extreme value distribution for each alternative, the choice model is logit. A variety of choice models exists because a variety of assumptions can be made about the distribution of the random terms. In all econometric work, the form of the *true* model remains unknown because the error structure is never precisely known. The selection of model type, therefore, is an approximation. For problems involving choice among a large number of alternatives such as dwellings or submarkets, multinomial probit is computationally intractable and inaccurate. The largest probit model estimated to date is the 14-alternative model by Miller and Lerman (1979), which explains the store location choices of clothing retailers in Boston. The authors show a strong similarity between this model and equivalent logit models that they also estimate. For choice problems with large numbers of alternatives, logit and its relatives are the only tractable choice models. Furthermore, even if the true probit coefficients were to be somehow known to us, all would still not be well since the calculation of probit probabilities requires a numerical integration procedure based on Clark's formula (1961), which becomes inaccurate for a large number of choice alternatives. The state-of-the-art belief is that logit and probit are close approximations of each other because of the close similarity between the extreme value and the normal distributions. For empirical and numerical confirmations, see Horowitz (1980) and Hausman and Wise (1978) and Table 4.5.

Ruling out probit and other as yet unknown choice models may introduce some specification error, but such errors are probably quite small. Larger and unavoidable errors can occur in specifying the variance–covariance of the error structure within a chosen model type. For example, selection of logit is inappropriate if the random terms for alternatives are correlated. If nested logit is selected, the precise nesting sequence for the alternatives must be decided. Decisions related to choice model type are, strictly speaking, not independent of decisions related to other sources of bias.

1.2. Objective Function

Although the literature on applied choice modeling has specialized in linear or loglinear utility (or other objective) functions, choice models can be specified with any type of objective function. Changes in the functional form of the utility function may necessitate changing the assumptions about the distribution of the random terms and thus changing the type of choice model. For problems with a large number of choice alternatives, the only tractable strategy for investigating the validity of alternative objective functional forms is to embed these into the logit family of models and to estimate these models. In addition, the effects of certain kinds of separability in the objective function can also be explored by estimating appropriately nested logit models. There is direct and indirect evidence from the literature that the form of the utility function can lead to large differences in the response measures (such as elasticities) of the estimated model. This evidence will be discussed more thoroughly in Sections 6 and 7, where empirical assessments of the sources of bias are performed.

1.3. Explanatory Attributes

The selection of explanatory attributes to be entered into the objective function (assuming the functional form of the objective function has been determined) is probably the most important source of bias in specifying a choice model. Missing variables excluded because of data limitations or an inadequate theoretical basis can seriously bias the estimated coefficients of the included attributes, frequently resulting in wrong signs. Inclusion of superfluous attributes can yield misleading results, and the use of proxy variables may result in noncausal models with uninterpretable elasticities or response measures. Missing attributes directly influence assumptions about error terms since the effects of all missing attributes must be included in the random terms. Important changes in model type may be implied if certain attributes are known to be missing from the objective function and are correlated across choice alternatives. In such cases, the nesting sequence and assumptions about random term covariances must be reconsidered. Inclusion–exclusion properties related to explanatory attributes will be discussed at a later point in this chapter.

1.4. Choice Alternatives

Definition of the choice alternatives is a fundamental problem. If one is interested in modeling housing choice, should one define alternatives as "geographic zones" or as "structural housing types"? Next, suppose one of the above is decided, how should one define zone boundaries or structural types? In all applications, it is necessary to make rather arbitrary decisions about the definition of alternatives. Judgment and experience are the primary guides in resolving the problem of alternative definition. To this author's knowledge, there is no empirical evidence demonstrating the effect of alternative definitions on the estimated coefficients of choice models.

1.5. Choice Sets

The choice set is a subset of the universe of alternatives. The alternatives in a choice set are those available for choice. Each chooser may have a different choice set because numerous unobserved constraints prevent that chooser from considering all alternatives. Such constraints can be complex and intractable. Economic theory has done little in identifying these constraints, and the problem of choice set formation has not been modeled as an endogenous part of the choice process. As a result, choice sets are specified by assumption, or all alternatives are entered into the choice set by assuming a state of perfect economic information.

1.6. Population Segmentation

Biases in population segmentation occur when certain choosers in a sample are assigned to the wrong segment and therefore the wrong choice model. The most commonly committed segmentation error arises from assuming that all choosers belong to a single segment, which corresponds to assuming that a single choice model applies to the entire population. Ideally, the segmentation of a population (the number and membership of each segment) must be decided jointly with the problem of model estimation. This can be done only by working through a complex and intractable analysis-of-variance approach combined with model estimation. It is no wonder, therefore, that most segmentation analysis relies on predetermined and intuitive definitions of segments, rather than on a fully analytic segmentation strategy.

1.7. Aggregation of Alternatives and Attributes

Often, we may not know precisely which alternative a chooser has chosen because choice alternatives may appear in aggregated form. For example, we may know the geographic zone chosen by each chooser without knowing the precise dwelling (or location) chosen within the zone, or we may know the mode of travel chosen without knowing the precise day on which the choice was made, and thus without knowing the precise attributes faced by the chooser at the time of choice. In such cases, when choices are identified as aggregations of alternatives, the attributes of alternatives are typically averaged over the same aggregation units. The use of averaged attributes to explain aggregated choices results in bias in the estimated coefficients of choice models. As will be discussed in more detail in this chapter, aggregation error occurs because the use of averaged attributes (instead of the disaggregate attribute data) reduces the variance in the estimation sample used in maximum likelihood estimation. As shown by McFadden and Reid (1975), the size of the aggregation error in the estimated coefficients is directly related to the size of aggregation units; the larger the units, the larger the variance of the aggregated attributes *within* the aggregation unit and thus the larger the errors in the estimated coefficients and their estimated standard errors. McFadden and Reid (1975) derive a closed form formula for obtaining the coefficients of a disaggregate binary probit model from the biased coefficients of an estimated aggregate binary probit model. Unfortunately, this derivation is not applicable in most cases because it is derived for the hypothetical case in which the variance–covariance matrix of the observed utility attributes is the same for *each* aggregation unit (spatial zone). This homogeneity assumption is never reasonable in locational choice analysis. Furthermore, the variance–covariance matrices of utility attributes within aggregation units are normally not observed in aggregated data sets. Other studies of the relationship between aggregate and disaggregate models are those by Koppelman (1976), Talvittie (1973), and Bouthelier and Daganzo (1979). All studies on this issue imply or demonstrate that corrections for aggregation biases in the estimated coefficients of logit models are expensive and require variance–covariance information that is not normally available. Some of these studies also provide analytical or empirical evidence that aggregation errors can be reasonably small if the aggregation units are small or nearly homogeneous internally.

The empirical results of this chapter support the above conclusion. We will argue that errors in coefficients resulting from aggregation appear to be comparable to or smaller than errors arising from model specification or other sources if the aggregation units are reasonably small. This argument and the inconclusiveness of the analytical efforts to resolve the aggregation problem enable the use of aggregated (relative frequency) data and averaged attribute data to estimate behaviorally valid choice models.

1.8.   Sampling of Choosers and Alternatives

To avoid bias, choice models can be estimated separately for each population segment by using a random sample of choosers from that segment *and* specifying the complete choice set of the chooser in the sample. The second of these requirements creates a serious difficulty because if the choice alternatives are many or if the full choice sets are not known, estimation becomes intractable or impossible. In the case of multinomial logit, there are several theorems that simplify estimation by allowing us to consistently estimate the model, using nonrandom samples of choosers and alternatives.

It has been proved by Manski and Lerman (1977) [see also Cosslett (1978)] that the logit model can be estimated based on a biased sample of choosers called a *choice based sample*. According to this method of sampling, the analyst may preselect a number of choice alternatives and then select a random sample of choosers for each alternative from those choosing that alternative *without* imposing the requirement that the sampling rate for each alternative be the same. The sample of choosers selected in this way is not a random sample, but maximum likelihood estimation applied to this sample determines the unbiased utility coefficients for all of the explanatory attributes with the exception of the alternative-specific dummy variables entered into the utility function. If such dummies are excluded from the utility function, however, the estimated coefficients will be biased for all explanatory variables. Manski and Lerman further demonstrate that the bias in the estimated dummy coefficients is eliminated by performing a simple adjustment that takes into account the proportion of the number of choosers in the sample choosing that alternative to the number of choosers in the population choosing the same alternative. The use of such an adjustment procedure will be demonstrated in this chapter. The primary advantage of choice based sampling is that it allows us to collect data via alternative-specific surveys aimed at the choosers of selected choice alternatives, rather than home based surveys aimed at the general population of choosers. A second advantage is that alternatives chosen by only a few choosers can be more thoroughly covered by sampling these at a higher rate.

Choice based sampling does not address the sampling of alternatives from each chooser's full choice set. McFadden (1978) has proven that equally fortunate results exist for consistently estimating multinomial logit models with nonrandom samples of choice alternatives. These results stem from the *independence from irrelevant alternatives* (IIA) property of logit models. It is shown by McFadden that models obeying the IIA property can be correctly estimated without knowing the full choice sets of choosers and by using any random or nonrandom sample of the choice alternatives in the full choice set. More precisely, McFadden proposes two rules for selecting alternatives from full choice sets. One of these is called the *uniform conditioning property* (UCP) and the other the *positive conditioning property* (PCP). To explain the use of these properties, we will first assume that a group of choosers have a common full choice set labeled C. The probability that one of these choosers will choose alternative i is given as $P(i|C, \overline{X}, \bar{\alpha})$, where $\overline{X}$ is a vector of attributes describing all alternatives and $\bar{\alpha}$, a set of utility coefficients. The problem the analyst faces is to define a choice set $D \subseteq C$, define choice probabilities $P(i|D, \overline{X}, \bar{\alpha})$, and then estimate the model using these choice probabilities. According to the UCP, the choice set D may be defined as a fixed subset of C repeated for each chooser or a random subset of C repeated for each chooser. Choice set D may also be defined to include the chosen alternative of a chooser plus one or more randomly chosen elements of C for each chooser. An example of the PCP occurs when D is defined to include the alternative chosen by a chooser plus one or more nonrandomly selected alternatives for each chooser. When the UCP holds, the coefficients can be consistently estimated via the maximization of the usual likelihood function. If, on the other hand, the PCP holds, the analyst can consistently estimate the model by maximizing a modified likelihood function or by maximizing the usual likelihood function in which alternative-specific dummy variables have been included in the utility function.

Although nonrandom sampling methods are extremely powerful means for estimating multinomial logit models in practice, it is important to recall that these sampling methods can be applied only when multinomial logit is the correct model specification, i.e., when all errors due to model specification have already been eliminated. In practice, multinomial logit may be the most robust and the best model statistically, but it is almost never exactly correct theoretically. As a result, different sampling techniques will yield different estimated coefficients, and a certain amount of care is required in selecting the appropriate sampling technique. Indeed, estimating the logit model with alternative nonrandom samples drawn from the same data provides a way of determining the robustness of the multinomial logit specification: if alternative samples yield very similar coefficients or elasticities, the "correctness" of the specification is confirmed and the validity of the IIA property determined. If, on the other hand, alternative samples yield sufficiently divergent coefficients or elasticities, the validity of multinomial logit may be doubted.

1.9. Measurement of Explanatory Attributes

An important source of bias in estimating choice models results from errors in measuring the explanatory attributes entered into the choice model's objective function. There are many examples of this problem, but probably the best known is that of "travel time" in travel demand models: should the analyst measure travel time as the time reported by individual travelers or as the travel time measured according to the techniques of the local transportation planning agency? If the latter is to be used, the problem is further complicated by the fact that different techniques for generating door-to-door travel times exist and are in use by different transportation agencies.

Similar problems also exist for the measurement of housing prices, rents, incomes, and many other variables to be used as explanatory attributes. In each case these may be reported, surveyed, or objectively measured, as in the case of housing prices obtained from actual sale transaction records.

It is confirmed by empirical studies that measurement problems will lead to substantial deviations in the estimated coefficients and the resulting choice probabilities. Two articles that reach this conclusion are those by Train (1978) and Talvittie and Dehgani (1979). Both studies obtain substantially changed travel time coefficients depending on the type of travel time attribute data entered into the models.

1.10. Estimation Method

The theoretically most appealing method for estimating probabilistic choice models is maximum likelihood. Occasionally, however, analysts may find a rationale for applying other estimation criteria such as least squares or maximum score estimation. In all econometric work, the choice of estimation method is an important decision and a major source of bias in the estimated coefficients. Fortunately, the strong rationale for maximum likelihood minimizes the existence of biases due to estimation method.

A more specific estimation method problem arises in connection with the estimation of the nested logit model. It was mentioned in Chapter 2 that this model is normally estimated in two steps, the first of which estimates the coefficients of the conditional choice part and the second of which estimates the coefficients of the marginal choice part and the inclusive value coefficients, given the preestimated coefficients of the conditional choice part. It is known that each step results in asymptotically consistent estimates. Two-step estimates will, in general, be different from the one-step maximum likelihood estimates, which are more difficult to compute. Since one-step estimation is the optimal method in principle, the use of the cheaper two-step method can introduce substantial bias in the estimated coefficients. An empirical comparison of the one-step and two-step estimation of a nested logit model will be performed in Section 6.

1.11. Meaningfulness, Usefulness, and Transferability of Probabilistic Choice Models

Taken together, the ten sources of bias discussed in this section can have a strong impact on the empirical estimates obtained in a specific application. Judgment remains to be exercised in order to minimize or reduce the resulting biases and in order to evaluate the validity of the resulting estimated coefficients and their suitability for policy analysis.

Research in choice modeling remains worthwhile in the hope that the combined effect of the ten sources of bias may be negligible or controllable in practice to the point where choice models estimated in partial ignorance are *meaningful, useful,* and *transferable* (from place to place and time to time). A choice model can be said to be meaningful if it confirms intuition and prior knowledge and if it aids understanding. Most of the published choice models have passed the test of meaningfulness: explanatory attributes often obtain the correct sign and exhibit elasticities that are within an acceptable range. Meaningful models may not be useful, however, unless they can produce unbiased and reasonably precise predictions of actual choices. The confident transferability of choice models appears conjectural at present: it is not known whether the lack of agreement between the coefficients of different models (estimated for different places and times) is due to the differential influence of the sources of error discussed above or due to real differences observed to occur in time and place. The transferability issue can only be resolved after a long term research program aimed at determining the relative importance of the various sources of bias and the compounded biases that result when two or more of the sources interact in the same empirical estimation. When such knowledge is attained, it will become possible to separate the biases due to specification and data from the real differences in the estimated coefficients.

At the end of this chapter, we will offer several conclusions drawn from the results of this chapter that occupy a small place within a long term investigation of the relative importance of the various sources of bias encountered in the estimation of probabilistic choice models.

2. THE DATA

The data used in this chapter originate from the household home interview information compiled as part of the 1970 U.S. Census of population, employment, housing, and commuting for the Chicago SMSA. The 1980 Census results were not available at the time of this study and will not be comparably tabulated until 1983 or 1985. Similar data for 1970 is available for most major metropolitan areas. The Census data's overall accuracy is superior to those of small sample surveys because the Census samples households and dwellings at the rate of 15% and 20%, projecting the results to the population.

The original Census survey is not available in disaggregate form in which households and dwellings are distinct observations, but it is aggregated to the level of quarter sections ($\frac{1}{2}$-mile by $\frac{1}{2}$-mile square zones) that form a roughly regular grid and cover the entire metropolitan area. Aggregations of these quarter sections form larger zones called sections (1-mile by 1-mile square zones) and groups of sections for which travel time and travel cost data are regularly computed and updated by the Chicago Area Transportation Study (CATS). This system of transportation planning oriented zones, known as the CATS zone system, is shown in Fig. 4.1. It consists of sections covering the entire city of Chicago and the inner suburbs and of larger square zones for the outer suburban and exurban areas. The boundary line AA' depicts the area that is the Census SMSA definition consisting of 4918 quarter sections. Census data are not tabulated for zones outside the line AA', but this is inconsequential because the area included extends 35–40 miles in any radial direction from the Chicago Central Business District (CBD). The inner line BB' is the legal city limit boundary of the city of Chicago.

For the purposes of this study, the Central Business District (CBD) is defined as a roughly 4-square-mile area centered on State and Madison streets and bordering on Lake Michigan. This small area contained nearly 20% of the jobs within the Census tabulation area defined by the line AA'. Of the 4918 quarter sections represented in the Census area, 4776 contained some residential dwellings, and 3073 (roughly 62%) were recorded as reporting some trips to the CBD.

The Census data consist of three parts or three sets of tabulations. The first of these is employment information that describes the characteristics of

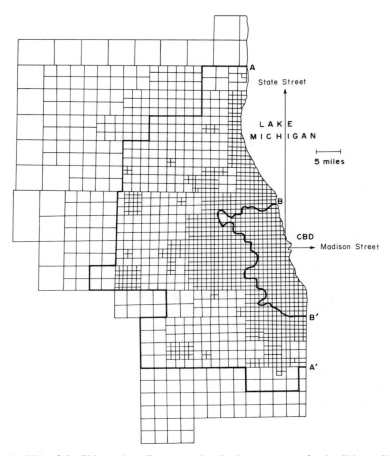

Fig. 4.1. Map of the Chicago Area Transportation Study zone system for the Chicago SMSA.

the jobs (employed persons) in each quarter section. More precisely, this data set consists of several frequency distributions of jobs by sex, occupation, and industry groups. The second part of the Census data describes the resident persons, households, and dwellings in each quarter section. This information can be grouped into two general categories: (1) socioeconomic characteristics describing the households and persons residing in each quarter section; and (2) physical and economic attributes describing the housing stock of each quarter section. The socioeconomic information consists of frequency distributions by family income, family size, age of household head, occupation and industry of household head, race of household head, household car ownership, etc. The housing stock information consists of frequency distributions for the number of rooms, age of housing, rent paid, reported value for owner occupied units, type of structure and proportion of occupied dwellings that are owned and those that are rented, proportion of dwellings that are vacant, etc. From these frequency distributions, means and standard deviations can be computed for each quarter section. All of this information forms the basis for most of the explanatory attributes to be used in the empirical estimations of the demand- and supply-side multinomial logit models.

The third part of the Census data is a tabulation of work trips by place of origin (residence), place of destination (employment), and mode of travel. More precisely, for each quarter section, the Census data provides the number of commuters originating at a residence within that quarter section and terminating at a workplace in each other quarter section and taking a particular mode. Trips are reported for eight modes: auto driver, auto passenger, commuter rail, bus, elevated or subway rapid transit, truck, taxi, walking, and other. Thus the entire origin–destination matrix consists of $4918 \times 4918 \times 8 = 193,493,792$ potential entries. Actually, many of these entries are zero because only 4776 quarter sections contain some housing, only about 3000 contain some employment, and a large number of origin–destination–mode combinations contain no trips. We denote the original matrix as $\{^\circ N_{ijm}\}$, where each element is the (observed) number of trips reported in the census; i, the origin quarter section (place of residence); j, the destination quartersection (place of work); and m, the mode of travel. The CBD travel matrix, which forms the focus of much of our attention in this chapter, is obtained by aggregating the above matrix by summing over the CBD destination quarter sections:

$$\{^\circ N_{im}^C\} \triangleq \{\sum_{k \in C} {}^\circ N_{ikm}\}, \tag{4.1}$$

where C denotes the CBD, e.g., the set of quarter sections within the 2-mile by 2-mile CBD definition. The non-CBD travel matrix, which will also be made use of, is defined as the matrix of trips terminating in all work places outside of the CBD and is defined as

$$(^\circ N_{im}^{\mathcal{C}}) \triangleq (\sum_{k \notin C} {}^\circ N_{ikm}), \tag{4.2}$$

where $\mathcal{C}$ denotes the set of quarter sections outside of the CBD. In this study we focus only on the five dominant modes, which are auto driver, auto passenger, commuter rail, bus, and rapid transit. Truck, taxi, walking, and other modes are aggregated into a sixth category called "other." This is reasonable since truck, taxi, walking, and all other modes are only 6% of the

TABLE 4.1

Distribution of 1970 Work Trips by Mode and Workplace in the Chicago SMSA

Travel modes	Location of workplace		Mode totals
	Inside CBD	Outside CBD	
Auto driver	129,995 (29%)	1,184,372 (61%)	1,314,367 (55%)
Auto passenger	28,251 (6%)	230,598 (12%)	258,849 (11%)
Commuter rail[a]	77,908 (17%)	26,665 (1%)	104,573 (4%)
Rapid transit[a]	83,092 (18%)	38,849 (2%)	121,941 (5%)
Bus[a]	108,400 (24%)	232,109 (12%)	340,509 (14%)
Other	26,050 (6%)	231,373 (12%)	257,423 (11%)
Total	453,696 (19%)	1,943,966 (81%)	2,397,662

[a] Primary mode utilized during the trip. Access to the primary mode may be by walking, bus, auto, or other means.

CBD-terminating trips and represent a small number of trips by zone, local trips of households living very near or within the CBD, or are not, for most cases, regularly used commuting alternatives but represent unusual choices during the day of the census survey. A precise tabulation of the aggregates of the CBD and non-CBD travel matrices is shown in Table 4.1. It is noteworthy that the dominant non-CBD travel modes are auto, bus, and "other" with rapid transit and commuter rail forming a mere 3% of these trips. The larger percentage (12%) of "other" trips to non-CBD destinations is explained by the thinner spatial distribution of non-CBD employment that enables increased access to it by bicycle, walking, and other modes.

Additional information on the characteristics of commuting is obtained from the travel time–travel cost data of the Chicago Area Transportation Study. These data consist of the average total travel time and travel cost of commuting from each residential quarter section to each employment quarter section by each of four modes: auto, bus, commuter rail, and rapid transit. It is important to recall that these four modes are the primary mode of a trip, but the costs and times of travel include any access, waiting, egress, line-haul, exit, and parking times and costs. Additional data such as the availability of park-and-ride facilities and the density of bus route miles by zone are also obtained from CATS.

Salient features of the data are tabulated in Table 4.2, which lists the average values by 2-mile rings surrounding the CBD. Figure 4.2 shows the profiles of eight important variables as a function of concentric ring averages centered around the CBD.

TABLE 4.2a

Socioeconomic and Housing Characteristics of the Chicago SMSA[a,b]

Distance from CBD (miles)	Annual household income ($)	Black-headed households (%)	Owner occupied dwellings (%)	Developed land (%)	Housing density (dwellings/ square mile)	Vacant dwellings (%)	Housing age (yr)	Rooms in house	Monthly Rent ($)	Value ($)	Cars per household	Work trips per household
0–2	11,923	24.9	19.9	91.2	7,055	13.43	24.3	3.2	157	29,387	0.43	0.84
2–4	7,978	28.9	24.0	87.2	10,450	8.99	29.0	4.2	99	16,777	0.52	0.92
4–6	8,167	35.3	28.7	90.7	9,888	7.44	31.1	4.4	101	16,882	0.60	0.95
6–8	9,188	24.2	35.4	91.1	8,472	5.48	30.4	4.3	113	21,159	0.71	1.02
8–10	11,392	23.1	48.9	91.4	5,822	2.64	27.5	4.8	132	25,277	0.95	1.14
10–12	12,767	15.4	68.4	85.1	3,501	2.46	22.9	5.1	131	26,718	1.17	1.25
12–14	13,579	7.4	73.8	85.4	2,599	1.95	20.5	5.3	145	28,267	1.29	1.24
14–16	15,666	3.2	75.7	76.1	1,942	2.19	17.0	5.5	150	32,550	1.42	1.21
16–18	15,299	4.6	76.1	70.4	1,485	2.93	17.7	5.5	154	30,650	1.44	1.24
18–20	14,169	7.1	76.6	65.8	1,676	3.05	16.4	5.4	144	28,627	1.45	1.17
20–22	15,861	1.3	84.1	60.7	1,348	4.58	13.3	5.8	184	32,119	1.56	1.26
22–24	16,621	1.3	82.1	58.7	1,437	4.01	14.4	5.9	175	33,511	1.53	1.25
24–26	15,617	2.2	79.4	53.8	1,362	4.65	14.0	5.9	159	33,638	1.53	1.20
26–28	14,438	4.6	78.3	44.2	1,510	4.80	14.8	5.9	136	30,586	1.47	1.26
28–30	14,566	0.3	83.7	35.9	1,373	3.67	15.2	5.7	142	27,509	1.51	1.26
30–32	14,383	3.3	79.4	31.5	1,392	4.26	18.0	5.8	136	28,859	1.51	1.10
32–34	11,562	10.2	65.2	43.4	1,554	4.33	23.1	5.1	112	22,507	1.28	1.80
>34	11,387	7.4	65.4	47.5	1,713	3.29	23.9	4.9	113	23,092	1.27	1.21
Mean	11,765	17.3	54.4	64.4	2,697	4.68	24.2	4.9	121	28,075	1.03	1.14

[a] Average values by distance from the CBD.

[b] Source: 1970 Census of Population and Housing.

TABLE 4.2b

Work Trip Characteristics of the Chicago SMSA for Commuters to the Central Business District (CBD)[a,b]

Distance from CBD (miles)	Trips per zone (quartersection) CBD					Bus mile density (miles/ square mile)	One-way times to CBD				One-way daily costs to CBD			
	Total	Auto	Rail	Transit	Bus		Auto time (min)	Rail time (min)	Transit time (min)	Bus time (min)	Auto cost ($)	Rail cost ($)	Transit cost ($)	Bus cost ($)
0–2	1177	104	0	43	237	67.3	13.6	46.6	21.9	21.1	1.65	1.12	0.53	0.45
2–4	1787	151	0.2	64	277	69.0	20.8	44.7	27.3	31.4	1.84	0.90	0.54	0.45
4–6	1890	156	0.6	86	194	53.6	29.6	49.9	30.6	39.0	2.05	1.00	0.56	0.45
6–8	1793	143	0.6	147	130	42.7	38.1	53.4	35.6	47.4	2.25	1.12	0.61	0.45
8–10	1463	135	15	109	90	32.7	45.9	53.1	40.0	56.6	2.44	1.18	0.61	0.54
10–12	921	74	26	34	27	23.4	54.8	55.1	43.8	61.6	2.63	1.13	0.67	0.55
12–14	673	46	33	17	10	18.2	63.4	59.7	51.1	71.2	2.88	1.19	0.77	0.66
14–16	425	28	31	4	3	13.4	68.3	61.0	57.9	82.1	3.09	1.25	0.90	0.60
16–18	326	19	29	1	0.8	9.9	72.9	62.9	66.1	85.8	3.32	1.28	1.06	0.55
18–20	319	15	23	0.7	1.0	9.7	76.9	66.6	69.8	54.0	3.47	1.36	1.06	0.45
20–22	252	13	25	0.3	0.1	8.3	83.3	68.6	86.1	75.0	3.70	1.42	1.54	0.95
22–24	259	11	27	0.3	0.1	10.4	85.0	74.9	54.6	—	3.91	1.50	0.87	—
24–26	217	9	17	0.1	0.0	5.4	91.3	76.9	94.8	—	4.11	1.54	1.72	—
26–28	207	8	16	0.0	0.0	4.0	94.7	82.1	—	—	4.34	1.69	—	—
28–30	139	5	7	0.0	0.0	2.1	95.7	85.2	—	—	4.51	1.78	—	—
30–32	107	2	5	0.0	0.0	2.4	96.6	—	—	—	4.56	—	—	—
32–34	314	2	5	0.0	0.0	7.6	105.5	—	—	—	5.01	—	—	—
>34	265	2	4	0.0	0.0	12.3	104.8	—	—	—	5.07	—	—	—
Mean	543	37	18	19.5	25.5	15.4	50.0	58.7	37.9	43.8	2.62	1.21	0.62	0.48

[a] Average values by distance from the CBD.

[b] Source: 1970 Census of Population and Housing; travel time/travel cost data of the Chicago Area Transportation study.

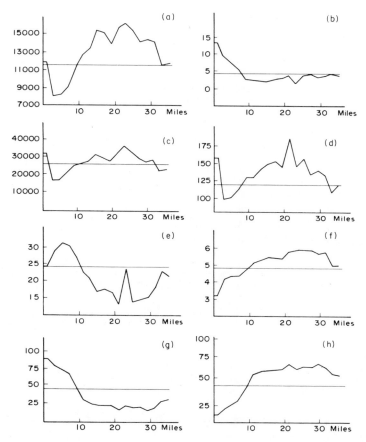

Fig. 4.2. Profiles of selected variables as a function of distance from the CBD. (a) Annual household income ($), (b) vacancy rate (%), (c) value of owner occupied units ($), (d) monthly rate for renter occupied units, (e) housing age (yr), (f) number of rooms, (g) renter occupied dwellings (%), (h) owner occupied dwellings (%). (Constructed from zonal averages. Horizontal line is position of SMSA mean.)

3. DEMAND-SIDE MODELS: CHOICE OF RESIDENTIAL LOCATION AND TRAVEL MODE

We now turn to the theoretical derivation of the demand-side multinomial logit models. In deriving these models for both the CBD and non-CBD commuters, we will consider the assumed error structure, the form of the aggregation error in these models, and the assumed form and separability of the utility function. First we discuss the theoretical derivation of an aggregated model suited for estimation from relative frequency data. Next we point out the difference between CBD and non-CBD models.

3.1. Derivation of an Aggregated Model

The utility function of a commuter with a *given* workplace is expressed as

$$\hat{U}_{imk} = U_{imk} + \zeta_{imk}, \tag{4.3}$$

where $\hat{U}_{imk}$ is the total utility of geographic zone (location) i, commuting mode m, and dwelling k [alternative (i, m, k)]. The first part, U_{imk}, is the measurable (or strict) utility of alternative (i, m, k), and the second part, ζ_{imk}, is the random, unobserved (or perceived) utility of alternative (i, m, k). A disaggregate logit model of joint zone, mode, and dwelling choice can be derived by assuming that the random terms are *independently* and *identically* distributed for each alternative (i, m, k) according to the Weibull distribution as discussed in Chapter 2. The only difference between the models discussed here and those of Chapter 2 is that in the current models, a choice alternative is a combination of zone, mode, and dwelling, whereas in Chapter 2, only zone–dwelling models were discussed. The logit model that corresponds to the current case is

$$P_{imk} = \exp(U_{imk}) / \sum_{j=1}^{J} \sum_{n=1}^{M_j} \sum_{p=1}^{S_j} \exp(U_{jnp}), \tag{4.4}$$

where J is the number of locations (geographic zones); M_j, the number of travel modes available to residents of zone j; S_j, the number of dwellings in zone j; and P_{imk}, the probability with which a randomly selected member of the workplace population will choose alternative (i, m, k) under assumptions of utility maximization. Various nested logit models can also be derived by assuming a correlation structure among the random terms for selected groups of dwellings and modes.

To achieve a transition from the disaggregate model to a workable aggregated model, we specify the utility function as

$$\hat{U}_{imk} = \sum_{w=1}^{W} \alpha_w X_{ikw} + \sum_{v=1}^{V} \beta_v X_{imkv} + \zeta_{imk}, \tag{4.5}$$

where X_{ikw} are $w = 1, 2, \ldots, W$ attribute measures that vary by zone and dwelling; X_{imkv} are $v = 1, 2, \ldots, V$ attribute measures that vary by zone, mode, and dwelling; and α_w, β_v are corresponding coefficients of the utility function.

Since dwelling-specific data are not observed, the attributes may be expressed as

$$X_{ikw} = \bar{X}_{iw} + e_{ikw}, \qquad w = 1, 2, \ldots, W \qquad (4.6)$$

and

$$X_{imkv} = \bar{X}_{imv} + e_{imkv}, \qquad v = 1, 2, \ldots, V, \qquad (4.7)$$

where $\bar{X}_{iw}$ and $\bar{X}_{imv}$ are observed zonal measures for attributes w and v and e_{ikw}, e_{imkv} are unobserved dwelling specific deviations from the zonal measures. The attribute measures X_{ikw} and/or X_{imkv} can be nonlinear functions of the underlying attribute data such as

$$X_{ikw} \equiv \log Y_{ikw} \qquad (4.8)$$

or

$$X_{imkv} \equiv \log Y_{imkv}. \qquad (4.9)$$

These are consistent with (4.6) and (4.7) if we define the attribute data Y_{ikw} or Y_{imkv} as

$$Y_{ikw} \equiv \bar{Y}_{iw} d_{ikw} \qquad (4.10)$$

and

$$Y_{imkv} \equiv \bar{Y}_{imv} d_{imkv}, \qquad (4.11)$$

where $\bar{Y}_{iw}$ and $\bar{Y}_{imv}$ are means over dwellings and d_{ikw}, d_{imkv} are multiplicative deviations from the means. Definitions (4.8) and (4.9) can now be written as

$$X_{ikw} = \log \bar{Y}_{iw} + \log d_{ikw} \qquad (4.12)$$

and

$$X_{imkv} = \log \bar{Y}_{imv} + \log d_{imkv}, \qquad (4.13)$$

which are of the same form as (4.6) and (4.7), with

$$\bar{X}_{iw} = \log \bar{Y}_{iw}, \qquad e_{ikw} = \log d_{ikw}, \qquad (4.14)$$

and

$$\bar{X}_{imv} = \log \bar{Y}_{imv}, \qquad e_{imkv} = \log d_{imkv}. \qquad (4.15)$$

The utility function can be rewritten as

$$\hat{U}_{imk} = \sum_{w=1}^{W} \alpha_w \bar{X}_{iw} + \sum_{v=1}^{V} \beta_v \bar{X}_{imv} + E_{imk}, \qquad (4.16)$$

where

$$E_{imk} = \sum_{w=1}^{W} \alpha_w e_{ikw} + \sum_{v=1}^{V} \beta_v e_{imkv} + \zeta_{imk}. \qquad (4.17)$$

We can now see that the utility function (4.3) consists of four essential parts and can be written as

$$\hat{U}_{imk} = U_i + U_{im} + \Theta_{imk} + \zeta_{imk}. \qquad (4.18)$$

These four parts are defined as follows:

$$U_i \equiv \sum_{w=1}^{W} \alpha_w \overline{X}_{iw}, \tag{4.19}$$

which is a function of zone-specific average attribute measures

$$U_{im} \equiv \sum_{v=1}^{V} \beta_v \overline{X}_{imv}, \tag{4.20}$$

which is a function of zone- and mode-specific average attribute measures

$$\Theta_{imk} \equiv \sum_{w=1}^{W} \alpha_w e_{ikw} + \sum_{v=1}^{V} \beta_v e_{imkv}, \tag{4.21}$$

which is a part of the utility that remains unobserved due to aggregation but that is not random over the population for each alternative. The final part, of course, is the random utility ζ_{imk}, which varies among the choosers in the population.

The problematic part of the utility function (4.18) is the third part, Θ_{imk}. This is problematic for two reasons: (1) it is a function of *unobserved* but non-random deviations from zonal means, and (2) it is a function of the utility coefficients that must be estimated. The Θ_{imk} are thus the sources of aggregation error.

The utility structure (4.18) is consistent with utility maximization for the sequential choice probability structure

$$P_{imk} = P_i P_{m|i} P_{k|im}, \tag{4.22}$$

where $P_{k|im}$ is the conditional probability of choosing dwelling k given the choice of zone i and mode m; $P_{m|i}$, the conditional probability of choosing mode m given zone i; and P_i, the marginal probability of choosing zone i. The logistic form of these choice probabilities is

$$P_i = \exp[U_i + (1 - \sigma)I_i] / \sum_{j=1}^{J} \exp[U_j + (1 - \sigma)I_j], \tag{4.23}$$

$$P_{m|i} = \exp[U_{im} + (1 - \delta)J_{im}] / \exp(I_i), \tag{4.24}$$

$$P_{k|im} = \exp(\Theta_{imk}) / \exp(J_{im}), \tag{4.25}$$

where the inclusive values I_j and J_{jn} are

$$I_j = \log \sum_{n=1}^{M_j} \exp[U_{jn} + (1 - \delta)J_{jn}], \tag{4.26}$$

$$J_{jn} = \log \sum_{s=1}^{S_j} \exp(\Theta_{jns}). \tag{4.27}$$

The same utility structure (4.18) is also consistent with utility maximization for the sequential choice probability structure

$$P_{imk} = P_i P_{k|i} P_{m|ik}, \qquad (4.28)$$

where $P_{m|ik}$ is the conditional probability of choosing mode m given the choice of zone i and dwelling k; $P_{k|i}$, the conditional probability of choosing dwelling k given the choice of zone i; and P_i, the marginal probability of zone choice. The logistic form of these choice probabilities is

$$P_i = \exp[U_i + (1 - \tau)L_i] / \sum_{j=1}^{J} \exp[U_j + (1 - \tau)L_j], \qquad (4.29)$$

$$P_{k|i} = \exp[\Theta'_{ik} + (1 - \theta)K_{ik}] / \exp(L_i), \qquad (4.30)$$

$$P_{m|ik} = \exp(\Theta'_{imk} + U_{im}) / \exp(K_{ik}), \qquad (4.31)$$

where $\Theta'_{ik} + \Theta'_{imk} = \Theta_{imk}$, and

$$\Theta'_{ik} \equiv \sum_{w=1}^{W} \alpha_w e_{ikw}, \qquad (4.32)$$

$$\Theta'_{imk} \equiv \sum_{v=1}^{V} \beta_v e_{imkv}. \qquad (4.33)$$

The inclusive values L_j and K_{js} are

$$L_j = \log \sum_{s=1}^{S_j} \exp[\Theta'_{js} + (1 - \theta)K_{js}], \qquad (4.34)$$

$$K_{js} = \log \sum_{n=1}^{M_j} \exp(\Theta'_{jns} + U_{jn}). \qquad (4.35)$$

The two choice probability structures differ in that the first one assumes a doubly nested logit model in which the choice of dwelling is conditional on the choice of mode, whereas the second structure assumes a doubly nested logit model in which the choice of mode is conditional on the choice of dwelling. In the first structure, the inclusive value coefficient δ measures the correlation among the random terms ζ_{jns} due to dwelling similarity within a zone and for the same mode. If this coefficient is zero, unobserved dwelling attributes may be assumed to be independently distributed within the zone; whereas if $\delta \doteq 1$, dwellings within the same zone are nearly identical in their unobserved attributes. Similarly, the inclusive value coefficient σ is a measure of correlation among unobserved travel mode related attributes within a zone, with $\sigma = 0$ denoting no correlation among the modes and $\sigma \doteq 1$ indicating nearly identical unobserved random attributes for the modes.

In the second choice probability structure, the inclusive value coefficients have a similar but reversed interpretation: the coefficient θ measures mode similarity in unobserved random attributes and the coefficient τ measures dwelling similarity in unobserved random attributes.

We will now consider the effect of aggregation assumptions on the form of these models. Aggregation becomes necessary because we are not able to observe choices of dwellings, but instead we observe aggregates of choices by zone and by zone and travel mode combinations. Explanatory variables are computed as zone and as zone–mode-specific averages, and intrazonal deviations from these averages are not observed in the data.

The effect of aggregation on the first choice structure (4.23)–(4.27) is to set the values of the Θ_{imk} equal to a constant for all k within each (i, m). The effect is to simplify the choice probability structure to the form:

$$P_{k|im} = 1/S_i, \tag{4.36}$$

$$P_{m|i} = \exp(U_{im})/\exp(I_i), \tag{4.37}$$

$$P_i = S_i^\gamma \exp[U_i + (1 - \sigma)I_i]/ \sum_{j=1}^{J} S_j^\gamma \exp[U_j + (1 - \sigma)I_j], \tag{4.38}$$

$$I_j = \log \sum_{n=1}^{M_j} \exp(U_{jn}), \tag{4.39}$$

$$\gamma \equiv (1 - \delta)(1 - \sigma). \tag{4.40}$$

The effect of aggregation on the second choice structure (4.29)–(4.35) may be observed by setting Θ'_{ik} and $\Theta'_{imk} = $ const for all k within each i and (i, m). Doing this simplifies the choice probability structure to the form:

$$P_{m|ik} = \exp(U_{im})/ \sum_{n=1}^{M_i} \exp(U_{in}), \tag{4.41}$$

$$P_{k|i} = 1/S_i, \tag{4.42}$$

$$P_i = S_i^\gamma \exp[U_i + (1 - \sigma)I_i]/ \sum_{j=1}^{J} S_j^\gamma \exp[U_j + (1 - \sigma)I_j], \tag{4.43}$$

$$I_j = \log \sum_{n=1}^{M_j} \exp(U_{jn}), \tag{4.44}$$

$$\gamma \equiv (1 - \tau), \tag{4.45}$$

$$\sigma \equiv 1 - (1 - \tau)(1 - \theta). \tag{4.46}$$

Comparing the two marginal choice structures, we find that these are of precisely the same form. We also note that the conditional part of the first choice structure, which is $P_{m|i}P_{k|im}$, is identical to the conditional part of the second choice structure, which is $P_{k|i}P_{m|ik}$. The product of the corresponding conditional parts expresses the joint choice of mode and dwelling given the choice of zone, e. g., $P_{mk|i} = P_{m|i}P_{k|im}$ in the case of model 1 and $P_{mk|i} = P_{k|i}P_{m|ik}$ in the case of model 2.

We must now review the extent to which the aggregation assumptions Θ_{imk} or Θ'_{ik} and Θ'_{imk} constant for each i, (i, m) may be justified. These will be satisfied if, for each alternative (i, m, k), the values of e_{ikw} and/or e_{imkv} multiplied by their respective utility coefficients balance out to yield a constant. Alternatively, the same conditions will be approximately satisfied, i.e., Θ_{imk} or Θ'_{ik}, Θ'_{imk} roughly invariant in each i, (i, m) if each e_{ikw} and e_{imkv} is small in value due to the smallness of the geographic zones (aggregation units). Thus the best safeguard against excessive aggregation error is to keep the units of aggregation as small as possible, as we choose to do in this study. Given any aggregation scheme, there will be a certain amount of aggregation bias in the estimated coefficients γ, σ, $\bar{\alpha} = (\alpha_1, \alpha_2, \ldots, \alpha_W)$ and $\bar{\beta} = (\beta_1, \beta_2, \ldots, \beta_V)$. If the units of aggregation are kept small, there is good reason to believe that the bias introduced because of aggregation will be smaller than the bias that would be introduced because of sampling errors in any disaggregate attribute data of a small sample survey.

3.2. Models for CBD and Non-CBD Commuters

The model derived above will be estimated for those commuters working in the CBD as well as for all other commuters working anywhere outside of the CBD. These two commuter segments receive identical treatment in every respect except for the manner in which two variables, "travel time" and "travel cost," are treated in aggregated form.

Suppose $_1\overline{X}_{ijm}$ and $_2\overline{X}_{ijm}$ are "the average travel time from employment zone j to residential zone i via mode m" and "the average travel cost from employment zone j to residential zone i via mode m," respectively. Each residential zone and each employment zone is a $\frac{1}{2}$-mile $\times$ $\frac{1}{2}$-mile quarter section. The average time and cost from each residential zone to the CBD and the non-CBD employment situations is computed as

$$_s\overline{X}^C_{im} = \frac{\sum_{j\in C} {_s\overline{X}_{ijm}}\,{^\circ N_{ijm}}}{\sum_{j\in C} {^\circ N_{ijm}}} \qquad \text{for CBD} \qquad (4.47)$$

and

$$_s\overline{X}^{\mathbb{C}}_{im} = \frac{\sum_{j\in\mathbb{C}} {_s\overline{X}_{ijm}}\,{^\circ N_{ijm}}}{\sum_{j\in\mathbb{C}} {^\circ N_{ijm}}} \qquad \text{for non-CBD}, \qquad (4.48)$$

where $s = 1$ represents travel time, $s = 2$ represents travel cost, and $°N_{ijm}$ is the number of commuters that live in residential zone i and commute to residential zone j by mode m.

The major difference between these averaged CBD and non-CBD times and costs is that the CBD is a spatially specific and contiguous small area of about 2 miles by 2 miles, whereas the spatially nonspecific non-CBD employment situation represents all other zones distributed throughout the metropolitan area. Thus while travel times and costs from any zone i and any mode m to the CBD have only a small variance, travel times and costs from any zone i and any mode m to a non-CBD employment zone have a much larger variance. Apart from this measurement of travel times and travel costs, the formulation of CBD and non-CBD models follows identical theoretical lines. The empirical results will be discussed in Sections 6 and 7.

4. THE SUPPLY-SIDE MODEL: CHOICE OF RENTAL VERSUS VACANCY STATUS

The owner of each dwelling faces the choices of offering the dwelling unit for rental at the current rental rate or keeping the unit vacant. This binary decision is resolved via profit maximization: if the differential profit that can be obtained from offering the dwelling unit for rent is positive, the unit will be offered for rental. If, on the other hand, the differential profit is negative because of high perceived maintenance costs for occupied dwellings, the magnitude of this *loss* must be compared to the cost of maintaining the same dwelling unit when it is vacant. More precisely, when the loss from an occupied unit is larger than the cost of maintaining a vacant unit, the landlord will prefer to keep the unit vacant.

The profit from dwelling n in zone j when that dwelling is occupied can be written as

$$\hat{\Pi}_{jn} = R_{jn} - C_{jn}, \tag{4.49}$$

where R_{jn} is the rent of the nth dwelling in zone j expected by the landlord and C_{jn}, the cost of maintaining that dwelling when it is occupied. When the same dwelling is vacant, the loss to the landlord is

$$\hat{\Pi}_{jn}^0 = -C_{jn}^0, \tag{4.50}$$

where C_{jn}^0 is the cost of maintaining the vacant dwelling.

The rent of the nth dwelling in zone j can be written as

$$R_{jn} = R_j + r_{jn}, \tag{4.51}$$

where R_j is the average rent of dwellings in zone j and r_{jn}, the deviation between the average zone rent and the rent of dwelling n. The maintenance costs are themselves functions of the various attributes of the zone and the dwelling. We assume that these are linear functions that can be written as

$$C_{jn} = \sum_{t=1}^{T} \eta_t X_{jnt} + \epsilon_{jn} \tag{4.52}$$

and

$$C_{jn}^0 = \sum_{t=1}^{T} \eta_t^0 X_{jnt} + \epsilon_{jn}^0, \tag{4.53}$$

where ϵ_{jn} and ϵ_{jn}^0 are random terms; X_{jnt} is the tth attribute (or the natural logarithm of the mean of the tth attribute Y_{jnt}, e.g., $X_{jnt} \equiv \log Y_{jnt}$); and η_t, η_t^0 are empirical coefficients. We can express each attribute as

$$X_{jnt} = \bar{X}_{jt} + e_{jnt}, \tag{4.54}$$

where $\bar{X}_{jt}$ is the zone average value of the tth attribute (or the natural logarithm of the mean of the tth attribute, e.g., $\bar{X}_{jt} \equiv \log \bar{Y}_{jt}$) and e_{jnt}, the deviation of the dwelling specific value of the tth attribute from the mean, e.g., $e_{jnt} \equiv X_{jnt} - \bar{X}_{jt}$. Using these definitions, we can rewrite the profit functions as

$$\hat{\Pi}_{jn} = R_j - \sum_{t=1}^{T} \eta_t \bar{X}_{jt} + r_{jn} - \sum_{t=1}^{T} \eta_t e_{jnt} - \epsilon_{jn} \tag{4.55}$$

and

$$\hat{\Pi}_{jn}^0 = - \sum_{t=1}^{T} \eta_t^0 \bar{X}_{jt} - \sum_{t=1}^{T} \eta_t^0 e_{jnt} - \epsilon_{jn}^0. \tag{4.56}$$

Each of these profit functions consist of two components:

$$\Pi_j \equiv R_j - \sum_{t=1}^{T} \eta_t \bar{X}_{jt} \tag{4.57}$$

and

$$\Pi_j^0 \equiv - \sum_{t=1}^{T} \eta_t^0 \bar{X}_{jt} \tag{4.58}$$

are the zonal average profit measures, and

$$\xi_{jn} \equiv r_{jn} - \sum_{t=1}^{T} \eta_t e_{jnt} - \epsilon_{jn}, \tag{4.59}$$

$$\xi_{jn}^0 \equiv - \sum_{t=1}^{T} \eta_t^0 e_{jnt} - \epsilon_{jn}^0 \tag{4.60}$$

are deviations in the profit of the nth dwelling from the average zonal profit. Thus the profit function can be rewritten as

$$\hat{\Pi}_j = \Pi_j + \xi_j \tag{4.61}$$

and

$$\hat{\Pi}_j^o = \Pi_j^o + \xi_j^o, \tag{4.62}$$

where ξ_j and ξ_j^o are random variables reflecting the unobserved part of perceived profit, which varies from dwelling to dwelling. As shown in (4.59) and (4.60), the randomness of ξ_j and ξ_j^o stems in part from purely unobserved dwelling-specific attributes, the effects of which are in $-\epsilon_{jn}$ and $-\epsilon_{jn}^o$. The remaining part of the unobserved profit comes from the unobserved part of the dwelling rent and the dwelling attributes entering the cost functions.

The probability Q_j that a randomly drawn dwelling in zone j will be offered for rent can be computed through stochastic profit maximization as

$$Q_j = \text{Prob}(\Pi_j + \xi_j > \Pi_j^o + \xi_j^o). \tag{4.63}$$

If we assume that ξ_j and ξ_j^o are identically and independently distributed and that the effect of aggregation introduced by the unobservability of r_{jn} and e_{jnt}, $t = 1, \ldots, T$, is small, we can derive the binary logit model

$$Q_j = \exp(\lambda \Pi_j)/[\exp(\lambda \Pi_j) + \exp(\lambda \Pi_j^o)], \tag{4.64}$$

which can also be written as

$$Q_j = \exp[\lambda(\Pi_j - \Pi_j^o)]/\{1 + \exp[\lambda(\Pi_j - \Pi_j^o)]\}, \tag{4.65}$$

where

$$\Pi_j - \Pi_j^o = R_j - \sum_{t=1}^{T} (\eta_t - \eta_t^o)\bar{X}_{jt}. \tag{4.66}$$

The binary logit model (4.65) can be estimated for the coefficients $-(\eta_t - \eta_t^o)\lambda$, $t = 1, \ldots, T$, and for λ.

The estimated coefficients of this supply-side model will contain some aggregation error because the rent and the cost function attributes are observed as zonal means. The resulting model is one which, given the average rent and average attributes of a zone, predicts the expected proportion of dwellings in that zone offered for rental. The expected proportion of dwellings that will be kept vacant is $1 - Q_j$.

5. SAMPLING, MAXIMUM LIKELIHOOD ESTIMATION, AND GOODNESS-OF-FIT MEASURES

5.1. Sampling Method

The multinomial logit models discussed in the previous section can be estimated via the maximization of appropriately defined likelihood functions. Before estimating these models, certain decisions must be made as to the sampling procedure that will be used to generate the estimation sample. The sampling theorems briefly summarized in Section 1.8 imply that *if the multinomial logit specification is correct*, the empirical coefficients of the joint multinomial logit model can be consistently estimated by random or non-random samples of the choice alternatives from the full choice set. For the demand models, the full choice set consists of the dwellings in all the geographic zones ($\frac{1}{2}$-mile by $\frac{1}{2}$-mile quarter sections) and all the modes available to these zones, where M_j^C is the number of modes available to the residents of zone j commuting to the CBD and $M_j^{\mathcal{C}}$ is the number of modes available to the residents of the same zone commuting to a non-CBD workplace.

We now consider the estimation sample. Suppose the vector $°N^C = \{°N_{11}^C \cdots °N_{1M_i^C}^C, °N_{21}^C \cdots °N_{JM_J^C}^C\}$ is the vector of the total number of trips by zone and mode terminating at the CBD, and let $°N^{\mathcal{C}} = \{°N_{11}^{\mathcal{C}} \cdots °N_{1M_i^{\mathcal{C}}}^{\mathcal{C}}, °N_{21}^{\mathcal{C}} \cdots °N_{JM_J^{\mathcal{C}}}^{\mathcal{C}}\}$ be the vector of the total number of trips by zone and mode terminating at non-CBD workplaces. An estimation sample drawn from the population vectors $°N^C$ and $°N^{\mathcal{C}}$ will be denoted as $\tilde{N}^C$ and $\tilde{N}^{\mathcal{C}}$. Demand models will be estimated with several different samples. These are (a) the entire observed data, namely $\tilde{N} = °N$; (b) samples in which the elements of $\tilde{N}$ are commuters chosen randomly from $°N$; (c) samples in which a random sample of the J zones has been selected and for which $\tilde{N}_{im} = °N_{im}$ for each m if i is a zone included in the sample *and* $\tilde{N}_{im} = 0$ for each m if i is a zone not included in the sample; and (d) samples in which a random sample of alternatives has been selected from the list of alternatives $\{1 \ldots M_1, 1 \ldots M_2, \ldots, 1 \ldots M_J\}$, and for which $\tilde{N}_{im} = °N_{im}$ if (i, m) is an alternative included in the sample and $\tilde{N}_{im} = 0$ if (i, m) is an alternative not included in the sample.

5.2. Likelihood Maximization

We will now consider the form of the likelihood function for the aggregated model given by (4.41)–(4.46). The probability of joint zone and mode choice for this model has the form to be given below, where $\bar{\alpha} \equiv (\alpha_1, \alpha_2, \ldots, \alpha_W)$, $\bar{\beta} \equiv (\beta_1, \beta_2, \ldots \beta_V)$ are the utility coefficients to be estimated, and $\overline{X}_i \equiv (\overline{X}_{i1}, \overline{X}_{i2}, \ldots, \overline{X}_{iW})$, $\overline{X}_{im} \equiv (\overline{X}_{im1}, \overline{X}_{im2}, \ldots, \overline{X}_{imV})$ are the mean attribute measures in vector form for each i and (i, m). The zone- and the zone–mode-specific part of utility can now be written in vector form as

$$U_i = \bar{\alpha}\overline{X}'_i, \tag{4.67}$$

$$U_{im} = \bar{\beta}\overline{X}'_{im}. \tag{4.68}$$

The joint choice expected probability can now be written directly as a function of the coefficients to be estimated, which are $\bar{\alpha}$, $\bar{\beta}$, γ, and σ. The probability is

$$P_{im} = P_i P_{m|i}$$

$$= \left[S_i^\gamma \exp(\bar{\alpha}\overline{X}'_i + \bar{\beta}\overline{X}'_{im} - \sigma I_i)\right] / \sum_{j=1}^{J} S_j^\gamma \exp\left[\bar{\alpha}\overline{X}'_j + (1 - \sigma)I_j\right], \tag{4.69}$$

where

$$I_j \equiv \log \sum_{n=1}^{M_j} \exp(\bar{\beta}\overline{X}'_{jn}), \qquad j = 1, \ldots, J. \tag{4.70}$$

The likelihood (or joint probability) function can now be written as

$$\mathscr{L} = \left[\tilde{N}! / \prod_{i,m} \tilde{N}_{im}!\right] \prod_{i,m} P_{im}(\bar{\alpha}, \bar{\beta}, \gamma, \sigma)^{\tilde{N}_{im}}, \tag{4.71}$$

where $\tilde{N} \equiv \sum_{i,m} \tilde{N}_{im}$. The log-likelihood function net of a constant term is

$$\log \mathscr{L} = \sum_{i=1}^{J} \sum_{m=1}^{M_i} \tilde{N}_{im} \log P_{im}(\bar{\alpha}, \bar{\beta}, \gamma, \sigma) + \text{const.} \tag{4.72}$$

The conditional probability of mode choice given the choice of zone is

$$P_{m|i} = \exp(\bar{\beta}\overline{X}'_{im}) / \sum_{n=1}^{M_i} \exp(\bar{\beta}\overline{X}'_{in}), \tag{4.73}$$

and the marginal zone choice probability is

$$P_i = S_i^\gamma \exp\left[\bar{\alpha}\overline{X}_i + (1 - \sigma)I_i\right] / \sum_{j=1}^{J} S_j^\gamma \exp\left[\bar{\alpha}\overline{X}_j + (1 - \sigma)I_j\right], \tag{4.74}$$

where

$$I_j \equiv \log \sum_{n=1}^{M_j} \exp(\bar{\beta}\overline{X}_{jn}), \qquad j = 1, \ldots, J. \tag{4.75}$$

Using the definition $P_{im} = P_i P_{m|i}$, the likelihood function (4.72) can be decomposed into

$$\log \mathscr{L} = \log \mathscr{L}_{\text{marg}} + \log \mathscr{L}_{\text{cond}} + \text{const}, \tag{4.76}$$

where

$$\log \mathscr{L}_{\text{marg}} = \sum_{i=1}^{J} \tilde{N}_i \log P_i(\bar{\alpha}, \bar{\beta}, \gamma, \sigma), \tag{4.77}$$

and

$$\log \mathscr{L}_{\text{cond}} = \sum_{i=1}^{J} \sum_{m=1}^{M_i} \tilde{N}_{im} \log P_{m|i}(\bar{\beta}), \tag{4.78}$$

where

$$\tilde{N}_i \equiv \sum_{m=1}^{M_i} \tilde{N}_{im}. \tag{4.79}$$

It has been observed by McFadden (1978) and others that the nested logit model can be estimated in two steps. In the first step, one maximizes the conditional part of the likelihood function, $\log \mathscr{L}_{\text{cond}}$, with respect to $\bar{\beta}$. In the second step, one maximizes $\log \mathscr{L}_{\text{marg}}$ to determine $\bar{\alpha}$, γ, σ, given the value of $\bar{\beta}$ determined in the first step. It has been demonstrated by Amemiya (1978) that this two-step estimation procedure yields consistent coefficient estimates. It is clear that this two-step estimation method is suboptimal to the one-step method, which maximizes (4.76) directly for $\bar{\alpha}$, $\bar{\beta}$, γ, and σ, although in most cases it is computationally efficient when compared to the one-step method. In separate studies, Ben-Akiva (1974) and Cosslett (1978) have confirmed that when a nested logit model is estimated by the two-step method, results are different from those obtained by applying the one-step method to the same estimation sample. We will provide our own confirmation of this result. Cosslett's results also provide empirical evidence that the one-step method does not always yield unique maximum likelihood estimates, whereas each step of the two-step suboptimal approach does yield unique estimates. In the special case of $\sigma = 0$, the multinomial logit model can be estimated directly by maximizing $\log \mathscr{L}$ (after setting $\sigma = 0$) to find the unique maximum likelihood estimates of $\bar{\alpha}$, $\bar{\beta}$, and γ.

That the two-step estimates can differ from the one-step estimates becomes clear by deriving and examining the first-order (necessary) conditions for the one-step and two-step maximization problems. These are as follows:

The one-step method requires that the following equations be solved simultaneously for $\bar{\alpha}^*$, $\bar{\beta}^*$, γ^*, and σ^*:

$$\frac{\partial \log \mathscr{L}}{\partial \beta_v} = \sum_i \sum_m (\tilde{P}_{im} - \hat{P}_{im}) \bar{X}_{imv}$$

$$- \sigma \left[\sum_i (\tilde{P}_i - \hat{P}_i) \sum_m \hat{P}_{m|i} \bar{X}_{imv} \right] = 0, \quad v = 1, \ldots, V, \tag{4.80}$$

$$\frac{\partial \log \mathscr{L}}{\partial \alpha_w} = \sum_i (\tilde{P}_i - \hat{P}_i) \bar{X}_{iw} = 0, \qquad w = 1, \ldots, W. \tag{4.81}$$

$$\frac{\partial \log \mathscr{L}}{\partial \gamma} = \sum_i (\tilde{P}_i - \hat{P}_i) \log S_i = 0, \tag{4.82}$$

$$\frac{\partial \log \mathscr{L}}{\partial \sigma} = \sum_i (\tilde{P}_i - \hat{P}_i) I_i = 0, \tag{4.83}$$

where $\tilde{P}_i \equiv \sum_m \tilde{N}_{im}/N$, $\tilde{P}_{m|i} \equiv \tilde{N}_{im}/\sum_m \tilde{N}_{im}$, $\hat{P}_i = P_i(\bar{\alpha}, \bar{\beta}, \gamma, \sigma)$, $\hat{P}_{m|i} = P_{m|i}(\bar{\beta})$, $N \equiv \sum_i \sum_m \tilde{N}_{im}$, and $I_i = \log \sum_m \exp(\bar{\beta}\overline{X}'_{im})$.

The two-step method requires that we first solve simultaneously the equations

$$\frac{\partial \log \mathscr{L}_{\text{cond}}}{\partial \beta_v} = \sum_i \tilde{P}_i \sum_m (\tilde{P}_{m|i} - \hat{P}_{m|i})\overline{X}_{imv} = 0, \quad v = 1, \dots, V \quad (4.84)$$

for $\bar{\beta}^*$ and subsequently solve the following equations simultaneously for $\bar{\alpha}^*$, γ^*, and σ^* after setting $\bar{\beta} = \bar{\beta}^*$:

$$\frac{\partial \log \mathscr{L}_{\text{marg}}}{\partial \alpha_w} = \sum_i (\tilde{P}_i - \hat{P}_i)\overline{X}_{iw} = 0, \qquad w = 1, \dots, W, \quad (4.85)$$

$$\frac{\partial \log \mathscr{L}_{\text{marg}}}{\partial \gamma} = \sum_i (\tilde{P}_i - \hat{P}_i) \log S_i = 0, \quad (4.86)$$

$$\frac{\partial \log \mathscr{L}_{\text{marg}}}{\partial \sigma} = \sum_i (\tilde{P}_i - \hat{P}_i)I_i^* = 0, \quad (4.87)$$

where $\hat{P}_i = P_i(\bar{\alpha}, \bar{\beta}^*, \gamma, \sigma)$, $\hat{P}_{m|i} = P_{m|i}(\bar{\beta}^*)$, and $I_i^* \equiv \log \sum_m \exp(\bar{\beta}^*\overline{X}'_{im})$.

Likelihood maximization for the supply-side model is examined next. This model can be written as

$$Q_i = \exp(\lambda R_i + \bar{\mu}\overline{X}'_i)/[1 + \exp(\lambda R_i + \bar{\mu}\overline{X}'_i)], \quad (4.88)$$

where $\bar{\mu} \equiv (\mu_1, \mu_2, \dots, \mu_T)$, $\mu_t \equiv -(\eta_t - \eta_t^0)\lambda$, $t = 1, \dots, T$, and $\overline{X}_i = (\overline{X}_{i1}, \overline{X}_{i2}, \dots, \overline{X}_{iT})$. The estimation sample for this model consists of a sample of observations on dwellings organized in vector form as $(\tilde{O}_1, \tilde{V}_1, \tilde{O}_2, \tilde{V}_2, \dots, \tilde{O}_J, \tilde{V}_J)$, where $\tilde{O}_i$ is the occupied sampled dwellings in zone i and $\tilde{V}_i$, the vacant sampled dwellings in zone i. The likelihood function for this supply-side model can be written as

$$\mathscr{L} = \prod_{i=1}^{J} \left[\frac{(\tilde{O}_i + \tilde{V}_i)!}{\tilde{O}_i!\tilde{V}_i!}\right] Q_i(\lambda, \bar{\mu})^{\tilde{O}_i}[1 - Q_i(\lambda, \bar{\mu})]^{\tilde{V}_i}, \quad (4.89)$$

and the log-likelihood net of a constant term is

$$\log \mathscr{L} = \sum_{i=1}^{J} \tilde{O}_i \log Q_i(\lambda, \bar{\mu}) + \tilde{V}_i \log[1 - Q_i(\lambda, \bar{\mu})] + \text{const}, \quad (4.90)$$

which can be maximized to find λ^*, $\bar{\mu}^*$.

5.3.   The Use of Alternative-Specific Constants

Probabilistic choice models are sometimes estimated with a set of "alternative-specific constants" or "dummy variables." A choice model with I

alternatives can be specified to include I-1 alternative specific constants as attributes in the utility function. The ith of these variables obtains the value one in the utility function evaluated for the ith alternative and obtains the value zero in the utility function evaluated for each of the other alternatives. The Ith alternative serves as the reference alternative, and it is not assigned an alternative-specific constant. In the utility function evaluated for this alternative, all I-1 alternative-specific constants obtain the value zero.

The specification of alternative-specific constants in the binary choice supply-side model is very simple: there are two choice alternatives, so only one constant is needed. This can be defined to obtain the value one for the alternative "offer for rent" and the value zero fro the alternative "keep vacant." Specification of alternative-specific constants in the demand-side models is more problematic because there are many alternatives and because each alternative is a combination of two underlying alternatives: mode and location (zone). Conceptually, it is possible to define an alternative-specific constant for each alternative (i, m) by defining the elements of the (i, m)-specific utility attribute vector $[\overline{X}_{im1}, \overline{X}_{im2}, \ldots, \overline{X}_{imV}]$ to include the appropriate number of zero–one variables. If (i, m) is the tth alternative and there is a total of I alternatives, the $V - (I - 1) + t$th variable is an alternative-specific constant that obtains the value one for alternative (i, m) and the value zero for any other alternative. Thus

$$\overline{X}_{jn,V-(I-1)+t} = \begin{cases} 1 & \text{if} \quad (j, n) = (i, m), \\ 0 & \text{if} \quad (j, n) \neq (i, m). \end{cases} \tag{4.91}$$

Here $t \equiv \sum_{j=1}^{i-1} M_j + m$, where M_j is the number of modes available to zone j.

It is clear that the number of alternative-specific constants needed in this way can be enormous for even a modest or a small sample of zones and modes from which the model is to be estimated. A practically equivalent way of specifying alternative-specific constants in the demand-side models is to specify separate constants for the conditional and marginal parts of these models. Thus, if the conditional part of the model describes the choice among M_j modes for zone j, the utility function evaluated for the jth zone will include $M_j - 1$ alternative-specific constants. Similarly, the marginal part of the choice model describing the choice among I geographic locations can be specified with $I - 1$ alternative-specific constants. The mode-specific constants of the conditional model are included in $\overline{X}_{im}$, and the location-specific constants of the marginal part are included in $\overline{X}_i$.

Alternative-specific constants are included in choice models in order to achieve two aims. First, these constants serve to capture the influence of attributes missing from the utility or profit function. In the mode choice problem, for example, travel time, travel cost, and other attributes of a trip are intended to capture the utility of that trip, whereas "comfort," "convenience," and other attributes that may be equally important in a measure of trip utility are typically not observed. Mode-specific constants can be included to capture their effects, albeit in a limited way. Second, alternative-specific constants *must*, as a rule, be included in models estimated from nonrandom samples of choosers (such as choice based samples) or in some cases, from nonrandom samples of choice alternatives. In such models, the constants serve the function of assuring that the estimated coefficients of the noncostant attributes will be free of bias. In fact, all of the bias arising from the use of a nonrandom sample becomes contained in the alternative-specific constants themselves. However, the biased values of these constants can be corrected by a simple adjustment procedure, which works as follows. Let $\hat{a}_i$ be the biased estimated value of an alternative-specific constant for the ith alternative, and let a_i^* denote the unbiased value of the same constant. These two values are related by

$$a_i^* = \hat{a}_i - \log(\tilde{H}_i/H_i), \tag{4.92}$$

where $\tilde{H}_i$ is the proportion of choosers in the sample (also called *market share*) choosing alternative i, and H_i the proportion of choosers in the population choosing alternative i.

Models estimated with alternative-specific constants have the property of generating perfect predictions of the aggregate market share of each alternative in the estimation sample. This property can be proved directly by observing the first-order conditions for likelihood maximization. From (4.81), if zone-specific constants are included in the location choice part of the demand-side model, then the corresponding $\overline{X}_{iw}$ obtains the value one for i and the value zero for other zones. This yields

$$\tilde{P}_i = \hat{P}_i, \tag{4.93}$$

which is precisely the condition of perfectly predicted market shares and, in this case, perfectly predicted expected choice probabilities for each zone. In such a model, the estimated coefficients (including the constants) are greater in number than the number of zones in the sample, and the model is a *saturated* one. Estimation of such a model is both unnecessary and impractical because of the large number of zones involved and the high computational cost incurred in estimating the coefficients of such a large number of constants. The effect of mode-specific constants on the market shares of the travel modes can be seen from the first-order condition (4.80). If the vth variable $\overline{X}_{imv}$ is a mode-specific constant for mode m, it obtains the value one for that mode in each zone and the value zero for other modes in each zone. This leads to

$$\sum_i \tilde{P}_{im} - \sum_i \hat{P}_{im} = \sigma\Big[\sum_i (\tilde{P}_i - \hat{P}_i)\hat{P}_{m|i}\Big]. \tag{4.94}$$

It is seen from this relationship that models of joint location–mode choice that obey the IID assumption and thus have $\sigma = 0$ will result in the perfect prediction of aggregate mode market shares, namely

$$\sum_i \tilde{P}_{im} = \sum_i \hat{P}_{im}. \tag{4.95}$$

Nested logit models (with $0 < \sigma < 1$) will generally exhibit a bias in aggregate mode market shares, and the right-hand side of (4.94) is a measure of this bias. Empirical measures of this bias will be discussed and evaluated in this chapter.

5.4. Standard Errors

The standard errors of multinomial logit coefficients estimated via maximum likelihood can be computed directly from the log-likelihood function. Thus, let the demand model's estimated coefficients be arranged into a vector $\bar{\phi}$ such that $\bar{\phi} = (\bar{\alpha}\bar{\beta}\gamma\sigma)$, with the maximum likelihood estimates denoted as $\bar{\phi}^* = (\bar{\alpha}^*\bar{\beta}^*\gamma^*\sigma^*)$. The variance–covariance matrix of these estimated coefficients can be estimated as

$$\sum_{\bar{\phi}^*} = \big[-\partial^2 \log \mathscr{L}(\bar{\phi})/\partial\bar{\phi}\,\partial\bar{\phi}'\big|_{\bar{\phi}=\bar{\phi}^*}\big]^{-1}, \tag{4.96}$$

where $\log \mathscr{L}(\bar{\phi})$ is the log-likelihood function, the variance–covariance matrix being the inverse of the Hessian of the log-likelihood function evaluated at the optimal values of the utility coefficients.

The standard error of the ith coefficient is simply estimated as the square root of the ith diagonal term in the Hessian of the log-likelihood, namely,

$$s_i = \big[\partial^2 \log \mathscr{L}(\bar{\phi})/\partial\bar{\phi}_i^2\big|_{\bar{\phi}=\bar{\phi}^*}\big]^{1/2}. \tag{4.97}$$

Since the estimated coefficients $\bar{\phi}^*$ are asymptotically distributed according to the multivariate normal distribution, the t test is applicable to each coefficient in order to test the hypothesis that the true coefficient is zero $(H_0: \phi_i = 0; H_1: \phi_i \neq 0)$. This t statistic is

$$t_i = \phi_i/s_i. \tag{4.98}$$

The standard errors and t statistics of models estimated with aggregated data will contain aggregation error because the aggregation of attributes within each zone reduces the overall variance of the data (because of replication in the observed choices) and thus somewhat inflates the underlying disaggregate t statistics. An empirical assessment of the size of this aggregation bias will be presented in this chapter.

5.5. Goodness-of-Fit Measures and Significance Tests

In order to compute goodness-of-fit measures, we must first identify the null model against which estimated aggregated models should be compared. The null model can be defined as the model in which $\gamma = 1$ (the housing supply coefficient is restricted to equal one) and all other estimated coefficients are set to equal zero, i.e., $\alpha = \bar{0}$, $\bar{\beta} = \bar{0}$, and $\sigma = 0$. Thus the null joint choice probabilities are

$$P_{im}^0 = S_i / \sum_j S_j M_j, \tag{4.99}$$

and the marginal and conditional null probabilities are

$$P_i^0 = S_i M_i / \sum_j S_j M_j \tag{4.100}$$

$$P_{m|i}^0 = 1/M_i. \tag{4.101}$$

Suppose $\tilde{N}_{im}$, $\tilde{N}_i$, and $\tilde{N}_{m|i}$ denote the observed number of commuters in a sample choosing (i, m), i, and $m|i$, and let $N_{im}^* = N P_{im}^*$, $N_i^* = N P_i^*$, and $N_{m|i}^* = N_i^* P_{m|i}^*$ be the predicted number of commuters based on the maximum likelihood (*) coefficients estimated from the sampled observations with $N \equiv \sum_i \sum_m \tilde{N}_{im}$. Various goodness-of-fit measures comparing the estimated and observed values can now be computed. While such fit measures can be computed for the conditional, marginal and joint models separately, for the sake of brevity we will discuss them for the joint model only. The measures for the conditional and marginal models have analogous forms.

First, one can compute the simple correlation coefficient between observed and predicted data. This is

$$R = \frac{\sum_{i,m}(\tilde{N}_{im} - \bar{N})(N_{im}^* - \bar{N})}{\{[\sum_{i,m}(\tilde{N}_{im} - \bar{N})^2][\sum_{i,m}(N_{im}^* - \bar{N})^2]\}^{1/2}}, \tag{4.102}$$

where $\bar{N} \equiv N/\sum_j M_j S_j$ and $0 < R \le 1$.

Second, the variance ratio can be computed to determine the extent to which the estimated model reduces or increases the actual variance in the data:

$$V = \frac{\sum_{i,m}(N_{im}^* - \bar{N})^2}{\sum_{i,m}(\tilde{N}_{im} - \bar{N})^2}, \tag{4.103}$$

with $V > 0$.

An information-theoretic measure of the proportion of data information explained by the maximized log likelihood can be constructed as

$$\Lambda = \frac{\sum_{i,m} \tilde{N}_{im} \log N_{im}^*}{\sum_{i,m} \tilde{N}_{im} \log \tilde{N}_{im}} \le 1. \tag{4.104}$$

The denominator of Λ is minus one times the entropy (randomness) or information in the data, whereas the numerator is the value of the maximized log likelihood less a constant. For the correlation coefficient, variance ratio, and information measure, a natural approach is to compute the corresponding null model values R^0, V^0, and Λ^0 and to compare the improvements over these null model values achieved by maximum likelihood estimation.

Another direct measure of fit is the value of the maximized log likelihood denoted as

$$\log \mathcal{L}^* = \sum_{i,m} \tilde{N}_{im} \log P_{im}^* < 0. \qquad (4.105)$$

Now let N_{im}^0 (and correspondingly N_i^0 and $N_{m|i}^0$) denote the predictions of the null model. Then the null log-likelihood value is

$$\log \mathcal{L}^0 = \sum_{i,m} N_{im}^0 \log P_{im}^0 < 0. \qquad (4.106)$$

Similarly, the saturated or perfect prediction value of the log likelihood for the estimation sample is denoted as

$$\log \mathcal{L}^{**} = \sum_{i,m} \tilde{N}_{im} \log \left(\frac{\tilde{N}_{im}}{N} \right). \qquad (4.107)$$

This is the likelihood value that would be obtained were it possible to add enough attributes into the model until the point is reached where the model becomes saturated and reproduces observed choices exactly. As discussed in Section 5.3, one way to achieve such a saturated model is to include an appropriate number of alternative-specific constants into the model.

The percentage of the saturated log-likelihood value explained by the estimated model is computed as the well-known rho-squared statistic, which is

$$\rho^2 = (\log \mathcal{L}^* - \log \mathcal{L}^0)/(\log \mathcal{L}^{**} - \log \mathcal{L}^0), \qquad (4.108)$$

with $0 \leq \rho^2 \leq 1$. The null model value of rho-squared is, of course, zero.

The overall significance of a choice model is usually tested by computing the asymptotically chi-squared distributed value

$$2(\log \mathcal{L}^* - \log \mathcal{L}^0) \sim \chi_K^2, \qquad (4.109)$$

where the degrees of freedom K is the number of coefficients in the estimated model. In a similar way, one can test the estimated model against the saturated model by computing the chi-squared distributed value

$$2(\log \mathcal{L}^{**} - \log \mathcal{L}^*) \sim \chi_{O-K}^2, \qquad (4.110)$$

where $O \equiv \sum_i (M_i - 1)$ is the number of sample points, with M_i the number of mode alternatives available in zone i. The χ^2 test may also be used to compare two models estimated from the same data set, one of which is specified with K_1 attributes, the other with $K_2 > K_1$ attributes, with the first K_1 attributes common to both models. To do this test, we must utilize

$$2(\log \mathscr{L}_2^* - \log \mathscr{L}_1^*) \sim \chi^2_{K_2 - K_1}. \tag{4.111}$$

Figure 4.3 shows a schematic view of the application of the χ^2 tests discussed here.

Another approach for comparing alternative models and for testing the significance of specific models is to use Hotelling's T^2 test for the significance of vectors or the equality of two vectors. This test is a generalization of the traditional t test, which is normally applied to each estimated coefficient to determine if it is significantly different from zero, as discussed in Section 5.4. We will first discuss the application of the T^2 test to determine whether an estimated vector of coefficients $\bar{\phi}^*$ is statistically different from an arbitrarily specified fixed vector $\hat{\phi}$ (possibly $\hat{\phi} = \bar{0}$). More precisely, we wish to test the formal hypothesis

$$H_0 : \bar{\phi}^* = \hat{\phi}, \qquad H_1 : \bar{\phi}^* \neq \hat{\phi}. \tag{4.112}$$

Now let the estimated variance–covariance matrix of $\bar{\phi}^*$ be $\Sigma_{\bar{\phi}^*}$; then the T^2 statistic is

$$T^2 = (\bar{\phi}^* - \hat{\phi})\Sigma_{\bar{\phi}^*}^{-1}(\bar{\phi}^* - \hat{\phi}), \tag{4.113}$$

and is distributed with an F value:

$$F = T^2(N - K)/(N - 1)K, \tag{4.114}$$

which is distributed with K and $N - K$ degrees of freedom, where N is the number of choosers in the sample and K the number of the coefficients in the estimated model. The T^2 test can also be used to compare the estimated coefficients of two identically specified choice models in which the coefficients of one are a subset of the other and in which the remaining coefficients obtain the value zero and assume zero variance and covariance with the other coefficients. To apply the test, we first pool the estimated variance–covariance matrices of the estimated vectors $\bar{\phi}_1^*$ and $\bar{\phi}_2^*$. The pooling yields

$$\Sigma_{\bar{\phi}} = [N_1/(N_1 + N_2)]\Sigma_{\bar{\phi}_1^*} + [N_2/(N_1 + N_2)]\Sigma_{\bar{\phi}_2^*}, \tag{4.115}$$

where $\Sigma_{\bar{\phi}}$ is the pooled variance–covariance matrix, and N_1 and N_2 are the sample sizes of the two models. We wish to test the formal hypothesis:

$$\begin{aligned} H_0 : \bar{\phi}_1^* - \bar{\phi}_2^* = 0, \\ H_1 : \bar{\phi}_1^* - \bar{\phi}_2^* \neq 0. \end{aligned} \tag{4.116}$$

The T^2 statistic is

$$T^2 = [N_1 N_2/(N_1 + N_2)](\bar{\phi}_1^* - \bar{\phi}_2^*)\Sigma_{\bar{\phi}}^{-1}(\bar{\phi}_1^* - \bar{\phi}_2^*)', \tag{4.117}$$

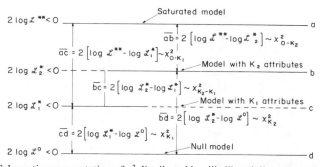

Fig. 4.3. Schematic representation of χ^2 distributed log-likelihood distances and corresponding tests. $\overline{cd}$: Is model with K_1 attributes significantly different from null model? $\overline{bd}$: Is model with $K_2 > K_1$ attributes significantly different from null model? $\overline{bc}$: Is model with K_2 attributes significantly different from model with K_1 attributes? $\overline{ac}$: Is model with K_1 attributes significantly different from saturated model? $\overline{ab}$: Is model with K_2 attributes significantly different from saturated model?

and the corresponding F value is

$$F = [(N_1 + N_2 - K)/(N_1 + N_2)K]T^2, \qquad (4.118)$$

which is distributed with K and $N_1 + N_2 - K$ degrees of freedom. Applications of the tests discussed here will be presented in Sections 6 and 7.

6. EMPIRICAL SPECIFICATION AND ESTIMATION RESULTS

Equipped with the arguments and discussions of the previous five sections, we are now ready to estimate the demand models for the CBD commuting population, for the non-CBD commuting population, and for the supply-side model. In presenting the empirical results, we will explore the effects of sampling, aggregation, and specification decisions on the estimated coefficients and their standard errors as well as on the elasticity estimates derived from the coefficients. We will also explore the various goodness-of-fit measures and statistical tests as well as the ability of the estimated models to produce aggregate predictions of acceptable quality.

6.1. The Effects of Sampling, Aggregation, Specification, and Estimation Method on the Conditional Model of Mode Choice

We now present empirical results for the model of mode choice for work travel to the CBD conditional on the choice of zone. The utility function is specified as

$$U_{im} = \beta_1 \log(R_i + C_{im}) + \beta_2 T_{im} + \beta_3 D_{i2} + \beta_4 D_{i3} + \beta_5 D_{i4}, \quad (4.119)$$

where R_i is the average annual rent per dwelling in zone i; C_{im}, the average annual cost of traveling to the CBD from zone i via mode m; T_{im}, the average daily one-way travel time from zone i to the CBD via mode m; and D_{i2}, D_{i3}, D_{i4} are three mode-specific (alternative-specific) constants such that $D_{im} = 1$ when the chosen mode is mode m and $D_{in} = 0$ for $n \neq m$. Mode 1 ($m = 1$) is auto driver, followed by rapid transit (elevated or subway) for mode 2 ($m = 2$), commuter rail for mode 3 ($m = 3$), and bus for mode 4 ($m = 4$). The reference mode is auto driver, described by $D_{im} = 0$ for $m = 2, 3, 4$. The average annual rent is computed as

$$R_i \equiv f_i r_i + (1 - f_i)V_i/10, \quad (4.120)$$

where f_i is the proportion of zone i's occupied dwellings that are renter occupied; r_i, the average annual rent of these renter occupied dwellings; and V_i, the average annual market value of the owner occupied dwellings in zone i. Dividing market value by ten annualizes it so that it can be combined with average rent. Definition (4.120), a rule of thumb commonly utilized in urban economics, is necessary in this study because travelers' choices in the data are identified by travel mode and zone but not by travel mode, zone, *and* tenure status (owner versus renter).

Tables 4.3 and 4.4 report the results of different estimations of the model based on the utility function (4.119). The form of the model is

$$P_{m|i} = e^{U_{im}} / \sum_{n=1}^{M_i} e^{U_{in}} \quad (4.121)$$

Model 3 in Table 4.4 differs from the others in that it includes one more attribute, "bus mile density," which is the total length in miles of the bus routes crossing a zone divided by the land area in square miles of that zone. This attribute enters the utility function via a sixth additive term ($\cdots + \beta_6 B_{im}$) and is treated as an attribute specific to the bus mode by setting B_{im} equal to "bus mile density" when $m = 4$ (bus) and setting $B_{im} = 0$ when $m \neq 4$.

It should be noted that the four modes "auto driver," "commuter rail," "rapid transit," and "bus" comprise 88% of the CBD work trips, as shown in Table 4.1.

Table 4.3 demonstrates the effect of sampling errors on the variability of the estimated utility coefficients. The table shows five estimations based on the following sampling procedure. First, a discrete probability distribution is defined over the number of zone–mode alternatives (i, m). The probability for

TABLE 4.3

The Effect of Sampling Variation on the Estimated Coefficients[a]

Attributes	1	2	3	4	5
Rapid transit	−1.12	−1.039	−1.475	−1.037	−0.9651
	(5.7)	(2.8)	(3.9)	(2.6)	(2.3)
Commuter rail	−0.599	−0.364	−0.8272	−0.7974	−0.3975
	(3.5)	(1.10)	(2.4)	(2.2)	(1.1)
Bus	−0.144	−0.138	−0.609	−0.062	−0.037
	(0.64)	(0.30)	(1.4)	(0.1)	(0.08)
Travel time	−0.04343	−0.03298	−0.03589	−0.05938	−0.04671
	(9.9)	(3.9)	(4.0)	(6.7)	(5.1)
log(rent + travel cost)	−1.77	−0.749	−2.854	−1.546	−1.998
	(3.1)	(0.7)	(2.6)	(1.3)	(1.6)
$\log \mathscr{L}^{**}$	−143	−30	−38	−32	−37
$\log \mathscr{L}^{*}$	−2077	−512	−527	−511	−516
$\log \mathscr{L}^{0}$	−2213	−549	−558	−553	−553
$2(\log \mathscr{L}^{*} - \log \mathscr{L}^{0})$; ($\chi^2_{\text{crit}} = 0.05$)	272(11)	73(11)	63(11)	83(11)	75(11)
$2(\log \mathscr{L}^{**} - \log \mathscr{L}^{*})$; ($\chi^2_{\text{crit}} = 0.05$)	3868(1049)	964(220)	978(212)	958(228)	958(222)
ρ^2	0.066	0.067	0.056	0.075	0.068
Auto (%)	0.34	0.36	0.34	0.35	0.30
Rapid transit (%)	0.19	0.15	0.19	0.21	0.21
Commuter rail (%)	0.21	0.21	0.20	0.20	0.22
Bus (%)	0.26	0.28	0.27	0.24	0.27
Time/log(rent + cost)[b]					
Auto	49.5/8.1	50.7/8.1	49.1/8.1	50.1/8.1	48.2/8.1
Rapid transit	45.0/7.7	45.6/7.7	44.7/7.8	44.9/7.7	44.7/7.7
Commuter rail	57.1/8.1	58.0/8.1	57.5/8.1	57.2/8.1	55.4/8.1
Bus	48.9/7.6	48.2/7.6	50.1/7.6	49.2/7.6	48.6/7.6

[a] *t* statistics in parentheses.

[b] Average values of attributes for the sample and for each travel mode. Sample size for model 1: 2000 trips; models 2–5: 500 trips each.

each (i, m) is set equal to the relative frequency of trips for that (i, m). Next, two thousand commuters are generated by selecting, each one independently, from the discrete probability distribution defined above. Since the data contain 397,620 trips to the CBD, this random sample of 2000 is a nearly 0.5% sample, and any subset of 500 travelers selected from this 2000 is a random sample of nearly 0.125%. Model 1 in Table 4.3 is estimated from these 2000 trips. Each of models 2–5 is estimated from a different subsample of 500 trips. Although the sampling rates represented in these estimations are very low, multinomial logit models of mode choice have been consistently

TABLE 4.4

Estimated Coefficients of the Conditional Model of Mode Choice for CBD Commuters

Attributes	Estimated coefficients[a]							
	0	1	2	3	4[b]	5[c]	6[d]	7[e]
Rapid transit	-0.4684	-0.7822	-1.12	-1.23	-1.28	-1.40	-0.645	-1.24
	(7.2)	(5.0)	(5.7)	(6.2)	(47.7)	(33.9)	(12.1)	(88.8)
Commuter rail	0.3744	-0.320	-5.99	-0.715	-0.982	-1.19	-0.639	-0.949
	(5.3)	(2.2)	(3.5)	(4.1)	(40.4)	(32.9)	(13.8)	(75.1)
Bus	0.1117	0.239	-0.144	-1.00	-0.149	-0.709	0.175	-0.259
	(1.8)	(1.3)	(0.64)	(3.9)	(4.9)	(14.9)	(2.9)	(16.0)
Travel time	—	-0.0444	-0.0434	-0.0430	-0.0518	-0.048	-0.0516	-0.0519
		(10.2)	(9.9)	(9.8)	(77.7)	(54.0)	(61.6)	(16.6)
log(rent + travel cost)	—	-0.694	-1.77	-2.08	-2.55	-3.69	-1.58	-2.46
		(1.7)	(3.1)	(3.7)	(33.2)	(32.2)	(10.2)	(61.5)
Bus mile density	—	—	—	0.01436	—	—	—	—
				(6.9)				
Number of trips	2,000	2,000	2,000	2,000	122,620	56,698	56,698	397,620
Degrees of freedom	977	975	975	974	1,397	704	704	5,843

Auto drivers[f] (%)		0.34		0.32		0.31	0.34
Rapid transit[f] (%)		0.19		0.21		0.25	0.19
Commuter rail[f] (%)		0.21		0.18		0.15	0.20
Bus[f] (%)		0.26		0.30		0.29	0.27
$\log \mathcal{L}^{**}$	-143	-143	-143	$-73{,}367$	$-49{,}507$	$-49{,}507$	$-335{,}900$
$\log \mathcal{L}^{*}$	$-2{,}144$	$-2{,}077$	$-2{,}052$	$-92{,}760$	$-59{,}910$	$-60{,}091$	$-412{,}000$
$\log \mathcal{L}^{0}$	$-2{,}213$	$-2{,}213$	$-2{,}213$	$-100{,}600$	$-63{,}090$	$-63{,}090$	$-441{,}000$
$2(\log \mathcal{L}^{*} - \log \mathcal{L}^{0})$	139	272	322	15,580	6,358	5,998	57,910
$\chi^2_{crit} = 0.05^{g}$	7.8	11.07	12.6	11.07	11.07	11.07	11.07
$2(\log \mathcal{L}^{**} - \log \mathcal{L}^{*})$	4,002	3,868	3,818	38,786	20,806	21,168	152,200
$\chi^2_{crit} = 0.05^{h}$	1,052	1,049	1,046	1,485	767	767	6,027
ρ^2	0.067	0.066	0.078	0.287	0.234	0.221	0.276

[a] t statistics in parentheses.

[b] Estimated from 122,620 trips randomly selected.

[c] Estimated from the 56,698 trips of a random sample of 433 zones.

[d] Estimated from the 56,698 trips of a random sample of 433 zones, in one step together with the marginal part.

[e] Estimated from all 397,620 trips.

[f] Mode splits of estimation sample.

[g] 5% chi-square value for $2(\log \mathcal{L}^{*} - \log \mathcal{L}^{0})$.

[h] 5% chi-square value for $2(\log \mathcal{L}^{**} - \log \mathcal{L}^{*})$.

estimated with samples as small as several hundred trips. It is widely believed that samples of 300 trips plus or minus a hundred or so provide an adequate basis for obtaining accurate estimates of the true utility coefficients. This presumed property of disaggregate models has resulted in a lack of interest in the stability of the coefficients obtained and in a presumption that disaggregate models will perform well when applied to aggregated prediction tasks. Table 4.3 shows that the presumption of small sample stability is generally unjustified. All of the estimated coefficients vary substantially due to sampling, with the coefficient of $\log(R_i + C_{im})$ being affected the most and quite substantially and the coefficient of T_{im} being affected the least. The resulting errors are, of course, attributable purely to sampling. Our purpose in documenting these errors is not only to challenge the questionable state-of-the-art presumption, but also to compare errors in these coefficients resulting from other sources to errors resulting purely from sampling. The market shares and average attribute measures of each sample are also listed in Table 4.3.

The results in Table 4.4 are intended to demonstrate four different effects. First, the model numbered zero is the market share model in which the only estimated coefficients are the mode-specific constants. Model 2 differs from model 0 in that two additional attributes, "travel time" and the "logarithm of rent plus travel cost," have been added to the market share model. In model 3, one more attribute, "bus mile density," is added. Each of these steps (from model 0 to models 2 and 3) improves on the previous step so that the added attributes significantly increase the log likelihood compared to the log likelihood of the null model as shown by the χ^2 test.

While models 0, 2, and 3 test the effect of attribute inclusion on the estimated coefficients when keeping the sample constant, model 1 compared to model 2 tests the effect of aggregation in one attribute. This is done by generating a disaggregate value for the attribute "rent" for each of the 2000 individuals in the sample. To do this, we utilize three relative frequency distributions for each zone, provided by the census data. The first of these is the proportion of owner occupied and renter occupied dwellings in each zone. For the owner occupied dwellings, the census data provide a discrete relative frequency distribution that gives the proportion of the owner occupied dwellings in each of a number of discrete market value categories. For the renter occupied dwellings, the census data provide a discrete relative frequency distribution that gives the proportion of the renter occupied dwellings in each of a number of discrete annual rental categories. Using these relative frequencies as probabilities, we generate a renter–owner tenure status for each individual. Subsequent to this, we probabilistically assign each renter to a rental interval and each owner to a market value interval. Finally, each renter's "rent" is taken to be the median rent of the relevant interval and each owner's "rent" is taken to be equal to one-tenth the market value of the relevant interval. Thus, while in model 2, "travel time" and "log(rent + travel cost)" are based on zone average data for each individual, in model 1, "travel time" and "travel cost" are still zone averages, but "rent" is a disaggregate attribute that has a different value for each individual in the sample; two or more individuals choosing the same zone have different values of "rent." Since the census data provide neither the within-zone covariances among zone-specific attributes such as rent, travel time, travel cost, etc., nor the within-zone variances of travel time and travel cost, disaggregation in attributes other than rent is not possible. Comparing models 1 and 2 in Table 4.4, we see that the coefficient of log(rent + travel cost) changes from -0.694 to -1.77, but the magnitude of this change is not larger than the corresponding changes that occur solely because of sampling variation, as shown in Table 4.3. Comparing models 2 and 3 of Table 4.3, for example, we see a change from -0.749 to -2.854, about twice as large in magnitude when compared to the change due to aggregation. The conclusion we may draw from this observation is that errors in the estimated coefficients arising from the aggregation of certain attributes (such as "rent") to the zonal level appear to be smaller or comparable in magnitude to errors arising purely from sampling.

Included in Tables 4.3 and 4.4 are the χ^2 tests, which show that each of the estimated models is significantly different from the corresponding null model but also significantly different from the corresponding saturated models. This pattern illustrates the well-known weakness of this type of χ^2 test when applied to choice models. To this author's knowledge, there is no case in the literature in which a similar χ^2 test was applied and in which the test revealed that the choice model was not significantly different from a corresponding null model.

The effect of another source of bias, the choice of model type, is shown in Table 4.5. This is done by estimating an IID probit and a logit model from a sample of 50 randomly generated trips from those zones in which all four modes are available for choice. The sample size was deliberately kept small to avoid the cost of a probit estimation. The two models yielded extremely similar results. Both models are significantly different from the corresponding null models as determined by the χ^2 test applied to $2(\log \mathscr{L}^* - \log \mathscr{L}^0)$.

The results of Table 4.5 demonstrate clearly that there is virtually no difference between MNL and IID probit. The MNL model should be preferred because of its computational simplicity. This result is in agreement with that of Hausman and Wise (1978), who also demonstrated that generalized probit formulations that allow non-IID assumptions can yield utility coefficients that are substantially different from those of MNL or IID probit.

Table 4.5

Comparison of the IID Probit Model to the Multinomial Logit Model Estimated from the Same Sample[a]

Utility attributes	MNL($\lambda\alpha$)	IID probit	Adjusted MNL[b] (α)
Rapid transit	-2.177	-1.766	-1.775
	(-2.00)	—	(-2.00)
Commuter rail	-1.110	-9.562	-0.9051
	(-1.41)	—	(-1.41)
Bus	-1.188	-0.9911	-0.9687
	(-1.01)	—	(-1.01)
Travel time	-0.0843	-0.0633	-0.0688
	(-2.7)	—	(-2.7)
log(rent + travel cost)	-4.487	-3.676	-3.659
	(-1.58)	—	(-1.6)
σ^2	—	1.097	1.097
$\log \mathscr{L}^0$	-69.31	-69.31	-69.31
$\log \mathscr{L}^*$	-63.00	-63.46	-63.00
$2(\log \mathscr{L}^* - \log \mathscr{L}^0)$	11.70	12.62	11.70
Trips	50	50	50
Observations	200	200	200

[a] t statistics in parentheses; (—), t statistics not computed.
[b] Adjusted by dividing the MNL coefficients (column 1) by $\lambda = (\pi/\sqrt{6})/\sigma$, where $\sigma^2 = 1.097$ and thus $\lambda = 1.2264$.

6.2. The Marginal Location Choice Model and the Joint Choice of Location and Mode

The marginal probability of location (zone) choice is a function of the coefficient vector $\bar{\beta}$, as well as the coefficient vector $\bar{\alpha}$, the inclusive value coefficient σ, and the housing supply coefficient γ. The precise form of this marginal choice probability is

$$P_i = \frac{S_i^\gamma \exp\left[\sum_w \alpha_w X_{iw} + (1 - \sigma) \log \sum_m \exp(\sum_v \beta_v X_{imv})\right]}{\sum_j S_j^\gamma \exp\left[\sum_w \alpha_w X_{jw} + (1 - \sigma) \log \sum_m \exp(\sum_v \beta_v X_{jmv})\right]}. \quad (4.122)$$

As we discussed in Section 5, the above model should be normally estimated in one step by maximizing the joint likelihood function and determing $\bar{\alpha}$, $\bar{\beta}$, σ, and γ, or in two steps by first estimating the conditional model first, to determine $\bar{\beta}$, and the marginal model next, to determine $\bar{\alpha}$, σ, and γ. In principle, the one-step estimation is the correct but computationally expensive approach. This approach generally involves search over several local optima in order to find the globally optimal point. The two-step approach has unique local optima at each step but will generally yield results different from the global optimum of the one-step method, although these can be achieved much more efficiently. The two-step approach is generally favored in the literature and is followed here, even though we make an effort to compare the results of a two-step model to its one-step equivalent.

Table 4.6 shows the estimated coefficients of eight models. Of these models, all have some difference in specification with the exception of models 7 and 8, which are specified identically and are both nested, with the difference that model 8 is estimated in one step and model 7 in two steps. All joint choice models in which $(1 - \sigma)$ is forced to equal one are estimated in a single step (these are models 3 and 5), whereas models 1, 2, 4, and 6, in which $(1 - \sigma)$ is unrestricted, are estimated in two steps. The table lists both the conditional and marginal choice coefficients since the values of the conditional choice coefficients influence the magnitude of the marginal choice coefficients regardless of whether one- or two-step estimation is used. The data used in estimating these models are the same and include all 56,698 trip observations in a randomly selected sample of 433 residential zones containing 1142 travel mode alternatives.

In arriving at the models in Table 4.6, a lengthy search was conducted in an effort to determine a set of estimations with consistent coefficient magnitudes and signs. The search produced meaningful estimations, only eight of which are reported in Table 4.6. We first comment on the definition and measurement of the utility attributes that were entered into the models. The three key explanatory attributes are "rent," "travel cost," and "travel time," already discussed in the previous section, which reviewed the estimation of the conditional choice model. Attribute 13, the average income of the zone resident households, serves as a proxy for social and public service amenities or the residential prestige of the location. Attributes 10 and 12 are the average number of rooms in the zone's housing stock and average age of the zone's housing, and attribute 9 is the total length of bus routes within a zone divided by the land area of the zone (a measure of bus availability). Attributes 1, 2, and 3 are the usual mode-specific dummies intended to capture unobserved mode attributes such as comfort–convenience. Attributes 16, 17, and 18 serve a similar purpose in capturing the unobserved attractiveness features of four circumferential rings in the metropolitan area, defined as 0–10 miles (almost coincident with the city of Chicago), 10–20 miles, 20–25 miles, and beyond 25 miles. Other location-correlated effects are captured by attribute 14 (straight line distance to the CBD) and attribute 15 (angular displacement in degrees from the Lake Michigan north shore).

The full empirical search, which will not be reported here, revealed

TABLE 4.6

Estimated Coefficients of the Travel Mode and Residential Location Choice Models[a]

Attributes	Estimated coefficients							
	1	2	3	4	5	6	7	8
1. Commuter rail	-0.279 (6.1)	-1.43 (31.3)	-0.362 (32.1)	-1.20 (33.6)	-0.548 (34.2)	-1.38 (37.4)	-1.195 (32.9)	-0.639 (12.1)
2. Rapid transit	4.06 (44.8)	1.79 (15.5)	2.40 (27.2)	2.52 (26.0)	2.35 (28.1)	2.34 (24.6)	-1.399 (33.9)	-0.645 (13.9)
3. Bus	4.48 (43.7)	1.76 (13.1)	2.85 (20.4)	2.76 (25.6)	2.83 (25.7)	2.69 (25.4)	-0.709 (14.9)	0.175[b] (2.9)
4. log(travel time)	-2.78 (55.4)	-2.21 (45.7)	-2.19 (42.8)	-2.65 (60.0)	—	—	—	—
5. Travel time	—	—	—	—	-0.048 (62.8)	-0.060 (62.7)	-0.048 (54.0)	-0.052 (61.6)
6. log(travel cost)	—	-1.30 (28.5)	—	—	—	—	—	—
7. log(travel cost + rent)	—	—	-0.698 (48.3)	-3.56 (30.6)	-0.662 (40.2)	-3.22 (27.2)	-3.69 (32.2)	-1.58 (10.2)
8. Travel cost + rent	-0.000044[b] (1.0)	—	—	—	—	—	—	—
9. Bus miles/square mile	0.100 (28.9)	0.107 (31.4)	0.066 (28.3)	0.103 (30.3)	0.051 (32.1)	0.074 (22.0)	—	—
10. log(rooms)	2.74 (49.9)	2.33 (40.8)	1.76 (28.9)	2.53 (46.0)	1.79 (35.5)	2.39 (44.9)	—	—

	(1)	(2)	(3)	(4)	(5)	(6)	(7)	(8)
11. Rent	—	-0.000138 (11.4)	—	—	—	—	—	—
12. log(age)	-0.146 (10.6)	-0.203 (13.9)	-0.257 (23.0)	-0.265 (19.0)	-0.264 (21.0)	-0.227 (15.7)	-0.214 (14.8)	-0.226 (16.0)
13. log(income)	0.814 (40.2)	0.954 (34.9)	0.803 (30.1)	0.886 (42.1)	0.872 (30.2)	1.08 (49.2)	1.100 (45.2)	1.175 (50.0)
14. log(distance)	0.323 (10.1)	0.609 (18.9)	1.48 (6.4)	0.148 (5.4)	1.22 (2.8)	0.152 (5.8)	0.032[b] (1.51)	0.398 (10.4)
15. log(angle)	0.081 (5.1)	0.042[b] (2.6)	-0.109 (8.9)	-0.117 (8.4)	-0.059 (6.4)	0.038[b] (2.4)	0.052[b] (3.3)	0.002[b] (0.15)
16. D1 (0–10 miles)	0.360 (12.8)	0.305 (11.0)	0.592 (20.1)	0.606 (24.3)	-0.051 (12.1)	0.262 (9.5)	0.235 (8.4)	0.054[b] (1.5)
17. D2 (10–20 miles)	0.061[b] (2.9)	0.040[b] (1.9)	0.162[b] (0.2)	0.172 (8.4)	-0.189[b] (3.8)	0.015[b] (0.7)	-0.011[b] (0.54)	-0.135 (5.1)
18. D3 (25+ miles)	-0.471 (16.4)	-0.404 (14.0)	-0.485 (14.5)	-0.548 (19.2)	-0.080 (13.0)	-0.450 (15.6)	-0.479 (16.7)	-0.347 (9.9)
19. $(1-\sigma)$	0.243 (16.4)	0.417 (26.3)	1.00	0.113 (12.7)	1.00	0.132 (13.6)	0.096 (11.4)	0.368 (20.1)
20. γ	1.17 (147.1)	1.11 (131.8)	1.00	1.00	1.09 (138.9)	1.17 (146.1)	1.16 (144.1)	1.12 (119.0)
$2(\log \mathcal{L}^* - \log \mathcal{L}^0)$	13,398	14,694	12,230	13,464	13,480	14,828	11,180	11,180
$\rho^2\ (\rho^{20} = 0)$	0.343	0.377	0.314	0.350	0.346	0.380	0.287	0.287
$\Lambda\ (\Lambda^0 = 0.931)$	0.955	0.957	0.953	0.955	0.955	0.957	0.951	0.951
$V\ (V^0 = 0.382)$	0.792	0.827	0.706	0.657	0.740	0.730	0.651	0.670
$R\ (R^0 = 0.757)$	0.879	0.869	0.867	0.881	0.873	0.892	0.823	0.830

[a] Asymptotic t statistics in parentheses.
[b] Insignificant or slightly significant coefficient.

interesting and logical inclusion–exclusion interactions among the explanatory attributes. These interactions are summarized as follows:

(1)   When "rent" and "average zonal income" (attributes 11 and 13) are both included in the marginal part, the inclusion of income is necessary to assure that the coefficient of rent obtains the correct negative sign. Thus the inclusion of income is important in controlling for the fact that households like to live in higher income neighborhoods, other things being equal. In the absence of income, "rent" tends to proxy the effects of residential prestige associated with "average zonal income."

(2)   Inclusion of "distance from the CBD" (attribute 14) is found necessary to proxy the radial variation in public services but also to assure that "travel time" (attribute 4 or 5) measures the intended commuting time effect separating this from the travel distance effect. If distance is excluded, travel time may obtain a positive sign and tends to measure public service quality instead of measuring commuting disutility. This change of sign will occur only in those models estimated in a single step. As shown in Tables 4.3 and 4.4, the change of sign will not occur in the conditional model when estimated separately since the conditional model explains the choice of mode while keeping zonal distance constant.

(3)   The "age of housing" (attribute 12) does not generally obtain the correct sign unless the "ring dummy variables" (attributes 16, 17, and 18) and "angular displacement" (attribute 15) are introduced to control for neighborhood quality effects that tend to decline counterclockwise from the Lake Michigan north shore and to improve from the city to successive suburban rings.

(4)   The ring dummy signs show that if one controls for public service effects through "distance to the CBD" and "angular displacement," the innermost ring is the most desirable area. This is probably a reflection of the high accessibility advantages of this central location for CBD commuters and the proximity of the area to downtown amenities.

(5)   A great deal of effort was spent in searching for a formulation that would give the "number of rooms" (attribute 10) the correct sign. It was found that this attribute has a negative correlation with the use of the rapid transit mode, perhaps due to the fact that many multifamily housing units (with few rooms) are located in proximity to the rapid transit lines. To obtain the correct sign for the "number of rooms," this attribute was treated as mode specific, entered into the utility functions of auto and commuter rail users only, and deleted from the utility functions of rapid transit and bus commuters. It is demonstrated in model 7, however, that this attribute is nearly superfluous as far as its effect on model 6 is concerned: excluding the

"number of rooms" changes the coefficient of travel time by a small amount and has most of its effect concentrated on attributes 13, 14, and 15, the last of which becomes insignificant. The coefficient of log(travel cost + rent) remains nearly the same.

(6) Eliminating rent from the model has a very small effect on the other coefficients except for the travel cost and the ring dummies, which change substantially in magnitude. This result implies that the introduction of a housing price measure may not be essential for obtaining unbiased estimates of travel demand and destination choice patterns. The result may be reversed, however, if choices are segmented by income and other socioeconomic characteristics related to rent paying ability.

Upon examining the models in Table 4.6, we see that most explanatory attributes, and certainly the key attributes, are generally significant. The coefficient of the inclusive value $(1 - \sigma)$ ranges from 0.096 to 0.417 and is significant. The housing supply term γ ranges from 1.09 to 1.17 and is also highly significant. Forcing γ to equal 1, however, as in models 3 and 5, has a small effect on other results and does not change the meaningfulness or usefulness of the models. Model 1 can be ignored as unsuccessful since the coefficient of "travel cost + rent" is too small and insignificant. This is the result of some specification error and implies that the quantity "travel cost + rent," which is a measure of locational expenditures, should not be entered into the model linearly. The remaining seven models are all generally acceptable specifications and cannot be readily rejected without more in-depth examination of their properties. The aggregate goodness-of-fit statistics $2(\log \mathcal{L}^* - \log \mathcal{L}^0)$, the variance ratio V, the ρ^2, and the correlation coefficient R all show significant improvements over the null model.

Table 4.7 shows the estimated coefficients of two additional models that are identical to model 7 in Table 4.6 but that include five additional attributes in the conditional part (attributes 6–10 in Table 4.7). Model 1 in Table 4.7 has its inclusive value coefficient $1 - \sigma$ forced to 1 and is estimated in one step, whereas model 2 in Table 4.7 does not restrict this coefficient and is estimated in two steps. Both models have their housing supply coefficients forced to 1. The five additional attributes are "bus mile density," entered as a bus specific attribute; attributes 7, 8, and 9, which are "the number of rapid transit stations" within $0-\frac{1}{2}, \frac{1}{2}-1$, and 1–2 miles from a zone's centroid, respectively; and attribute 10, which is "the number of commuter rail stations" within one mile of a zone's centroid. Attributes 7, 8, and 9 are entered as rapid-transit-specific, while attribute 10 is entered as commuter-rail-specific. Inclusion of these attributes is intended to improve the policy responsiveness of the choice models in Table 4.6. Indeed, these attributes create substantial and

TABLE 4.7

*Estimated Coefficients of Improved CBD Choice Models with Station
Accessibility Attributes*

	Estimated coefficients	
Utility attributes	Model 1 (nonnested)	Model 2 (nested)
1. Commuter rail (CR)	−0.406 (21.1)[a]	−0.846 (23.0)
2. Rapid transit (RT)	−1.090 (43.0)	−1.701 (39.0)
3. Bus	0.173 (6.9)	−0.636 (12.3)
4. log(travel time)	−1.619 (49.8)	−2.392 (55.5)
5. log(travel cost + rent)	−0.265 (7.6)	−1.488 (12.4)
6. Bus miles/square mile	0.0089 (40.6)	0.020 (54.4)
7. Number of RT stations (0–0.5 mile)	0.234 (20.2)	0.294 (20.9)
8. Number of RT stations (0.5–1 mile)	0.075 (6.6)	0.134 (9.9)
9. Number of RT stations (1–2 miles)	0.221 (24.4)	0.246 (23.2)
10. Number of CR stations (0–1 mile)	0.334 (27.1)	0.349 (19.9)
11. log(housing age)	−0.121 (8.3)	−0.188 (14.0)
12. log(zone income)	1.059 (43.6)	1.015 (53.2)
13. log(distance)	1.049 (42.1)	0.447 (18.4)
14. log(angle)	0.176 (11.8)	0.001[b] (0.08)
15. $D1$ (0–10 miles)	0.150 (5.7)	0.490 (19.6)
16. $D2$ (10–20 miles)	−0.080 (3.8)	0.122 (6.0)
17. $D3$ (>25 miles)	−0.473 (16.4)	−0.591 (20.6)
18. Inclusive value $1 - \sigma$	1.000 (—)	0.277 (30.7)
19. Housing supply γ	1.000 (—)	1.000 (—)
$2(\log \mathscr{L}^* - \log \mathscr{L}^0)$	14,854	16,508
$\rho^2 \ (\rho^{20} = 0)$	0.378	0.420
$\Lambda \ (\Lambda^0 = 0.931)$	0.957	0.959
$V \ (V^0 = 0.382)$	0.866	0.856
$R \ (R^0 = 0.757)$	0.877	0.882

[a] Asymptotic t statistics in parentheses.
[b] Coefficient not significant statistically.

significant improvement in the χ^2 distributed $2(\log \mathscr{L}^* - \log \mathscr{L}^0)$, in the ρ^2, and in the variance ratio V. The formulation of the "number of stations" attribute is not simply an integer count of the stations but is defined as $n' = n - \delta \log(n - 2)$, where n is the number of stations within the relevant interval $(n = 0, 1, 2, \ldots)$; $\delta = 0$ if $n \leq 2$, and $\delta = 1$ when $n \geq 3$; "log" is the natural logarithm; and n' is the value of the attribute entered into the model. This formula is intended to correct for the rare situations in which a zone located very near the central business district where many transit lines converge has four or more rapid transit stations within the relevant distance interval. It is clear that the marginal utility or perceived usefulness of additional stations declines rapidly, and a zone with five subway stations within 2 miles is not five times as attractive as a similar zone with only one station within 2 miles. This discounting results in the following values for n' given n:

n	n'	n	n'
0	0	4	3.3
1	1	5	3.9
2	2	6	4.6
3	3		

Commuter rail stations are rarely encountered within the city of Chicago but are relatively widely spaced along suburban rail lines.

It is seen from Table 4.7 that these station proximity attributes have the correct positive signs: clearly proximity to stations is important in influencing the probability of choosing to commute by transit. The availability of stations within a zone's immediate vicinity is also a rough measure (or proxy) of the access time (or out-of-vehicle time) in commuting by transit.

6.3. Non-CBD Models of Joint Mode and Location Choice

As explained in Section 3.2, the specification of non-CBD models follows lines similar to those described for the CBD models. Two models and their associated goodness-of-fit statistics are shown in Table 4.8. In both of these models, the housing supply coefficient γ is forced to one. Model 1 has $\sigma = 0$ and is estimated in one step, whereas model 2 has an unrestricted σ and is estimated in two steps. It can be seen from Table 4.1 that commuter rail and rapid transit are 1% and 2% of non-CBD work trips, respectively. Because of this, the non-CBD models have been specified only for the two major modes "auto driver" and "bus," which together comprise 73% of all the non-CBD work trips. "Auto driver" is treated as the reference mode, and one dummy attribute is used for the second mode "bus" (attribute 1 in Table 4.8). The non-CBD models are estimated from the same sample of 433 randomly selected zones used to estimate the CBD models.

6.4. The Supply-Side Model

The supply-side stochastic profit maximization model derived in Section 4 is also estimated from the randomly drawn 433 zone sample. The results are shown in Table 4.9. The chief attributes included in this model are the "average rent of the zone" (attribute 2) and attributes 3–8, which are socio-economic characteristics of the zones, intended to proxy the differential cost

TABLE 4.8

Estimated Coefficients for the Non-CBD Models

	Estimated coefficients	
Utility attributes	Model 1 (nonnested)	Model 2 (nested)
1. Bus	-1.837 $(183.0)^a$	-2.627 (175.0)
2. log(travel time)	-0.211 (10.1)	-0.910 (25.7)
3. log(travel cost + rent)	-0.099 (6.2)	-5.461 (42.6)
4. Bus miles/square mile	0.010 (66.6)	0.017 (70.5)
5. log(housing age)	-0.030 (4.5)	-0.097 (14.5)
6. log(income)	0.331 (24.8)	-0.117 (8.4)
7. log(distance)	0.354 (40.4)	0.426 (47.9)
8. log(angle)	0.076 (9.8)	-0.206 (23.0)
9. $D1$ (0–10 miles)	-0.129 (9.5)	0.287 (20.2)
10. $D2$ (10–20 miles)	0.040 (4.1)	0.296 (29.9)
11. $D3$ (>25 miles)	0.103 (9.7)	0.132 (12.3)
12. log(rooms)	—	1.194 (62.0)
13. Inclusive value $(1 - \sigma)$	1.000 (—)	0.045 (15.3)
14. Housing supply γ	1.000 (—)	1.00 (—)
$2(\log \mathscr{L}^* - \log \mathscr{L}^0)$	108,670	121,129
ρ^2 $(\rho^{20} = 0.0)$	0.743	0.828
Λ $(\Lambda^0 = 0.942)$	0.985	0.990
V $(V^0 = 1.145)$	0.937	0.754
R $(R^0 = 0.553)$	0.865	0.928

^{a} Asymptotic t statistics in parentheses.

of maintaining occupied and vacant housing units. Attribute 1 is a dummy variable for the "offer for rent" alternative. The results show that the coefficient of "rent" is positive as expected and ranges from 0.00042 to 0.00012.

The attributes that enter the differential cost function are $\mu_1–\mu_6$ and are themselves functions of $\eta_1–\eta_6$ and $\eta_1^0–\eta_6^0$, such that $-\mu_i = (\eta_i - \eta_i^0)\lambda$. We can estimate $-\mu_i$, but η_i, η_i^0 remain unidentified. The estimated values imply that the cost of maintaining an occupied unit relative to the cost of maintaining that unit when it is vacant *increases* as the "proportion of black households in the zone" (attribute 3) increases, but *decreases* as either the average age of the zone's housing, the percent of the zone's land that is developed, the percent of the zone's housing that is single family, or the zone's counterclockwise proximity to the south side of the city increases. These are plausible results, if not the only sensible ones, and cannot be rejected without reestimating the model with better data.

It should be noted that the resulting supply probabilities are a very flat function of the average zone rent. This result suggests that landlords pay

TABLE 4.9

Estimated Coefficients and Asymptotic t Statistics of Supply-Side Models

Profitability attributes	Estimated coefficients			
	1	2	3	4
1. Dummy	3.019	2.193	−0.532	−0.679
	(946.0)[a]	(245.9)	(12.5)	(17.2)
2. Rent, λ	—	0.00042	0.00012	0.00013
		(93.6)	(17.4)	(19.5)
3. % black, μ_1	—	—	−0.0035	−0.0035
			(0.032)	(0.32)
4. % developed, μ_2	—	—	0.0112	0.0108
			(0.054)	(0.55)
5. % single family, μ_3	—	—	0.019	0.0172
			(1.005)	(1.09)
6. log(housing age), μ_4	—	—	0.506	0.471
			(51.7)	(48.1)
7. Angle/100, μ_5	—	—	0.123	0.075
			(18.6)	(11.1)
8. Distance, μ_6	—	—	−0.005	—
			(9.2)	
$2(\log \mathscr{L}^* - \log \mathscr{L}^0)$	2,232,000	2,242,000	2,268,000	2,268,000
ρ^2	0.0	0.121[b]	0.458	0.458

[a] *t* statistics in parentheses.

[b] The ρ^2 values are computed relative to the market share model reported in the first column.

small attention to rent in deciding whether to withhold or supply dwellings but place a stronger emphasis on the *costs* of supplying as determined by the various socioeconomic risks of a particular location. Many of these risk measures, such as local crime, vandalism, and arson rates, are not available in the data but are at least in part proxied by the dummy variable and the attributes that have been included in the model.

7. EVALUATION OF ELASTICITIES AND THE QUALITY OF AGGREGATE PREDICTIONS

A preliminary assessment of the meaningfulness of estimated models can be done by evaluating the elasticities obtained from the estimated coefficients. We will focus on the demand elasticities of three policy-sensitive attributes: rent, travel cost, and travel time. Elasticities with respect to these attributes are evaluated and discussed for the estimated coefficients of the demand models in Tables 4.6, 4.7, and 4.8. The predictive performance of the demand models is also discussed in this section.

7.1. Rent, Travel Cost, and Travel Time Elasticities of the Estimated Demand Models

We let $E_{im}^{R_i}$, $E_{im}^{T_{im}}$, and $E_{im}^{C_{im}}$ denote the elasticity of the demand for alternative (i, m) with respect to the rent of zone i, the travel time to zone i via mode m, and the travel cost to zone i via mode m, respectively. Each elasticity measures the percentage decrease in the estimated demand (or relative choice frequency) for (i, m) given a unit percentage increase in the relevant attribute from a prespecified level. We must first derive the elasticities for each of the specifications that we have estimated by applying the definition

$$E_{im}^X = \frac{\partial P_{im}/\partial X_{im}}{P_{im}/X_{im}}. \tag{4.123}$$

When rent is specified as linear, the rent elasticity of demand is simply

$$E_{im}^{R_i} = \beta_{R+C}(1 - \sigma)(1 - P_i)R_i. \tag{4.124}$$

When rent is specified loglinearly, as in $\log(R_i + C_{im})$, the rent elasticity becomes

$$E_{im}^{R_i} = \beta_{R+C}\left\{\frac{R_i}{R_i + C_{im}} + \left(\sum_n \frac{R_i P_{n|i}}{R_i + C_{in}}\right)\left[-\sigma - (1 - \sigma)P_i\right]\right\}, \tag{4.125}$$

and the travel cost elasticity is

$$E_{im}^{C_{im}} = \beta_{R+C}\left[1 - (1 - \sigma)P_{im} - \sigma P_{m|i}\right]C_{im}/(R_i + C_{im}), \tag{4.126}$$

where β_{R+C} is the estimated coefficient of $\log(R_i + C_{im})$.

When travel time or travel cost enter utility in linear form, the elasticities are

$$E_{im}^{T_{im}} = \beta_T\left[1 - (1 - \sigma)P_{im} - \sigma P_{m|i}\right]T_{im} \tag{4.127}$$

and

$$E_{im}^{C_{im}} = \beta_C\left[1 - (1 - \sigma)P_{im} - \sigma P_{m|i}\right]C_{im}, \tag{4.128}$$

with β_T and β_C the estimated time and cost coefficients, respectively. When the same attributes enter loglinearly as $\log T_{im}$ or $\log C_{im}$, the elasticities are

$$E_{im}^{T_{im}} = \beta_T\left[1 - (1 - \sigma)P_{im} - \sigma P_{m|i}\right] \tag{4.129}$$

and

$$E_{im}^{C_{im}} = \beta_C\left[1 - (1 - \sigma)P_{im} - \sigma P_{m|i}\right], \tag{4.130}$$

with β_T and β_C again the estimated coefficients.

Using these formulas, we compute the rent, travel time, and travel cost

TABLE 4.10

Weighted Average Elasticities for the CBD Demand Models Reported in Table 4.6

	Choice model							
	1	2	3	4	5	6	7	8
Attributes	$(\sigma \neq 0)$	$(\sigma \neq 0)$	$(\sigma = 0)$	$(\sigma \neq 0)$	$(\sigma = 0)$	$(\sigma \neq 0)$	$(\sigma \neq 0)$	$(\sigma \neq 0)$
Rent (R)								
Specification	$(R + C)$	(R)			$\log(R + C)$			
All modes	-0.060	-0.269	-0.529	-0.303	-0.503	-0.321	-0.317	-0.441
Auto	-0.060	-0.270	-0.409	-0.226	-0.390	-0.167	-0.269	-0.180
Rail	-0.080	-0.406	-0.564	-0.496	-0.536	-0.484	-0.427	-0.506
Transit	-0.060	-0.243	-0.580	-0.567	-0.550	-0.557	-0.528	-0.551
Bus	-0.050	-0.214	-0.592	-0.637	-0.561	-0.616	-0.605	-0.583
Time (T)								
Specification		$\log(T)$				(T)		
All modes	-1.97	-1.70	-2.19	-1.73	-2.19	-1.78	-1.462	-1.787
Auto	-2.05	-1.76	-2.19	-1.82	-2.22	-1.92	-1.483	-1.783
Rail	-1.76	-1.56	-2.19	-1.46	-2.90	-1.87	-1.483	-2.046
Transit	-2.14	-1.81	-2.19	-1.92	-1.90	-1.73	-1.427	-1.711
Bus	-1.86	-1.63	-2.19	-1.63	-2.90	-1.63	-1.356	-2.046
Cost (C)								
Specification	$(R + C)$	$\log(C)$			$\log(R + C)$			
All modes	-0.020	-1.01	-0.169	-0.564	-0.159	-0.509	-0.573	-0.282
Auto	-0.040	-1.04	-0.289	-0.939	-0.272	-0.867	-1.007	-0.498
Rail	-0.020	-0.92	-0.134	-0.378	-0.126	-0.329	-0.369	-0.206
Transit	-0.010	-1.07	-0.118	-0.402	-0.111	-0.369	-0.437	-0.203
Bus	-0.010	-0.97	-0.106	-0.332	-0.100	-0.296	-0.325	-0.162

elasticities corresponding to the estimated demand models reported in Tables 4.6, 4.7, and 4.8. The results are listed in Tables 4.10, 4.11, and 4.12. In each case, the reported elasticity value is the weighted average elasticity over all alternatives (i, m) evaluated at the observed values of the variables (i.e., the estimation sample). Thus the weighted average rent elasticity, for example, is computed as

$$E^R \equiv \sum_i \sum_m E_{im}^{R_i} P_{im}^*, \tag{4.131}$$

where the summation is over the alternatives (i, m) in the estimation sample and $E_{im}^{R_i}$, P_{im}^* are evaluated using the estimation sample values of the attributes and the estimated utility coefficients. The tables also list elasticity values for each mode. These are defined as

$$E_m^R \equiv \sum_i E_{im}^{R_i}(P_{im}^* / \sum_i P_{im}^*). \tag{4.132}$$

TABLE 4.11

Weighted Average Elasticities for the CBD
Demand Models Reported in Table 4.7

Attributes	Choice model	
	1 $\sigma = 0$	2 $1 > \sigma > 0$
Rent (R) Specification	log(R + C)	
All modes	−0.202	−0.314
Auto	−0.157	−0.077
Rail	−0.213	−0.395
Transit	−0.220	−0.408
Bus	−0.226	−0.436
Cost (C) Specification	log(R + C)	
All modes	−0.061	−0.246
Auto	−0.105	−0.445
Rail	−0.051	−0.186
Transit	−0.042	−0.177
Bus	−0.035	−0.134
Time (T) Specification	log(T)	
All models	−1.612	−1.694
Auto	−1.614	−1.803
Rail	−1.618	−1.541
Transit	−1.610	−1.788
Bus	−1.608	−1.588

The rent elasticities shown in Table 4.10 range from −0.060 to −0.529. If we eliminate models 1 and 2 because of their unsatisfactory linear specification of rent, the range is narrowed substantially and goes from −0.303 to −0.529. Models 3–8, which give this narrower range, have the same specification of utility as loglinear in rent plus cost and are consistent with urban economic theory, where locational expenditures such as rent plus travel cost are entered into the model together, and the marginal utility of money (or disutility of locational expenditure) is not constant. The range is narrowed even further if we remove models 3 and 5, in which the inclusive value

TABLE 4.12

Weighted Average Elasticities for the Non-CBD Demand Models Reported in Table 4.8

Attributes	Choice model	
	1 $\sigma = 0$	2 $1 > \sigma > 0$
Rent (R) Specification	$\log(R + C)$	
All modes	-0.082	-0.205
Auto	-0.081	-0.144
Bus	-0.086	-0.510
Cost (C) Specification	$\log(R + C)$	
All modes	-0.017	-0.256
Auto	-0.017	-0.202
Bus	-0.013	-0.525
Time (T) Specification	$\log(T)$	
All modes	-0.210	-0.251
Auto	-0.210	-0.167
Bus	-0.211	-0.666

coefficient has been set equal to zero ($\sigma = 0$). When this is done, the range is from -0.303 to -0.441. Thus the effect of forcing $\sigma = 0$ decreases the estimated value of the rent elasticity by about 56% (comparing model 5 to 6) and 75% (comparing model 3 to 4) if the nested models ($\sigma \neq 0$) are estimated in two steps. Estimating the model in one step increases the rent elasticity by 39% (comparing model 7 to model 8). Entering travel time linearly versus loglinearly decreases the rent elasticity by 5% (comparing model 3 to model 5) for the $\sigma = 0$ case, and increases it by 6% (comparing model 4 to model 6). We can conclude from these empirical investigations that the specification of travel time has a small effect on the estimated rent elasticity, that the estimation of the nested model ($\sigma \neq 0$) in one step has a larger and possibly substantial effect, and that the specification of the choice model as nested versus nonnested ($\sigma = 0$) has the largest and most powerful effect on the estimated rent elasticity of demand. It is important to recall once again, however, that these ranges in the elasticity estimates, which are purely due to specification error keeping the estimation sample the same, are not wider than the ranges that can be observed in the same elasticities when the specification is kept constant and the estimation sample is varied, as was done to obtain the results of Table 4.3.

Lerman's disaggregate model (1977), estimated with Washington, D.C., data, produced elasticities very close to those of models 3 to 8 in Table 4.10. Since Lerman's model was similar in specification but used disaggregate data, we can conclude that the estimation uncertainty due to data aggregation is probably not very large and compares well with the uncertainty due to model specification. There is, of course, good reason to believe that this comparison will not hold if the aggregation units are larger zones. Thus a great deal of the success in estimating policy-sensitive choice models depends on the analyst's ability to select small aggregation units and to estimate the choice models from these units.

Comparing model 3 of Table 4.10 to model 1 of Table 4.11, we find that the rent elasticity of the latter model is 38% of the former. On the other hand, comparing model 4 of Table 4.10 to model 2 of Table 4.11, we find that the latter elasticity is only 3.6% higher than the former. These two comparisons reveal another important specification influence. The first comparison shows the effect of introducing station accessibility attributes into a nonnested ($\sigma = 0$) model: the effect on the rent elasticity is substantial. If, however, the same attributes are introduced into the nested model, the effect on the rent elasticity is quite small.

The results clearly demonstrate that the rent elacticity of demand obtained from these logistic models is well below 1 (i.e., between -1 and 0) and probably between $-\frac{1}{2}$ and $-\frac{1}{4}$. This finding revises the now rarely held belief in urban economics that the rent elasticity of housing demand may be around -1.

Travel cost elasticities in Table 4.10, excluding the linear specifications 1 and 2, range from -0.169 to -0.564. Specifying travel time as linear or loglinear (compare model 3 to model 5) changes the elasticity by 6%, but when the model is nested (compare model 4 to model 6) the change is about 11%. The cost elasticity of nested models (compare 4 to 3 and 6 to 5) is about 320%–333% higher. Estimating the nested model in one versus two steps (compare 7 to 8) halves the elasticity. Again the relative importance of the three sources of specification bias on the cost elasticity appear to be as follows: specifying the model as nested versus nonnested increases the elasticity the most, estimating it in two steps also has a strong impact, but the specification of the travel time attribute as linear or loglinear has a very small impact. Thus the cost elasticity is affected in a way that is similar to the way the rent elasticity is affected.

Travel time elasticities listed in Table 4.10 vary from -1.462 to -2.19, a percentage range much narrower than those for the rent and cost elasticities. The effect of specifying travel time as linear versus loglinear (model 3 versus 5 or 4 versus 6) has a negligible effect on the elasticity of travel time. Estimating the nested model in one versus two steps decreases the time elasticity by 19%.

Introducing the station accessibility attributes into the utility function (models in Table 4.11) has a strong effect on the elasticity of travel cost: the elasticity is reduced by about 56% for the nested model and by 64% for the nonnested model. The effect of the station accessibility attributes on the time elasticities is smaller: the elasticity of the nested model is reduced by about 2% and that of the nonnested model is reduced by 27%.

Our travel time and travel cost elasticities can be compared not only to Lerman's model (1977) but also to other disaggregate mode choice models that do not include housing prices. We compare our results to those by Charles River Associates (CRA), Inc. (1967), Atherton *et al.* (1975), and Train (1976, 1977). The CRA model was estimated with 1967 data from San Francisco; the Atherton, Suhrbier, and Jessiman publication reports a model estimated at Cambridge Systematics (CSI), Inc. (1977) by Moshe Ben-Akiva and Richard Albright using 1968 data from Washington, D.C., and the papers by Train report a model estimated by Daniel McFadden and Kenneth Train using 1975 San Francisco data. These three models have been compared to each other in a recent publication by Goméz-Ibanéz and Fauth (1980) in terms of the magnitude of their elasticities and in terms of performance within a simulation framework. Comparing these models by transferring them to Boston, Goméz-Ibanéz and Fauth found that cost elasticities range from -0.12 to -1.16 for transit and -0.33 to -2.69 for the drive-alone mode. The in-vehicle time elasticity ranges from -0.36 to -1.40 for transit and -0.55 to -1.77 for the drive-alone mode. Out-of-vehicle time elasticities range from -0.23 to -2.7 for transit and are -0.42 for the drive-alone mode in the CSI model. The CRA model and McFadden–Train do not estimate out-of-vehicle time elasticities for the auto mode. These differences in elasticities are either due to specification differences in model, in explanatory attributes, in utility functional form, or in sampling method, or else due to real differences in preferences by time and place. Lerman's model estimated for Washington, D.C., using data from the sixties was evaluated in Anas (1981a) by transferring the estimated coefficients to the same Chicago data used in this chapter. Lerman's model, thus transferred, produces travel cost and total travel time elasticities that are fairly similar to those of the CSI model. Comparing all of these results to our results reported in Tables 4.10 and 4.11, we find that keeping data aggregation and data sampling constant but varying model specification, as we have done, creates travel cost and travel time ranges that are *within* the range of the above-mentioned models. Our travel time elasticities have a narrower range than those of the above-mentioned models. This range falls slightly beyond the *in-vehicle* time elasticities of the models by Lerman, McFadden and Train, CRA, CSI. It should be recalled, however, that our models were estimated in the absence of data pertaining to out-of-vehicle times. If such data were available, our time elasticities would come into closer agreement with those of the other models. Indeed, our total travel time elasticities agree most closely with those of the CRA model, which does not include out-of-vehicle times as a separate attribute in the specification, either.

Comparing the non-CBD demand model elasticities of Table 4.12 to the corresponding elasticities of the CBD demand model listed in Table 4.11, we find that the rent and cost elasticities agree strongly for the nested model but are much smaller for the nonnested non-CBD model than for the nonnested CBD model. Non-CBD travel time elasticities are about 14% of the CBD travel time elasticities. At least part of this difference is to be explained by the fact that the average income of non-CBD workers is much lower than that of CBD workers, who theoretically have a higher value of time.

7.2.   The Quality of Aggregate Predictions

The selection of useful choice models must be based not only on an evaluation of key policy relevant elasticities, but also on a direct evaluation of the estimated model's ability to predict aggregate quantities. There are several aspects of aggregate prediction that are of interest. First is the ability of the estimated models to replicate the sample aggregate market shares of the travel modes in the estimation sample. Second is the ability of the estimated models to replicate the zone-specific market shares of the travel modes in the estimation sample. Finally, the influence of the estimation sample on the predictive ability of the model can be tested by using the estimated model to make predictions for the population from which the estimation sample was drawn. Each of these examinations of predictive ability will be discussed below.

Let $\tilde{N}_m \equiv \sum_i \tilde{N} \hat{P}_{im}$ be the trips by mode m in the estimation sample predicted by the maximum likelihood estimated coefficients, where $\tilde{N}$ is the total number of trips in the sample and $\hat{P}_{im}$ are the predicted choice probabilities. It can be seem from Eq. (4.94) that the maximum likelihood value of the mth mode-specific constant will adjust in such a way that the error in the prediction of the aggregate trips by mode m will be

$$\tilde{N}_m - \hat{N}_m = \sigma\left[\sum (\tilde{P}_i - \hat{P}_i)\hat{P}_{m|i}\right]\tilde{N}. \tag{4.133}$$

We note from this equation that when $\sigma = 0$, i.e., the model is not nested, then $\tilde{N}_m = \hat{N}_m$ and there is no prediction bias for each mode m. For sequential

TABLE 4.13

Percentage Error[a] and Simple Correlation Coefficient[b] between Predicted and Observed Trips

CBD choice models (Table 4.6)	1	2	3	4	5	6	7
			Percentage Error				
Auto	+1.4%	+1.3%	0%	+2.2%	0%	+1.1%	−0.1%
Rail	+4.7%	+4.1%	0%	+5.9%	0%	+4.1%	+4.6%
Transit	−2.5%	−2.9%	0%	−2.8%	0%	−2.2%	−1.1%
Bus	−1.7%	−0.9%	0%	−2.9%	0%	−1.4%	−1.3%
F statistic[c]	2.69	1.49[d]	—	6.38	—	2.40	1.34[d]
			Simple Correlation Coefficient				
Auto	0.848	0.854	0.893	0.856	0.914	0.904	0.903
Rail	0.607	0.644	0.570	0.585	0.615	0.637	0.604
Transit	0.935	0.930	0.912	0.930	0.914	0.931	0.882
Bus	0.889	0.877	0.859	0.878	0.858	0.884	0.826
All modes	0.879	0.869	0.867	0.881	0.873	0.892	0.823

[a] Percentage error = [(predicted aggregate trips − observed aggregate trips)/observed aggregate trips] × 100. Computed for the estimation sample.

[b] Simple correlation coefficient between predicted and observed trips by mode for the estimation sample of 433 zones.

[c] F statistic for the hypothesis that the mode-specific constants of the adjusted model do not differ from the constants of the estimated (unadjusted) model.

[d] Adjusted constants not different from the estimated constants at the 5% level of significance.

representations of choice via a nested logit model $(0 < \sigma < 1)$, the right side of (4.133) measures the over- or underprediction of the sample market shares of each mode. This bias is totally due to the marginal (zone) choice structure because it can be shown that the conditional (mode) choice structure will result in the exact reproduction of the sample market shares by mode. As discussed in Section 5.3, if zone-specific constants were to be included in the marginal choice model, the marginal model would adjust and the estimated model would become saturated so that exact predictions would be generated for each alternative (i, m). Since our marginal choice models are unsaturated, they will have some bias in the prediction of the aggregate trips by mode. These biases are listed in Table 4.13 as percentage over- or underpredictions by mode for the nested CBD models of Table 4.6. Table 4.13 also lists the correlation coefficients between the observed and predicted zonal trip vectors by mode and for trips by all modes. Table 4.14 lists the same statistics for the CBD and non-CBD models of Tables 4.7 and 4.8. The percentage errors in the aggregate predictions are reasonably small for each of

Table 4.14

Percentage Errors in Aggregate Predicted Trips and Simple Correlation Coefficients between Predicted and Observed Trips[a]

Choice models	CBD (Table 4.7)		Non-CBD (Table 4.8)	
	1	2	1	2
	Percentage Error			
Auto	$0\%^a$	$-0.75\%^a$	$0\%^a$	$-0.29\%^a$
Rail	0%	$+4.09\%$	0%	—
Transit	0%	-3.57%	0%	—
Bus	0%	1.72%	0%	$+1.47\%$
	Simple Correlation Coefficient			
Auto	0.914^b $(0.787)^c$	0.886^b $(0.806)^c$	0.804^b $(0.900)^c$	0.871^b $(0.927)^c$
Rail	0.708 (0.735)	0.706 (0.748)	—	—
Transit	0.875 (0.781)	0.927 (0.848)	—	—
Bus	0.864 (0.755)	0.859 (0.794)	0.680 (0.509)	0.868 (0.794)
All modes	0.877 (0.787)	0.882 (0.806)	0.809 (0.911)	0.880 (0.938)

[a] Percentage error computed from the estimation sample of 433 zones.
[b] Simple correlation coefficient between predicted and observed trips by mode for the 433 zone estimation sample.
[c] Simple correlation coefficient between predicted and observed trips by mode for the 1690 zone simulation system.

the nested models (Table 4.13 or 4.14). In order to test the statistical significance of the aggregate biases by mode for the nested models in Table 4.13, we first minimized the sum of squares function:

$$\operatorname*{Min}_{\beta_1, \beta_2, \beta_3} S = \sum_{m=1}^{4} \left[\tilde{N}_m - \sum_i \tilde{N} P_{im}(\bar{\beta}, \bar{\alpha}^*, \sigma^*, \gamma^*) \right]^2, \qquad (4.134)$$

where $\bar{\beta} = (\beta_1, \beta_2, \beta_3, \beta_4^*, \ldots; \beta_{10}^*)$ and $\bar{\alpha}^*, \sigma^*, \gamma^*, \beta_4^*, \ldots, \beta_{10}^*$ are the maximum likelihood estimates, and $\beta_1, \beta_2, \beta_3$ are the mode-specific constants. Minimization of S eliminates all biases in the prediction of the sample market shares by finding adjusted mode-specific constants $\beta_1^{**}, \beta_2^{**}, \beta_3^{**}$ such that when $\beta_j = \beta_j^{**}, j = 1, 2, 3$; then each of the four squared deviations in S become zero. Having found $\beta_j^{**}, j = 1, 2, 3$, we now use the T^2 test to determine whether the maximum likelihood vector $\bar{\delta}^* \equiv (\bar{\beta}^* \bar{\alpha}^* \gamma^* \sigma^*)$ is different from the adjusted vector $\bar{\delta}^{**} \equiv (\beta_1^{**} \beta_2^{**} \beta_3^{**} \beta_4^* \cdots \beta_{10}^* \bar{\alpha}^* \gamma^* \sigma^*)$. The formal hypothesis we wish to test is

$$H_0 : \bar{\delta}^* = \bar{\delta}^{**}, \qquad H_1 : \bar{\delta}^* \neq \bar{\delta}^{**},$$

where the adjusted vector $\bar{\delta}^{**}$ is treated as a constant (nonrandom) vector and $\bar{\delta}^*$ is a random vector with a variance–covariance matrix $\bar{V}$ estimated via maximum likelihood. The T^2 statistic is

$$T^2 = (\bar{\delta}^* - \bar{\delta}^{**})\bar{V}^{-1}(\bar{\delta}^* - \bar{\delta}^{**})' \tag{4.135}$$

and is distributed with an F value

$$F = T^2(\tilde{N} - p)/(\tilde{N} - 1)p \tag{4.136}$$

and a 0.05 critical value of $F \cong 1.66$ for p, the number of estimated coefficients (elements of $\bar{\delta}^*$), and $N = 399{,}395$, the number of trips in the estimation sample. The F values listed in Table 4.13 show that the aggregate prediction biases of models 2 and 7 are not significant at the 0.05 level, whereas the biases of the remaining models *are* significant at the 0.05 level. The biases reflect an incompleteness in the marginal part of the estimated nested logit models. It is noteworthy that the bias is largest for the commuter rail mode. This is probably because of missing variables such as those describing access to commuter rail stations and the availability of parking at these stations. If such variables are introduced, the biases may decrease and become insignificant. Alternatively, the bias may be attributed to specification error in the assumed nesting structure of the four modes. If, for example, the commuter rail mode is removed from this nesting structure, its market share will be perfectly predicted while the remaining biases in the auto, bus, and transit modes can become smaller and insignificant.

The final step of our evaluation of the estimated models consists not of making predictions for the estimation sample of the 433 zones but of readjusting the constants via (4.134) and of making predictions for the 1690 zones that comprise the zone system to be used in the policy analysis of the next chapter. These 1690 zones are $\frac{1}{2}$-mile by $\frac{1}{2}$-mile square zones within the city of Chicago and 1-mile by 1-mile or larger traffic zones in the suburban area. The simple correlation coefficients between the observed and predicted trips for these 1690 zones are included in Table 4.14 in parentheses next to the correlation coefficients computed for the estimation sample of 433 zones. The magnitudes of these two sets of correlation coefficients are generally comparable, although some biases can be discerned. In both non-CBD models, for example, the predictions for auto trips increase in accuracy while the predictions for bus trips decrease in accuracy (and substantially so in the case of the nonnested model) when the estimated coefficients are transferred from the estimation sample to the simulation zone system.

Table 4.15 shows the adjusted values of the mode-specific constants used to perform the above-mentioned predictions. Column a lists the values of these constants estimated from the 433-zone estimation sample. Column b lists the values obtained when those of column a are adjusted according to

Table 4.15

Effect of Adjustments on the Estimated Mode-Specific Constants of the CBD Models[a]

	a	b	c	d
	Model 1 (Table 4.7)			
Rapid transit	−1.089	−1.273	−1.148	−1.344
Commuter rail	−0.406	−0.144	−0.448	−0.645
Bus	0.173	0.105	0.179	−0.017
	Model 2 (Table 4.7)			
Rapid transit	−1.701	−1.885	−1.695	−1.908
Commuter rail	−0.846	−0.584	−0.883	−1.132
Bus	−0.636	−0.704	−0.582	−0.790

[a] a, estimated from 433-zone sample; b, adjustment to correct for estimation sample error (Eq. 4.92); c, adjustment to eliminate mode market share errors in the predictions for the 1690 simulation zone system; d, adjustment as in c, but auto mode includes auto drivers plus auto passengers.

Eq. (4.92), the purpose of this adjustment being the correction of any influence arising from the nonrandomness of the estimation sample. The values in column c are those that produce perfect predictions of the aggregate trips by each mode for the 1690 zone simulation data set. Finally, the values in column d are adjusted in such a way that the prediction for auto trips includes the sum of auto driver trips (from which the model was estimated) and auto passenger trips and also in such a way that the prediction of aggregate trips by each mode is perfect for all four modes. These adjustments indicate that the rapid transit and bus constants are stable for the nested model, while the commuter rail constant is less stable. For the nonnested model, the rapid transit and commuter rail constants are fairly stable, while the bus constant is less so. In both cases, however, it is encouraging to see that the values of columns a and c are quite similar, indicating small changes as the model estimated from the 433 zones is transferred to the 1690 zones.

8. CONCLUSIONS

The chief purpose of this chapter was to formulate, empirically estimate, and evaluate the choice models needed to perform the equilibrium policy simulations of the next chapter.

In performing these empirical estimations, we reached several conclusions that are relevant to the literature on location and mode choice modeling and to the methodological practices within this literature. These conclusions can be summarized as follows:

(1) Choice models estimated from small area data can be at least as *meaningful*, *useful*, and *transferable* as equivalent choice models estimated from disaggregate data. The recent emphasis on the use of disaggregate data is apparently exaggerated and can motivate many researchers to bypass useful and easily accessible data sets based on small aggregation units. Disaggregate models are particularly unjustified when the objective of the analyst is to perform aggregative prediction and equilibrium simulation in order to examine policy issues.

(2) Comparison of the elasticities for rent, travel cost, and travel time of our aggregate models to the same elasticities of disaggregate models estimated by others shows that there is no discernible persistent difference. Differences among the elasticities of our estimated models can be substantial and due to specification decisions, yet the ranges of our elasticities compare extremely well with the ranges of the estimated elasticities generated from disaggregate models. When these ranges do not overlap extremely well, differences are logically explained by missing attributes, as in the case of the effect of including out-of-vehicle travel time on the elasticity of total travel time. To summarize, specification error affects disaggregate and aggregate data in similar and important ways, and errors due to specification seem to be easily more important than errors due to aggregation when the aggregation units are small as in our study.

(3) Our study confirms that IID probit and multinomial logit models yield virtually identical results. Thus the source of bias due to the choice between these two IID specifications is clearly the least important source. The next least important source of bias is probably that of the specification of our key policy-sensitive attributes, which are rent, travel cost, and travel time: the form in which these are entered into the model makes little difference, with the exception of the theoretically unsatisfactory linear rent and cost specifications. Much more important are errors due to the choice of a nested versus nonnested logit model, to the one-step or two-step estimation of the nested model, and to pure sampling error when the model is estimated with a very small sample of consumers, as is commonly done in disaggregate modeling. Errors due to attribute measurement and choice set definition are probably also important, but these were not studied in detail in this study.

(4) Although both nested and nonnested logit demand models perform quite well in elasticities and in aggregate prediction, the nested logit models

appear to be substantially more robust in prediction and to yield coefficients that are more stable in the face of specification changes.

(5)   Important inclusion–exclusion relationships among the explanatory attributes govern the specification of location–mode choice models. Attributes measuring or proxying public services, neighborhood quality, and location are important in obtaining acceptable estimates of the coefficients of rent, travel cost, and travel time.

(6)   Research into the transferability of choice models should focus on the comparative evaluation of the ten sources of error discussed in Section 1 of this chapter. From the work reported in this paper and other work to which our results are compared, it appears that errors due to aggregation should not unduly hamper efforts to achieve transferability. Future research should focus on discovering the most transferable choice model specification. Given the complexity of the specification issue and the influence of the other sources of error, the transferability problem may not become empirically resolved for a long time.

(7)   The work reported in this chapter and the methodological approach demonstrates that urban economists can usefully detach their attention from bid rent analysis and its numerous empirical shortcomings discussed in Chapter 1, and focus their attention on the discrete choice modeling of demand. The theoretical arguments favoring such a shift in emphasis were proposed in Chapter 2; the empirical estimation has been performed in this chapter. To complete the proposition, we need to develop and empirically test an efficient equilibrium simulation model based on the results of this chapter.

In closing this chapter, it is important to recall some of the limitations of our data and the resultant restrictions we needed to place on our estimated models. Two limitations need specific attention. First is the limitation arising from having to pool homeowners with renters because data on the separate choices of owners and renters are not readily available in the compiled form of the census data. Were such data available, the current models can be extended to represent the interactions of travel mode—residential location—housing tenure choices, while at the same time treating rentals and housing prices as separate attributes. A second limitation arises from not having more detailed data on the choices of households and their members: the only models that are estimable are those in which the disaggregate unit is the commuter—worker, and the aggregated choices are work trips rather than household choices. It is clear that both of the above limitations will introduce some bias into the estimated models, but it is doubtful that the magnitude of these biases will invalidate the results of the prototypical policy simulations to be reported in Chapter 5.

CHAPTER 5

EQUILIBRIUM ANALYSIS OF URBAN TRANSPORTATION POLICY

In this chapter, the demand- and supply-side choice functions estimated in Chapter 4 are combined into a multisubmarket locational equilibrium model. This model is then applied to the analysis of public transportation finance policy and specific transit projects proposed for the Chicago SMSA.

The Chicago SMSA is divided into 1690 small geographic residential zones forming a grid pattern. The city of Chicago contains 763 $\frac{1}{2}$-mile by $\frac{1}{2}$-mile square residential zones, while the suburban SMSA is divided into 927 residential zones of 1 mile by 1 mile or larger. The demand side represents the utility-maximizing dwelling location and travel-to-work choices of commuters classified by workplace. Because our primary concern is the analysis of CBD-oriented multimodal transportation policies, two workplace classifications are used. The first is the Chicago downtown (CBD), which in 1970 generated 20% of the SMSA work trips. The second is a locationally unspecified non-CBD classification containing *all* employment outside of the CBD. Downtown commuters choose between auto, commuter rail, rapid transit, and bus, whereas non-CBD commuters choose between auto and bus. Each geographic zone is treated as a distinct housing submarket.

The model determines a locational equilibrium by finding the unique zonal average market rents that equate the number of dwellings demanded for occupancy in each zone with the number of existing dwellings offered for occupancy in that zone. The model also determines the commuting modal splits of each zone's CBD and non-CBD residents, each zone's housing vacancy rate at equilibrium, and changes in the consumer welfare for the CBD and non-CBD commuters.

The travel demand side of the model is consistent with state-of-the-art transportation planning methodology, and it goes beyond it to include the simultaneity of travel and residential location choices. In this way, the model marries the urban economic theory of location market equilibrium developed in this book with behavioral travel demand modeling. Given an exogenously determined zonal housing stock distribution, exogenously given CBD, non-CBD employment levels, and multimodal transportation system characteristics, the model solves for the market equilibrium allocation of households to dwellings assuming that the estimated preference structure remains stable.

The stability of the preference structure implies several assumptions. First, the estimated utility and profit function coefficients should remain constant. Second, the statistical distribution of the unobserved parts of the utility and profit functions should remain constant for each choice alternative. Third, and most importantly, the alternative-specific constant parts of the utility and profit functions should be estimable for each *new* choice alternative introduced as part of policy.

Section 1 of this chapter discusses current issues in urban transportation finance, and in particular the financing of public transportation deficits from local economic resources. The rationales for gasoline and parking taxes, efficient fare structures, and the taxation of windfall gains in the real estate market are discussed and compared.

Section 2 presents the data that serve as an input into the equilibrium model. The assumptions and limitations of the equilibrium model are also discussed. Section 3 formulates the model mathematically, proves the uniqueness and stability of the equilibrium, proposes a computational algorithm, and examines the properties of the model analytically to the extent that this is tractable. Comparative static results regarding the impact of travel time improvements on the distribution of housing rents between city and suburb are derived, and these shed light on the model's internal structure.

The remaining sections focus on empirical policy simulations for the 1690-equation zone system. Section 4 compares the predictions generated by the alternative logistic demand models estimated in Chapter 4 and selects one of these models for policy analysis. Sensitivity analysis on this model's key coefficients is also performed in this chapter. It is shown that equilibrium elasticities can differ greatly from preequilibrium estimated elasticities, and gross errors in policy conclusions can occur if an equilibrium model is not used. Section 5 applies the equilibrium model to an investigation of alternative gasoline and parking tax schemes aimed at covering the Chicago public transportation system's projected deficit for 1981. Fare-free public transit alternatives are also examined. Section 6 evaluates three heavy rail rapid transit lines that have been proposed for implementation in Chicago's Southwest corridor. The viability of these proposed investments is examined from the ridership, commuter-welfare, and housing-rent-distribution viewpoints. The possibility of financing the operating and capital costs of these projects via a combination of gas, parking, and real estate windfall taxes is discussed. The Gulf Mobile & Ohio rail project is selected for detailed analysis, and its system characteristics and assumed market conditions are varied in search of a cost effective configuration.

The findings and policy conclusions of this chapter are summarized in Section 7.

1. ISSUES IN URBAN TRANSPORTATION FINANCE

Since the emergence of the "new urban economics" in the early seventies, urban economists have shown a strong but narrowly specialized interest in urban passenger transportation finance issues. It can be said without exaggeration that only one issue in urban transportation finance has attracted the concerted attention of urban economists. This is the issue of highway congestion pricing and the associated land use planning problem of the allocation of land to roads. Interest in the benefits of highway investments goes back to the early sixties (see Mohring and Harwitz, 1962), and the problem of congestion pricing predates "the new urban economics" and stems from observations by Vickrey (1965) and others that congestion tolls should be levied on highway travel in order to achieve a socially optimal congestion level and allocation of land to roads. Alonso-type spatial equilibrium models were first applied to this problem by Strotz (1965), Mills and Deferranti (1971), Solow and Vickrey (1971), Mills (1972a), and Solow (1972). Many other articles on the same topic continued to flood the leading urban economics journals throughout the rest of the seventies.

The conclusions derived from these extensive, and often repetitive, analyses can be summarized briefly. First, all articles agree that ideally a toll on highway travel is necessary to force travelers to pay their marginal cost, thus internalizing the congestion externality they impose on other travelers. If this is not done, travelers pay only their average cost, which is less than their marginal cost. The toll, if it can be implemented, helps achieve a socially efficient level of congestion that is less than the untolled congestion level. It is implied, therefore, that urban areas should allocate less land to roads and more land to residential and other land uses.

The policy implications of the highway congestion analysis have been that during the extensive growth of American metropolitan areas since World

War II, highway travel was underpriced, and more than optimal amounts of land were allocated to roads, leading to excessive urban sprawl. Semi-empirical analyses and numerical simulations of this problem can be found in the articles by Mills (1972a), Muth (1975), Henderson (1975), and others.

While the theoretical significance and historical importance of the highway congestion problem cannot be denied, it should be understood that this issue has lost much of its initial "timeliness." Most large and mature American metropolitan areas are no longer building urban highways and have entered an era of decline and internal decentralization and reorganization (see Leven, 1978). Furthermore, the extensive work on congestion tolling has confirmed the belief that the benefits to be derived from instituting congestion tolls are not significant and that the distortive effects of untolled congestion on land use are probably minor. Urban transportation is now plagued by new and more serious economic difficulties that are a symptom of the general process of central city decline and metropolitan decentralization. Hardest hit by this decline have been the urban public mass transportation systems. Ironically, urban economists have paid little attention to public transportation system pricing and to the interactions of subway and transit systems with land use. Alonso-type investigations of public transportation systems are those by Capozza (1973), Haring *et al.* (1976), Anas and Moses (1979), and Kim (1979), who applies the linear programming model by Mills (1972b).

The most important current problem in urban mass transit is the viability of mass transit as a financially self-supporting proposition. Up until the late 1960's, most metropolitan transit systems (bus lines and fixed rail transit) were generally self-sufficient: fare box revenues were high enough to cover operating and maintenance, if not capital improvement costs. Two fundamental processes have put an end to this viability. The first process is that of employment and population suburbanization, which has drained central cities—where transit services are generally concentrated—of their transit patronage potential. Early tabulations of the 1980 census published in the popular press indicate that despite substantial increases in the price of gasoline and fairly stable or declining real transit fares, large cities are continuing to show declining transit ridership patterns, obviously because of the movement of jobs and population to suburban and exurban areas. The problem is further compounded in that most of the suburbanizing population is of higher and middle income brackets, and the lower income and minority groups who are the most transit dependent continue to increase in proportion within the transit served areas of the central cities. Thus the average real income of potential transit users is dropping, and fare increases are becoming increasingly difficult to justify from the welfare, economic, and political viewpoints. The second process that has put an end to transit's financial viability is the skyrocketing operating maintenance and capital improvement costs.

Costs in general, but primarily transit operator wages, have increased to the point where fare box revenues are not sufficient to cover them. Tables 5.1 and 5.2 illustrate the transit deficits projected into the mideighties for the Chicago metropolitan transit system managed by the Regional Transportation Authority (RTA). A more detailed analysis of RTA's financial problems can be found in a report of the Metropolitan Housing and Planning Council (December, 1980).

The steady growth of transit deficits during the seventies led to growing Federal involvement in the subsidization of metropolitan transit operations. High proportions of the cost of existing and new projects are being borne by Federal subsidies. Since these subsidies come from general tax revenues, mass transit operations nationwide are being paid for, in large measure, by the average taxpayer. This financing scheme places a disproportionate burden on those who do not use transit. The gross economic inefficiency that results from this subsidization provides the rationale for seeking more efficient alternatives for financing metropolitan mass transit operations. Some transit finance alternatives that *do* exist and are workable in principle are the following: (1) efficient transit fare structures, (2) taxes on gasoline purchased by automobile users, (3) taxes on the use of automobile parking spaces, (4) taxes on local real estate, and (5) state or local income taxes.

Of these alternatives, the last one is preferable to Federal subsidization because it shifts the burden of financing transit from the nation as a whole to the populations of the urbanized states and municipalities where a larger percentage of people rely on transit systems. While such a scheme somewhat reduces the inefficiency of Federal subsidization, it is still the least efficient of the alternatives proposed above. The most efficient of the above alternatives is a public transportation fare structure that would have each transit rider pay his or her marginal cost. Thus transit fares must be set in a way that internalize any congestion externalities present on the metropolitan transit network and at such levels that the cost of transit operations plus the cost of efficiently planned improvements is covered. Although this approach is of eminent economic rationality, it is clear that pursuing it to its ultimate conclusion would lead to extensive transit disinvestment and service cuts. To balance revenues and costs, transit agencies would be forced to cut the latter by discontinuing those transit lines and services that are most heavily subsidized, while keeping those that break even or generate a surplus. Alternatively, if fares are raised to high levels to cover costs, ridership would decline sharply, forcing transit agencies to discontinue certain very sparsely utilized transit lines. While economically rational, this approach would depress the welfare of low income central city populations, thus creating other social externalities and distributional issues that are politically undesirable. Nevertheless, some "trimming" of inefficient transit networks is

TABLE 5.1

Systemwide Operations of the Regional Transportation Authority[a,b]

	1969	1974	1979	Percent change (1974–79)
Operating revenues	230.3	269.2	307.7	+14.3
Operating costs	213.7	350.9	557.6	+58.9
Surplus (+) or deficit (−)	+16.6	−81.7	−249.9	+205.9
Annual vehicle miles	178.5	173.7	177.1	+2.0
Annual passengers	722.6	713.3	815.5	+14.3
Revenue/mile	1.29	1.55	1.74	+12.3
Cost/mile	1.20	2.02	3.15	+55.9
Passengers/mile	4.05	4.11	4.60	+11.9
Cost/passenger	0.30	0.49	0.68	+38.8

[a] Millions.
[b] Source: "Regional Transportation Authority: Future Financing, Structure and Operations," The Metropolitan Housing and Planning Council, Dec. 1980, p. 8.

TABLE 5.2

Financial Outlook for the Chicago SMSA's Public Transportation System Administered by the Regional Transportation Authority[a,b]

	1981	1982	1983	1984	1985
	Status quo outlook				
Total costs	834.4	951.4	1035.3	1148.3	1288.0
Revenues					
Fare box	326.1	329.9	333.8	337.9	341.9
Sales tax	292.5	317.9	345.4	375.5	408.1
Federal subsidies	88.3	88.3	88.3	88.3	88.3
Deficit	128.0	215.3	267.8	346.6	449.7
	Balanced financing outlook				
Total costs	834.4	951.4	1035.3	1148.3	1288.0
Revenues					
Fare box (45% recovery)	375.5	421.1	465.9	516.7	579.6
Sales tax	292.5	317.9	345.4	375.5	408.1
Federal (Section 5)	80.7	80.7	80.7	80.7	80.7
State subsidy (12% of costs)	100.1	114.2	124.2	137.8	154.6
Local subsidy (3% of costs)	—	28.5	31.1	34.4	38.6
Surplus (+) or deficit (−)	+14.4	+11.0	+12.0	−3.2	−26.4

[a] Millions.
[b] Source: "Regional Transportation Authority: Future Financing, Structure and Operations," The Metropolitan Housing and Planning Council, Dec. 1980, p. v.

probably unavoidable in the near future. A less efficient but politically more acceptable fare structure is "average cost pricing," and this is similar in principle to transit fare structures currently in use. Under such a scheme, a transit user is charged the average cost of an individual transit line or the average cost of a part of the system or the entire system, with appropriate adjustments for peak and off-peak travel and, possibly, for distance traveled. The only advantage this option offers over perfect marginal cost pricing is that it is slightly easier to administer and implement. Under this option, too, extensive cuts in metropolitan transit services would probably become necessary in order to balance costs and revenues. An efficient way to administer the above transit pricing options is for the public transit authorities to manage each separate transit line or transit service as a profit-maximizing or loss-minimizing operation. Ideally, this may be achieved by setting up competitive public operators who independently decide the fare structure and other aspects of the services that are within their responsibility. Unsuccessful operators are eventually forced out of the "market," while successful ones break even or achieve profit margins that are, in turn, allocated into capital improvements. Such market like situations do exist in Tokyo, Seoul, and other large cities around the world where many transit service companies or railroad firms compete with each other in an oligopolistic setting.

The above fare structures would improve the efficiency of metropolitan transit finance but would not eliminate the huge deficits that currently plague the typical transit system in the mature American metropolis. Transit operators would find themselves minimizing losses rather than maximizing profits. Subsidies or extensive service cuts or both would be needed to maintain a socially acceptable yet economically viable level of public transit.

Given that a great deal of subsidization will be necessary, which is the most efficient way of raising these subsidies? This is the question that is of immediate practical importance if metropolitan transit as we know it is to survive without future Federal involvement. The answer is to be found in finance alternatives 2, 3, and 4 enumerated above. Alternative 4 involves real estate taxation, and its rationale will be discussed last. Alternatives 2 and 3 involve taxing automobile travel. The rationale behind taxing auto travel is as follows: If society is in favor of maintaining subsidized metropolitan transit systems, it must have a reason for it. One reason is that providing public transportation to the mobility deprived, the poor, the unemployed, the elderly, and the handicapped is socially desirable. A second reason for taxing auto travel is that the use of the automobile, even in the absence of congestion, creates certain externalities such as pollution, noise, and, possibly overconsumption of gasoline. Externalities arise from the lack of market pricing mechanisms in each case. This is clearly the case for noise and pollution. In the case of gasoline consumption, artificial constraints and regulations and the uncertainty about worldwide oil supplies may contribute to keeping the price of gasoline much below its socially optimal level, leading to overconsumption. A tax on gasoline at the pump can lower this gap, raising the cost of using an automobile to its socially optimal level. Auto users would respond by driving less and making more trips by transit or by switching to more efficient vehicles. Higher transit fare box revenues together with the gas tax revenues cover a portion of the subsidy needed to maintain the transit system. Because drivers predominate over transit riders in American cities, it would be feasible to set a gas tax that covers the projected transit deficits, but it is probably the case that such a tax would set the gross price of gasoline to the consumer above its socially desirable level, thus forcing people to consume less gasoline than is socially desirable. It is important to keep in mind that only a certain increment of a gas tax may be used to subsidize transit, while other increments may be used to pay for highway maintenance and highway improvements, which are also becoming extremely costly in the 1980s. Furthermore, gas tax revenues must be efficiently allocated among the different transit operations. For example, the portion of the gas tax revenues generated by daily downtown rush hour traffic can be allocated to the subsidization of the rush hour costs of the transit lines serving the downtown. A drawback of a gas tax policy is that many commuters who have no easy access to transit systems will be unable to avoid the tax by choosing to travel by transit.

The parking tax works in a way that is similar to the gas tax, with the difference that it does not directly discourage gasoline consumption. Thus the parking tax is not an efficient way to achieve socially optimal gasoline consumption levels, nor is it intended to do that. Instead, the parking tax is a good way to alleviate localized automobile congestion and pollution effects and to discourage the overallocation of land to parking lots. Again, a sufficiently high tax on rush hour downtown parking can probably cover all subsidies needed by the rush hour downtown transit service. The rush hour downtwon parking tax would certainly have a serious adverse effect: it would reduce the desirability of the downtown for businesses and would thus encourage the suburbanization of even more downtown employment. The rush hour parking tax would also lead to some, perhaps excessive, staggering or work hours. All things considered, it would appear that gas and parking taxes, coupled with efficient fare structures, provide a basis for maintaining socially desirable and financially viable public transit services without Federal involvement.

One other finance alternative remains to be discussed. This is the option of taxing urban real estate in order to subsidize public transit systems. In this vein, there is an idea popularly known as "value capture" in Federal and local transportation circles. Value capture is a cencept that dates back to the highway era but that has been recently revived and popularized by Sharpe (1974) in a study sponsored by the Urban Mass Transportation Administration. According to this idea, urban transportation systems impact urban real estate by creating changes in its market price. Since parts of these net real estate price changes are caused by public manipulations of the transportation system, they are taxable in the public interest and can be used to defray all or part of the cost of the public transit system. Taxation should be typically achieved by a legally permissible *lump sum incremental tax* levied as a one-time special assessment to be paid by the current owner in annual increments and the balance in full upon the resale of the property. The value of this tax would be highest at those locations where real estate prices are increased the most and would equal the amount of the increase in price. Presumably, there will be locations where real estate prices will decrease because of the transportation policies. These locations will be levied a *lump sum incremental rebate*, and the current owners would thus be compensated.

Value capture policy has been recently examined from the marketing, financial, legal, and urban planning viewpoints (Sharpe, 1974; Hagman and Misczynski, 1978), and had won the endorsement of the Federal government. An extension of the value capture idea is known as "joint development." This is the idea that public transportation authorities should participate in the urban land market by buying and selling, building, redeveloping, or converting real estate around new and improved transportation systems in order to cash in on the real estate price increases. Alternatively, zoning variances, construction subsidies, and other public actions can be coordinated with the transportation policies in order to maximize the value capture potential of the land that is developed jointly with a new transportation service, such as a transit line.

Experience with new rapid transit systems (subways, at-grade, or elevated lines) such as Philadelphia–Camden, San Francisco BART, and Washington, D.C., METRO indicates that most of the benefits are of a long term nature: land use in mature metropolitan areas may require years or decades before it can make major adjustments in response to new transit systems. There are statistical studies that have demonstrated significant property value increases around new transit investments for the Philadelphia–Camden (Mudge, 1972; Boyce and Allen, 1973), Toronto (Dewees, 1976) and Washington, D.C., METRO projects (Lerman *et al.*, 1977). In each case, the investigators do not claim impacts that are very powerful. Despite the lack of overwhelming evidence in favor of a rail transit development policy, Atlanta, Baltimore, Miami, and Buffalo had broken new ground for rail projects during the

Carter administration. Other cities, such as SanDiego, Detroit, Los Angeles, Portland, and Honolulu, have been planning for new rail systems, and cities like Chicago, New York, Cleveland, and Boston are studying plans to upgrade or expand their aging rail systems. The capital costs of these projects are staggering: $70 million per mile for D.C.'s 100-mile METRO, $1.7 billion for a "starter" line in Los Angeles, and $800 million for the small projects of Miami and Baltimore. These already high costs appear to be rising much more rapidly than planners can prepare and implement their plans. It was generally understood and was part of policy that the Carter administration would have underwritten 90% of the costs of many of these rail systems. The 1974 Amendment to the Urban Mass Transportation Act and subsequent policy positions of the Department of Transportation (see Federal Register, 1976, 1978, 1979) clearly supported the development of new rail transit systems and proposed to help fund such systems, particularly if urban areas are able to show that land use policies will be closely coordinated to speed up the impact on land development. The Federal government also sponsored the writing of a report that provided an evaluation of recent experience with completed and ongoing rail projects and related land use and taxation policies (Committee Print, U.S. Congress, 96–7, 1979).

Value capture policy is sound economic practice if pursued in the appropriate manner, with taxation and compensation through lump sum levies and rebates. The policy may run into difficulty because of the problems involved in accurately estimating and implementing the correct levies. Real estate market analyses carried out by Callies *et al.* (1976) claimed that 20–40% of the capital improvement cost of rail systems can be raised by the joint development of the immediate vicinity of the transit stations. If these figures are good estimates, they are encouraging, but they ignore a possibly big part of the story: locations away from stations decrease in value, thus requiring compensation. Wipeout losses, if taken into account, may substantially reduce or even exceed windfall gains.

In summary then, if fare box revenues must be supplemented by local subsidies to cover costs, the public authority has three chief instruments at its disposal: gas taxes, parking taxes, and value capture. The potential success and relative effectiveness of these three instruments in the central focus of the empirical analyses of this chapter.

2.   THE SIMULATION ASSUMPTIONS AND DATA

Although "simulation" literally means the replication or imitation of a phenomenon, simulation models in the social sciences are never complete. Numerous deficiencies related to data and computational constraints will normally restrict the completeness of a simulation model. Thus simulation results should always be interpreted in light of the assumptions made. A simulation model will predict the changes that will occur, assuming that aspects of the real world remain constant or do not affect the process being simulated. In many cases, the aspects of the real world that are excluded from the model may be important sectors of the economy or entire behavioral processes. Simulated situations may be both hypothetical and unrealistic. The success of policy analysis with simulation models depends to a large extent on how the effects of those aspects that are excluded from the simulation would have influenced the results if they could have been included. Some judgment needs to be brought to bear on the interpretation of the simulation results in order to compensate for the effects of the excluded aspects. Despite this problem of judgmental interpretation, even the crudest simulation model is often a significant improvement over alternative methods for analyzing the effects of complex policies. Furthermore, if the simulation model is estimated from real data, it enables the analyst to reach quantitatively valid conclusions. When complex systems such as urban areas are the object of study, sensible quantitative conclusions are often impossible without a simulation model. Finally, the output of a simulation model is useful in indicating the likely errors resulting from the aspects not included in the model. The excluded effects are generally second- or third-order effects. Estimating the magnitudes of these effects usually becomes much easier once the first-order effects are correctly modeled and estimated.

Perhaps the biggest shortcoming of the state of the art in simulation modeling is that models developed to date have aimed at a great deal of comprehensiveness and completeness and too little empirical accuracy or precision. As a result, errors from those aspects that are included in the model are substantial or possibly even larger than the errors resulting from those aspects which are excluded. A prime example of this problem may be the NBER urban simulation model (Ingram *et al.*, 1972; Kain *et al.*, 1976). It is designed to test policies at a very high level of spatial aggregation and also a very high level of socioeconomic (demand-side) disaggregation. It is aimed at a complete and comprehensive view of the entire housing market, but the accuracy of each submodel is questionable because of the quality of the data used in estimating these submodels and because of the excessive aggregation. The quantitative conclusions of the model may be in error even though the main qualitative results may be correct. Despite its shortcomings, the NBER model is of value because it represents an investigation of the structural problems encountered in housing market simulation modeling and because it introduces a substantial degree of economic analysis into the art of urban simulation modeling. At the other extreme from the NBER model, we have the models by Lowry (1964), Goldner (1968), and Putman

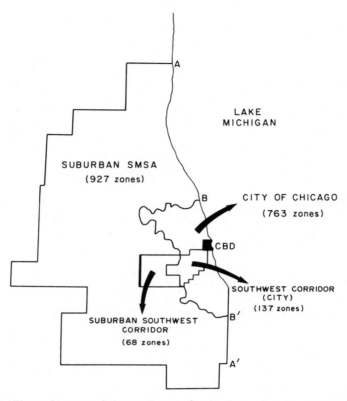

Fig. 5.1. The study area and the zone system for the Chicago SMSA and the Southwest corridor.

(1974), which are lacking in economics and also crude in aggregation, specification, and estimation. "Behavioral" simulation models based on accurate estimation and designed for sufficiently detailed economic policy analyses have not been developed prior to this study. It is generally the case that urban economists do not leave the realm of pencil-and-paper analysis and enter the realm of simulation modeling with ease.

The data set we use to perform the policy simulations of this chapter consists of a 1690 zone representation of the Chicago SMSA. As shown in Fig. 5.1, 763 of these zones are within the legal boundary of the city of Chicago, and the remaining 927 zones are in the suburban area, which is bounded by the line AA′ shown in Fig. 5.1. The city of Chicago zones are all $\frac{1}{2}$-mile by $\frac{1}{2}$-mile quartersections, whereas the suburban zones correspond to the Chicago Area Transportation Study (CATS) zone system. A few of these zones are quartersections, most of them are sections (1 mile by 1 mile), and the remaining few are larger in area but generally not larger than $1\frac{1}{2}$ or 2 square miles, with the exception of a few zones that are at the boundary line AA' of the study area and are thus far removed from the central business district (CBD). Figure 5.1 also shows the boundary line of the Southwest Corridor Study Area (SCSA), which consists of 205 zones, 137 of which are in the city of Chicago, with the remaining ones in the suburban part of this area.

The Census data that exist for this zone system are the same ones used to estimate the models described in Section 2 of Chapter 4. These 1970 data form the initial situation that is the benchmark against which specific policy analyses are carried out. Salient features of these data are illustrated in Fig. 4.2 of Chapter 4. Relevant aggregate aspects of these data for the SMSA study area are listed in Table 5.3.

The major assumptions of the simulation model, the mathematical structure of which is discussed in the next section, are the following:

(1)   The location of jobs for the CBD and the non-CBD categories and the number of jobs in each of these two categories are exogenously given. Because the non-CBD category is locationally dispersed, it is necessary to assume that when the total non-CBD jobs change, the distribution of these jobs among the many non-CBD job locations remains unchanged. The model is thus intended to study the effects of transportation policies on location housing market equilibrium *given* the total employment levels for the CBD and non-CBD categories and *given* a fixed relative frequency distribution of non-CBD employment among non-CBD job center locations.

(2)   The quantity of housing at each location is exogenously given. The current model does not determine the building of new housing but is intended to study the equilibria that will result *given* a predetermined housing stock distribution. Housing maintenance and quality change responses are also excluded from the model.

(3)   The problem of tenure choice, i.e., the choice of owned versus rented housing, is not within the scope of the model because, as discussed in Chapter 4, the form of the data does not enable us to estimate discrete choice models of joint tenure, location, and mode choice decisions. As a result, owner and renter occupied housing is aggregated, and owner occupied housing values are annualized to determine a housing "rent" for each zone in the SMSA, as discussed in Chapter 4.

(4)   Although the choice of housing and residential location is primarily a household decision, the data do not identify the choices of households but only the choices of each commuter. Thus the model has been estimated from data on individual trips, and fixed ratios of work trips per household are necessary, as shown in the next section, in order to compute the demand in

TABLE 5.3

Aggregate Data Descriptive of the 1970 Initial Situation in the Chicago SMSA Study Area[a]

Housing

	Rent ($/yr)	Housing stock	Vacant units	Vacancy rate (%)
City	1,859,632,333 (42.1)	1,197,370 (54.2)	70,344 (68.3)	5.87
Suburban	2,556,541,980 (57.9)	1,013,781 (45.8)	32,682 (31.7)	3.22
Total	4,416,174,314 (100.0)	2,211,151 (100.0)	103,026 (100.0)	4.66

Work trips[b]

	Auto	Commuter rail	Rapid transit	Bus	Other	Total
CBD	158,246 (35.0)	77,908 (17.0)	83,092 (18.0)	108,400 (24.0)	26,050 (6.0)	453,696 (19.0)
Non-CBD	1,414,970 (73.0)	26,665 (1.0)	38,849 (2.0)	232,109 (12.0)	231,373 (12.0)	1,943,966 (81.0)
Total	1,573,216 (66.0)	104,573 (4.0)	191,492 (5.0)	340,509 (14.0)	257,423 (11.0)	2,397,662 (100.0)

Travel time and cost for work trips[c]

	Auto	Commuter rail	Rapid transit	Bus	Total
CBD travel time	7,976,401	4,601,530	3,155,762	4,719,653	20,453,346
Non-CBD travel time	50,124,207	[d]	[d]	7,608,463	[d]
CBD travel cost	208,888,515	47,580,759	25,865,238	25,861,800	308,196,313
Non-CBD travel cost	1,559,869,108	[d]	[d]	52,400,825	[d]

[a] Numbers in parentheses indicate percentages.
[b] Daily, one-way.
[c] Daily, one-way times (min); annual two-way costs ($).
[d] Not available.

households. Empirical examinations we have performed indicate that this is a minor problem and that if the model were estimated from household data, very similar results would have been obtained.

(5) The decisions of households regarding nonwork travel such as shopping, recreational, and educational, are not included in the model. Residential location choice is explained solely as a function of commuting travel (time and cost) by mode, housing rent, and other fixed housing quality and public service characteristics of the zones. Some of the explanatory attributes included in the utility function are proxies for public service quality and locational accessibility and will indirectly capture the effects of nonwork travel, proximity to schools, etc.

(6) As discussed in Section 2 of this chapter, the key policy attributes are travel cost and travel time. The times and costs from each residential zone and for each employment category are exogenously given. Thus the possibility of traffic congestion, which would require that equilibrium travel costs and travel times be adjusted endogenously, is not taken into account. The empirical results of this chapter will demonstrate, however, that the potential for congestion is rather small as most policies do not disturb the initial equilibrium travel choices and modal splits by a great deal, thus changing only slightly the traffic loads of the highway and transit networks.

(7) Work trips other than auto, commuter rail, rapid transit, and bus amount to only 6% of CBD trips and are treated as fixed. The number of such trips from each zone to the CBD is exogenously fixed and not subject to change in response to the policies examined. Similarly, 15% of the non-CBD trips, which consist of commuter rail trips, (1%) rapid transit trips (2%) and all "other" trips (12%) are also treated as fixed and remain unaffected by policy changes that influence bus and auto trips. Reason and some experimental evidence indicate strongly that this is a good assumption indeed. If these fixed trips were to be made endogenous, their effect on the simulation results and policy conclusions to be reported would be quite small.

(8) The major policy simulations are with respect to the 1970 initial situation, and they should be viewed as comparative statics performed on that initial situation. The same policies carried out in 1975 or 1980 would have quite different effects, but thanks to known trends in the development of Chicago and other large SMSA's during the 1970s, extrapolating the effects of these policies is fairly straightforward. Indeed, through appropriate adjustments to the 1970 data, we were able to create a data set that bears strong similarity to the current situation, and results with this data set will be reported in Sections 5 and 6 of this chapter. Since data after the 1970 situation were not available at the time of this study, it is not possible at this time to provide a dynamic validation of the predictions and policy conclusions of the simulation model. Limited experiments of this nature may

become possible once the 1980 Census data become available in comparable form circa 1983–1985.

Subject to the assumptions summarized above, the simulation model is designed to predict changes resulting from exogenous travel cost and travel time, transit station location, and bus mile density inputs. The changes that can be predicted are (a) changes in equilibrium rents in each zone, (b) changes in housing vacancies in each zone, (c) changes in the CBD–non-CBD mix of each zone's resident population, (d) changes in the modal splits of a zone's CBD and non-CBD resident populations, (e) changes in aggregate rents by city and suburb, (f) changes in aggregate travel times and travel cost commuting expenditures by mode, and (g) changes in the consumer utility or surplus of the CBD and non-CBD employees.

3. THE EQUILIBRIUM MODEL AND ITS PROPERTIES

In this section we present the mathematical structure of the equilibrium model and we examine its properties analytically, to the degree that such examination is tractable. The topics discussed are the equilibrium formulation, correction of the model's specification errors, the effect of the unobserved attributes, some restrictive properties of demand predictions when the demand model of location–mode choice is not nested multinomial logit, the uniqueness and stability properties of the equilibrium solution, the computational algorithm and its cost, and some comparative static analyses of equilibrium predictions generated by the model.

3.1. Structure of the Equilibrium Model

Chapter 4 was devoted to the estimation of the demand- and supply-side models. Combining the demand and supply sides into an equilibrium framework follows naturally: the demand side determines the expected number of households that will choose each location (zone), and the supply side determines the expected number of housing units that will be offered for rent or sale by their owners, in each zone. At equilibrium, the expected number of housing units demanded in each zone will equal the expected number of housing units supplied in that zone. Thus an equilibrium formulation for an urban area of I zones is a system of I simultaneous equations in I endogenous variables. The I endogenous variables are the mean rent of each zone, namely the elements of the vector $\bar{R} \equiv (R_1, R_2, \ldots, R_I)$. The values of these endogenous variables must be determined in such a way as to keep the urban area at equilibrium, given predetermined values of all exogenous variables, policy instruments, and estimated coefficients.

In principle, all exogenous attributes entering the demand- and supply-side models can be treated as policy instruments. In this book, however, we focus on the transportation related attributes only. These are the travel time and travel cost from each zone to the CBD and to the "average" non-CBD employment location, the bus mile density in each zone, the number of rapid transit stations within $\frac{1}{2}$, $\frac{1}{2}$–1, and 1–2 miles of a zone's centroid, and the number of commuter railroad stations within 2 miles of a zone's centroid. As discussed in Chapter 4 and as reported in Tables 4.7 and 4.8, these attributes enter the demand-side models, and they are the chief policy instruments from which equilibrium changes will result. If the model is to be used to test the effect of specific transportation projects, the new values of the above policy instruments must be computed from the transportation system characteristics of the proposed project. This will be demonstrated in Section 5, which examines rapid transit projects proposed for Chicago's Southwest corridor.

The expected demand for each zone i can be computed as

$$D_i = \left[N^C P_i^C(\bar{R}, \bar{E}_P^C, \bar{E}_F^C, \bar{G}^C) + N^\mathcal{C} P_i^\mathcal{C}(\bar{R}, \bar{E}_P^\mathcal{C}, \bar{E}_F^\mathcal{C}, \bar{G}^\mathcal{C}) + N_i^F \right] \delta_i, \quad (5.1)$$

where N^C is the number of CBD work trips that use auto, commuter rail, rapid transit, or bus, $N^\mathcal{C}$, the number of non-CBD work trips that use auto or bus; and N_i^F the number of all other CBD and non-CBD trips. The value N_i^F is a *fixed* part of demand that is independent of the endogenous rent adjustment. The fixed trips amount to only 6% of CBD and 15% of non-CBD travel. Our policy analysis deals with CBD-focused radial transportation systems, and our policy tests are essentially unaffected by non-CBD travel. The coefficient δ_i is the zonal household per work trip (employed persons) ratio. It serves as a corrective factor necessary because the demand models of Chapter 4 are, because of data limitations, estimated from commuter rather than household choices. The vector $\bar{R}$ is the endogenous average zonal rent vector, E_P^C and $\bar{E}_P^\mathcal{C}$ are the CBD and non-CBD exogenous policy instrument attribute vectors, $\bar{E}_F^C$ and $\bar{E}_F^\mathcal{C}$ are the exogenous CBD and non-CBD attribute vectors that are treated as fixed, and $\bar{G}^C$, $\bar{G}^\mathcal{C}$ are vectors of adjustments performed to eliminate specification errors from the CBD and non-CBD demand models. These adjustments will be discussed in Section 3.2. P_i^C and $P_i^\mathcal{C}$ are the CBD and non-CBD choice models. Computed from (5.1), D_i is an estimate of the expected number of households choosing to locate in zone i. The expected number of dwellings in zone i offered for rent are

$$O_i = S_i Q_i(R_i, \bar{E}_i^S, H_i), \quad (5.2)$$

where S_i is the fixed number of dwellings in zone i; Q_i, the expected probability that a dwelling in zone i will be offered for rent given the zonal rent R_i; $\bar{E}_i^S$, a vector of the supply-side attributes of zone i that are treated as exogenous; and H_i, an adjustment that eliminates specification error in the supply-side model.

An equilibrium average rent vector $\bar{R}^*$ must satisfy the following conditions:

$$\mathcal{E}_i = \left[N^C P_i^C(\bar{R}^*) + N^{\mathcal{C}} P_i^{\mathcal{C}}(\bar{R}^*) + N_i^F \right] \delta_i - S_i Q_i(R_i^*) = 0, \qquad i = 1, \ldots, I. \quad (5.3)$$

The choice relative frequencies P_i^C and $P_i^{\mathcal{C}}$ are the nested or nonnested logit models given by equation (4.122) in Chapter 4, and Q_i is the profit-maximizing model given by Eq. (4.64). The I equations in (5.3) measure the excess expected demands for each zone i. The empirical analysis to be presented in this chapter uses the estimated coefficients of Table 4.7 for the CBD choice model P_i^C, the coefficients of Table 4.8 for the non-CBD choice model $P_i^{\mathcal{C}}$, and the fourth model of Table 4.9 for the supply-side choice probability Q_i.

3.2. The Use of Alternative-Specific Constants to Correct for Specification Error and the Influence of Unobserved Attributes

The choice models in Chapter 4 cannot generate perfect predictions of the observed relative frequencies from which they are estimated because of the sources of bias that affect the estimated coefficients. The most important prediction bias comes from missing variables and from the assumed form of the utility function. Fortunately, the analytical convenience of logit and nested logit models allows a direct computation of the relative magnitude of the specification error for each alternative (i, m). To see this, let $°N_{im}$ and $°N_{jm}$ be the observed CBD or non-CBD trips choosing alternatives (i, m) and (j, n). Now let G_{im} and G_{in} be the measures of total specification error in the utility functions of the conditional mode choice model for the choice of modes m and n given the choice of zone i. The ratio of observed choices of the modes within the same zone can now be expressed as

$$°N_{im}/°N_{in} = \exp(U_{im} + G_{im})/\exp(U_{in} + G_{in}). \quad (5.4)$$

The relative specification error $G_{im} - G_{in}$ is obtained from (5.4) and is

$$G_{in}^* - G_{im}^* = U_{im} - U_{in} - \log(°N_{im}/°N_{in}). \quad (5.5)$$

Next let G_i and G_j be the measures of specification error in the marginal choice model. The ratio of observed zone choices is

$$\frac{\sum_m °N_{im}}{\sum_m °N_{jm}} = \frac{\exp(U_i + G_i - \sigma I_i^* + U_{im} + G_{im}^*)}{\exp(U_j + G_j - \sigma I_j^* + U_{jn} + G_{jn}^*)}. \quad (5.6)$$

The relative specification error $G_i - G_j$ is obtained from (5.6) and is

$$G_j^* - G_i^* = U_i - U_j - \sigma(I_i^* - I_j^*)$$

$$+ U_{im} - U_{jn} + G_{jm}^* - G_{jn}^* - \log \frac{\sum_m {}^\circ N_{im}}{\sum_m {}^\circ N_{jm}}, \qquad (5.7)$$

where the inclusive values are

$$I_i^* = \log \sum_p \exp(U_{ip} + G_{ip}^*) \qquad (5.8)$$

and

$$I_j^* = \log \sum_p \exp(U_{jp} + G_{jp}^*). \qquad (5.9)$$

The zonal specification error H_i of the supply-side model can be computed from

$$(S_i - {}^\circ V_i)/{}^\circ V_i = \exp(\lambda \Pi_i + H_i)/\exp(\lambda \Pi_{i0}), \qquad (5.10)$$

where ${}^\circ V_i$ are the observed number of vacant dwellings in zone i; and Π_i, Π_{i0}, the estimated profit levels for the "rent" and "keep vacant" alternatives, respectively. Solving (5.10),

$$H_i^* = \log[(S_i - {}^\circ V_i)/{}^\circ V_i] - \lambda(\Pi_i - \Pi_{i0}), \qquad i = 1, \ldots, I. \qquad (5.11)$$

Thus all relative specification errors can be precomputed. Setting $G_j^* = 0$ and $G_{in}^* = 0$ for any one zone j and any mode n in any one zone i, a precise value can be uniquely determined for all remaining specification errors. Incrementing zone-specific utilities with G_i^*, zone–mode-specific utilities with G_{im}^*, and supply-side profits with H_i^*, we can eliminate all specification errors from the model and produce perfect predictions of observed choices for each alternative (i, m).

The interpretation of adjusting for specification errors in this way is the following: The constants G_i^* and H_i^* are functions of missing zone-specific attributes, and G_{im}^* is a function of missing zone–mode-specific attributes. When policy analysis is performed on the attributes included in the utility and profit functions, the values of H_i^*, G_i^*, and G_{im}^* will remain unchanged, as long as the unobserved attributes missing from the estimation remain unchanged. On the other hand, if the system is equilibrated without any correction for specification errors [i.e., $H_i^* = 0$ and $G_i^* = 0$ for each i, and $G_{im}^* = 0$ for each (i, m)], the equilibrium rent vector $\bar{R}^*$ may be biased because it will adjust to absorb part of the effect of the specification error as well as to balance supply and demand in each zone.

Once the CBD and non-CBD choice models and the supply-side choice models are adjusted for specification error, as shown in (5.1)–(5.3), the observed rent vector from which the choice models are estimated provides a good starting point for any policy analysis that involves a change in the exogenous attributes. As a result, the computational algorithm proposed in Section 3.4 finds the new equilibrium within a small number of iterations.

The use of alternative-specific constants to correct for prediction error is not without its problems. When the unobserved attributes excluded from the choice models remain unchanged or are uninfluenced by a specific change in the policy instruments included in the choice models, the use of alternative-specific constants is appropriate. Consider a hypothetical change that is a 10% increase in the price of gasoline. It may be safely conjectured that while this change will establish new zone-to-zone auto costs, it will not noticeably alter unobserved attributes. The travel and location choices of commuters and households can still be predicted under the assumption that the values of the unobserved attributes and their distribution remain constant for each choice alternative.

Now consider a different example. Suppose that a city has only two travel modes, automobile and public bus, and that a choice model has been estimated to predict travel mode and location choices in this city. Suppose that this model is to be used to predict travel mode and location choices for a new situation in which a fixed guideway rail system is introduced into the city. Clearly, the utility function estimated from auto and bus choices can be used to predict auto, bus and rail choices. The travel time, travel cost, and other observed attributes can be computed for the new rail system and entered into the choice model, the choice set of which is now expanded to include the rail alternative; but what are the unobserved attributes influencing the choice of rail, i.e., the constant terms in the rail utility function? In a study of the Bay Area Rapid Transit (BART) system, precisely this problem was encountered by the investigators in the Urban Travel Demand Forecasting project at Berkeley (McFadden *et al.*, 1979). The authors were forced to use a mode choice model estimated with pre-BART data using the auto and public bus choices of commuters. In using this model to predict BART's projected ridership for a sample of San Francisco's population, they assumed that the value of the BART alternative-specific constant was equal to the value of the estimated bus constant. While this was clearly the most reasonable assumption for that case, the model overpredicted actual post-BART ridership by 200%. Since the value of the BART specific constant plays a major role in controlling the market share of BART, it is probably the case that the error was in large measure due to the assumption that the BART constant equals the bus constant. It is fortunate that in a model such as the one used in this study, involving many location–mode alternatives and four different major travel modes, the problem of estimating the alternative-specific constants of "new" alternatives is substantially simpler than that encountered by the investigators of the BART study.

In Section 6 of this chapter, we will evaluate the impact of *new* rail transit alternatives proposed for the Chicago SMSA's Southwest corridor. Currently, rail transit service within this corridor is very sparse and geographically restricted because the corridor is mainly served by public bus and private automobile. If alternative-specific constants are precomputed for each zone–mode combination using the current data, then all the zones that currently do not generate any rail transit trips will receive large negative alternative-specific constants for the transit mode and will be predicted to generate no transit trips regardless of the characteristics of the proposed rail transit systems. To avoid such absurd predictions, one must be able to *estimate* the rail transit constants (i.e., the effect of the unobserved attributes missing from the utility function) for those zones that currently generate no transit trips. In our study, we do not have to assume that the rail transit constant of a zone equals the bus constant of that zone. Because our data contain many zones served by both auto, bus, and rail transit, it is possible to utilize statistical methods such as linear regression analysis to predict the values of the rail transit constants from the values of zone-specific independent variables or from the constants of other modes. The use of such a procedure will be demonstrated in Section 6.

3.3. Uniqueness and Stability of the Equilibrium Solution

We now prove a proposition dealing with the uniqueness and stability of the rent vector $\bar{R}^*$ in the equilibrium formulation (5.3).

Proposition 1. The equilibrium vector $\bar{R}^*$ of (5.3) is unique and satisfies local and Hicksian stability conditions if for each i,

$$\frac{\partial \mathscr{E}_i}{\partial R_j} = \begin{cases} <0 & \text{for} \quad j = i, \quad -\infty \le R_j \le R_{j\max} > 0 \\ >0 & \text{for} \quad j \ne i, \quad -\infty \le R_j \le R_{j\max} > 0 \end{cases} \tag{5.12}$$

and $\lim_{R_j \to R_{j\max}} D_j(\bar{R}) = N_j^F \delta_j < S_j Q_j(R_{j\max})$ for each $i = 1, \ldots, I$, namely, all zones (submarkets) are *strict gross substitutes* in the allowable rent ranges ($R_{j\max} = +\infty$ without any loss of generality).

Proof. The proof is a well-known result in multimarket Walrasian analysis and the stability of multimarket equilibrium. It is clear that the excess demand functions (5.3) are strict gross substitutes as long as $\partial P_i^C / \partial R_i < 0$, $\partial P_i^C / \partial R_i < 0$, and $\partial Q_i / \partial R_i > 0$. This will occur when the nested or non-nested choice models are estimated and it is found that the empirical coefficient associated with rent is negative in the CBD and non-CBD demand models and positive in the supply model, and any inclusive value coefficients in the nested models are between zero and one ($0 \le \sigma < 1$). Recalling that

$P_i = \sum_{m=1}^{M_i} P_{im}$ for either the CBD or the non-CBD model, it follows that $\partial P_i/\partial R_j = \sum_{m=1}^{M_i} \partial P_{im}/\partial R_j$, and for the nested model we have

$$P_{im} = \frac{\exp(U'_i + U'_{im} - \sigma I_i)}{\sum_j \exp[U'_j + (1 - \sigma)I_j]}, \tag{5.13}$$

$$I_i = \log \sum_m \exp(U'_{im}), \tag{5.14}$$

$$U'_{im} = \beta_{R+C} \log(R_i + C_{im}) + K_{im}, \tag{5.15}$$

where β_{R+C} is the estimated coefficient; C_{im}, travel cost, and K_{im}, the remaining part of the zone–mode-specific utility. The (') on U_i and U_{im} denotes that they have been adjusted for specification errors G_i^* and G_{im}^*. The derivatives of P_{im} computed from the above are

$$\frac{\partial P_{im}}{\partial R_i} = \beta_{R+C} P_{im} \left\{ \sum_m \frac{P_{m|i}}{(R_i + C_{im})} [-\sigma - (1 - \sigma)P_i] + \frac{1}{(R_i + C_{im})} \right\}, \tag{5.16}$$

where $\beta_{R+C} < 0$ and $0 \le \sigma < 1$; and, for $j \ne i$,

$$\frac{\partial P_{im}}{\partial R_j} = -\beta_{R+C}(1 - \sigma)P_{im}P_j \sum_m \frac{P_{m|j}}{R_j + C_{jm}}. \tag{5.17}$$

From (5.16) and (5.17) we can derive

$$\frac{\partial P_i}{\partial R_i} = \beta_{R+C}(1 - \sigma)(1 - P_i) \sum_m \frac{P_{im}}{R_i + C_{im}} < 0 \tag{5.18}$$

and, for $j \ne i$,

$$\frac{\partial P_i}{\partial R_j} = -\beta_{R+C}(1 - \sigma)P_i \sum_m \frac{P_{jm}}{R_j + C_{jm}} > 0. \tag{5.19}$$

From the supply model we verify that

$$\frac{\partial Q_i}{\partial R_i} = \lambda Q_i(1 - Q_i) > 0, \qquad \text{recalling} \quad \lambda > 0. \tag{5.20}$$

An alternative uniqueness proof can be obtained by demonstrating that the transpose of the Jacobian of the excess demand system has a dominant negative diagonal. To see this, let a_{ij} denote the ijth element of the Jacobian of (5.3). It can then be shown by utilizing (5.18)–(5.20) that for any column i,

$$|a_{ii}| - \sum_{j \ne i} |a_{ji}| = \lambda S_i Q_i(1 - Q_i) > 0. \tag{5.21}$$

It follows from this that $(-1)^I|J'| = (-1)^I|J| > 0$, where J is the Jacobian matrix.

The above proofs did not place a lower limit on rents in each zone. In reality, rents are bound from below at zero. It is thus worthwhile to consider what occurs if such a restriction is placed on rents. In this case, the system that must be examined is

$$\mathscr{E}_i(\bar{R}^*) = 0, \qquad i = 1, \ldots, I,$$
$$R_i^* - \theta_i^2 = 0, \qquad i = 1, \ldots, I, \tag{5.22}$$

where θ_i^2 are I additional nonnegative variables introduced to reflect the fact that $R_i^* \geq 0$ for each i. The Jacobian matrix of this system is

$$A = \begin{bmatrix} & J & & & 0 & & \\ \hline 1 & \cdots & 0 & -2\theta_1 & \cdots & 0 \\ & 1 & & & -2\theta_2 & & \\ \vdots & & \ddots & \vdots & \vdots & & \ddots & \vdots \\ 0 & \cdots & 1 & 0 & \cdots & -2\theta_I \end{bmatrix}, \tag{5.23}$$

where J is the Jacobian of the excess demand system. In this case, the transpose of A has a negative dominant diagonal only when

$$\lambda S_i Q_i (1 - Q_i) > 1 \qquad \text{for each} \quad i, \tag{5.24}$$

but these conditions are relevant only if the rent vector has at least one zero element. Thus if we encounter an equilibrium solution in which at least one zone has zero rent, we may find that the equilibrium is nonunique. If, on the other hand, the equilibrium has the property that $R_i^* > 0$ for each i (an interior solution), such an equilibrium is unique and stable. In all realistic policy simulations, the equilibrium will be an internal equilibrium, and thus the possiblitty of $R_i^* = 0$ will be encountered only very rarely, if ever.

3.4. The Computational Algorithm and Computational Cost

Having proved that a unique equilibrium exists as a solution of $\mathscr{E}_i(\bar{R}^*) = 0$, $i = 1, \ldots, I$, when $\bar{R}^* > 0$, we now propose an efficiently convergent algorithm for finding the equilibrium vector $\bar{R}^*$ given an arbitrary initial vector $\bar{R}_1$. The equilibrium vector is found iteratively via a rent adjustment procedure that begins with $\bar{R}^1$ and adjusts the rent vector until, at the final iteration, the adjusted rent vector is arbitrarily close to the equilibrium vector $\bar{R}^*$.

Let the iterations be numbered as $k = 1, \ldots, K$ such that $\bar{R}^K \simeq \bar{R}^*$. The adjusted rent vector for the $k + 1$ iteration is computed from the vector of the kth iteration according to the following procedure:

$$\bar{R}^{k+1} = \bar{R}^k - \left[\partial \mathscr{E}_i(\bar{R})/\partial R_j \big|_{\bar{R} = \bar{R}^k} \right]^{-1} \left[\mathscr{E}_i(\bar{R}^k) \right], \qquad k = 1, \ldots, K - 1, \tag{5.25}$$

where $[\cdot]^{-1}$ is the Jacobian of the excess demand system evaluated at $\bar{R} = \bar{R}^k$ and $[\cdot]$ is the vector of excess demands also evaluated at $\bar{R} = \bar{R}^k$. The computational cost of each of the above iterations is excessive because of the cost of evaluating and inverting the Jacobian at every iteration. A much cheaper iterative method can be obtained by ignoring all off-diagonal elements in the Jacobian. In this case, the rent of each zone can be adjusted independently by

$$R_i^{k+1} = R_i^k - \mathscr{E}_i(\bar{R}^k)/[\partial\mathscr{E}_i(\bar{R})/\partial R_i|_{R=R^k}], \qquad k = 1,\ldots,K-1. \quad (5.26)$$

If procedure (5.26) is used, the cost of each iteration is many times less than the cost of one iteration according to (5.25). Thus the unique equilibrium can be obtained much more efficiently via procedure (5.26).

The criterion for achieving convergence is that the approximate equilibrium vector $\bar{R}^K$ be within a very small neighborhood of the true equilibrium vector $\bar{R}^*$. In the policy experiments of this chapter, we will use the criterion that the absolute values of the excess demands at convergence be less than 0.1% of the number of housing units in each zone. Thus

$$|\mathscr{E}_i(\bar{R}^K)|/S_i \leq 0.001 \qquad \text{for each} \quad i \quad (5.27)$$

provides an extremely accurate approximation of the true equilibrium allocation of households to dwellings and therefore of the equilibrium vector $\bar{R}^*$.

The computational cost of this algorithm is low. One equilibrium simulation for a 1690 zone (or equation) system typically converges within 2–5 iterations, takes 42–47 sec of CPU time and costs \$4.00–\$4.50 as overnight priority on Northwestern University's CDC 6600, *given* the tight tolerance level of 0.1% of the number of housing units in each zone. A single iteration of the 1690 zone system takes about 2.6 sec and costs 18.3¢ on overnight priority. 72%–88% of the total cost is due to input–output and summary procedures. This computational efficiency is in large measure due to the effectiveness of the model's adjustment for specification error and the use of the observed rent vector as a starting point in the iterative algorithm. It is, of course, the case that policy simulations that introduce large changes in travel cost, travel time, and other policy instruments require a larger number of iterations, but the increase in cost is marginal.

3.5. Some Properties of Logistic Demand

Logit and nested logit models of demand have several properties that can be fully examined analytically. The properties we examine are relevant to policy-analytic issues because they pertain to changes in predicted demand that follow from certain systematic changes in exogenous policy variables.

Consider first the zone choice probabilities (relative frequencies) given by

$$P_i = \frac{e^{U'_i}(\sum_m e^{U'_{im}})^{1-\sigma}}{\sum_j e^{U'_j}(\sum_m e^{U'_{jm}})^{1-\sigma}},$$ (5.28)

where U'_i, U'_{im} are the utilities adjusted for specification error. Now suppose that the utility function U'_{im} is given as

$$U'_{im} = \beta_T \log T_{im} + K_{im},$$ (5.29)

where T_{im} is the travel time by mode m to zone i; β_T, the estimated travel time coefficient; and K_{im}, an abbreviation for the remaining part of the utility function. The choice model (5.12) can now be written as

$$P_i = \frac{e^{U'_i}\left[\sum_m (T_{im})^{\beta_T} e^{K_{im}}\right]^{1-\sigma}}{\sum_j e^{U'_j}\left[\sum_m (T_{jm})^{\beta_T} e^{K_{jm}}\right]^{1-\sigma}}.$$ (5.30)

It can be seen from (5.30) that multiplying all travel times by a factor a does not affect the choice probabilities P_i. Thus we can state the following properties:

(1)   Consider an attribute that enters utility in loglinear form. Any policy that multiplies this attribute by a constant for *each choice alternative* leaves all choice probabilities unchanged.

(2)   Consider an attribute that enters utility in linear form. Any policy that adds a constant amount to this attribute *for each choice alternative* leaves all choice probabilities unchanged.

We will now examine what occurs in the nonnested logit model ($\sigma = 0$) if the travel times by one mode m are scaled by a factor of a while the times of the other modes remain unchanged. The new choice probabilities will be denoted with a superscript A, and the old ones (prior to the scaling) with a superscript B. The following computations follow:

$$P_i^A = \frac{\exp(U'_i)\left[(aT_{im})^{\beta_T}\exp(K_{im}) + \sum_{n \neq m}(T_{in})^{\beta_T}\exp(K_{in})\right]}{\sum_j \exp(U'_j + I_j)},$$ (5.31)

$$I_j = \log \sum_k \exp(U'_{jk}),$$ (5.32)

$$P_i^A = \frac{\exp(U'_i)\left[\sum_n (T_{in})^{\beta_T}\exp(K_{in}) - (1 - a^{\beta_T})(T_{im})^{\beta_T}\exp(K_{im})\right]}{\sum_j \exp(U'_j + I_j)}$$ (5.33)

$$= \frac{\exp(U'_i + I_i) - (1 - a^{\beta_T})\exp(U'_i + U'_{im})}{\sum_j \exp(U'_j + I_j) - (1 - a^{\beta_T})\sum_j \exp(U'_j + U'_{jm})}.$$ (5.34)

Dividing both numerator and denominator by $\sum_j \exp(U'_j + I_j)$,

$$P_i^A = \frac{P_i^B - (1 - a^{\beta_T})P_{im}^B}{1 - (1 - a^{\beta_T}) \sum_j P_{jm}^B}, \tag{5.35}$$

$$\frac{P_i^A}{P_i^B} = \frac{1 - (1 - a^{\beta_T})P_{m|i}^B}{1 - (1 - a^{\beta_T}) \sum_j P_j^B P_{m|j}^B}, \tag{5.36}$$

where $\sum_j P_j^B P_{m|j}^B$ is the weighted average probability of choosing mode m given the choice of zone. Recalling that $\beta_T < 0$, we can now see from (5.36) that if $a < 1$, i.e., the travel time of mode m is improved, then

$$P_i^A < P_i^B \qquad \text{if} \quad \sum_j P_j^B P_{m|j}^B > P_{m|i}^B,$$

$$P_i^A > P_i^B \qquad \text{if} \quad \sum_j P_j^B P_{m|j}^B < P_{m|i}^B. \tag{5.37}$$

If $a > 1$, i.e., the travel time of mode m is increased, then

$$P_i^A < P_i^B \qquad \text{if} \quad \sum_j P_j^B P_{m|j}^B < P_{m|i}^B,$$

$$P_i^A > P_i^B \qquad \text{if} \quad \sum_j P_j^B P_{m|j}^B > P_{m|i}^B. \tag{5.38}$$

Finally, if $a = 1$, then of course

$$P_i^A = P_i^B. \tag{5.39}$$

The above result can be generalized to the case where the travel times of more than one mode are changed. Thus let $n \in S$ be an element of the set S of modes the travel times of which are changed by a factor of a. Then we find

$$\frac{P_i^A}{P_i^B} = \frac{1 - (1 - a^{\beta_T}) \sum_{n \in S} P_{n|i}^B}{1 - (1 - a^{\beta_T}) \sum_j P_j^B \sum_{n \in S} P_{n|j}^B}. \tag{5.40}$$

Note that when the set S includes all the modes, then $\sum_n P_{n|i}^B = 1$ and $P_i^A = P_i^B$. Now suppose that mode n is the only mode the travel time of which is not changed, and let the travel times of the other modes be scaled by n. From (5.40), we get

$$\frac{P_i^A}{P_i^B} = \frac{1 - (1 - a^{\beta_T})(1 - P_{n|i}^B)}{1 - (1 - a^{\beta_T}) \sum_j P_j^B(1 - P_{n|j}^B)} \tag{5.41}$$

$$= \frac{a^{\beta_T} - (a^{\beta_T} - 1)P_{n|i}^B}{a^{\beta_T} - (a^{\beta_T} - 1) \sum_j P_j^B P_{n|j}^B} \tag{5.42}$$

and, dividing both numerator and denominator by a^{β_T}, we find

$$\frac{P_i^A}{P_i^B} = \frac{1 - [1 - (1/a)^{\beta_T}]P_{n|i}^B}{1 - [1 - (1/a)^{\beta_T}]\sum_j P_j^B P_{n|j}^B}. \tag{5.43}$$

From (5.42) and (5.43) we can state that scaling the travel times of all modes but one by a produces exactly the same effect on all choice probabilities as scaling the travel times of only the remaining mode by $1/a$. More generally, if the travel times of any subset of the modes are scaled by a, the effects are the same as those we obtain when we scale the travel times of the remaining modes by $1/a$. As an example of this property, consider reducing the CBD travel time of auto by 10% in every zone ($a = 0.90$). This change would create exactly those demands that we would obtain if we increased the travel times of the remaining CBD modes (bus, transit, commuter rail) by $a = 1/0.90$. To obtain these properties, we assumed that the model was not nested ($\sigma = 0$). Thus these properties are a direct result of the independence from irrelevant alternatives (IIA) feature of the multinomial logit model. Knowing the existence of these properties and knowing that they do not hold for the nested model ($0 < \sigma < 1$) is helpful in selecting the latter model for policy analysis.

3.6. Analytical Comparative Statics: The Effect of Transportation Improvements on Housing Rents

Although the equilibrium model is intended for numerical solution on the computer, some of its salient properties can be obtained directly through comparative statics analysis of a simplified version. Suppose that there are only two zones available for residential choice. The first zone is "the city" and the second one is "the suburbs." Each zone can be commuted to via several modes, and for simplicity we assume all employment to be located in the city center. We wish to analyze this simple two-zone version of the model to determine the impact of travel time improvements on aggregate housing rents and on the rent level of city and suburb.

We let A denote aggregate housing rents. The system to be solved consists of three equations F_1, F_2, F_3 in three endogenous variables R_1, R_2, and A and exogenous variables $T_{1m}, T_{2m}, m = 1, \ldots, M$, the travel times of the M travel modes for zones 1 and 2, respectively. The three equations are

$$F_1 = A - NP_1 R_1 - NP_2 R_2 = 0,$$
$$F_2 = NP_1 - S_1 Q_1 = 0, \tag{5.44}$$
$$F_3 = NP_2 - S_2 Q_2 = 0,$$

where N is the number of households; S_1 and S_2 are the city and suburban housing stocks, respectively; $P_i = \sum_m P_{im}$, $i = 1, 2$, are the zone choice relative frequencies; and Q_1 and Q_2 are the relative frequencies of the city and suburban housing stocks that are offered for rent. The first equation in (5.44) gives the aggregate rent, while the next two equations are the equilibrium equations for the two zones.

Total differentiation of these three equations yields

$$
\begin{bmatrix} dA \\[1em] dR_1 \\[1em] dR_2 \end{bmatrix} = \begin{bmatrix} 1 & \dfrac{\partial F_1}{\partial R_1} & \dfrac{\partial F_1}{\partial R_2} \\[1em] 0 & \dfrac{\partial F_2}{\partial R_1} & \dfrac{\partial F_2}{\partial R_2} \\[1em] 0 & \dfrac{\partial F_3}{\partial R_1} & \dfrac{\partial F_3}{\partial R_2} \end{bmatrix}^{-1} \begin{bmatrix} -\sum_i \sum_m \dfrac{\partial F_1}{\partial T_{im}} dT_{im} \\[1em] -\sum_i \sum_m \dfrac{\partial F_2}{\partial T_{im}} dT_{im} \\[1em] -\sum_i \sum_m \dfrac{\partial F_3}{\partial T_{im}} dT_{im} \end{bmatrix}. \tag{5.45}
$$

Letting the P_{im}, joint mode–zone probabilities, be given by the nested logit model, it can be shown that $|J|$, the determinant of the Jacobian of (5.44), is

$$
|J| = -\beta_{R+C}(1 - \sigma)N\left[S_1 Q_1(1 - Q_1)P_1\left(\sum_m \frac{P_{2m}}{R_2 + C_{2m}} \right) \right.
$$
$$
\left. + S_2 Q_2(1 - Q_2)P_2\left(\sum_m \frac{P_{1m}}{R_1 + C_{1m}} \right) \right]
$$
$$
+ \left[S_1 S_2 Q_1 Q_2(1 - Q_1)(1 - Q_2) \right] > 0, \tag{5.46}
$$

where $\beta_{R+C} < 0$ is the coefficient of $\log(R_i + C_{im})$ in the utility function.

Solving the system (5.45) for dA, we find

$$
dA = \beta_T(1 - \sigma)N[P_2(P_{1m}/T_{1m})\, dT_{1m} - P_1(P_{2m}/T_{2m})\, dT_{2m}]B|J|, \tag{5.47}
$$

where $\beta_T < 0$ is the coefficient of $\log T_{im}$ in the utility function and

$$
B = [S_1 S_2 Q_1 Q_2(1 - Q_1)(1 - Q_2)(R_1 - R_2)
$$
$$
+ NP_1 S_2 Q_2(1 - Q_2) - NP_2 S_1 Q_1(1 - Q_1)]. \tag{5.48}
$$

It now follows from (5.46)–(5.48) that if $Q_1 = Q_2$ and $R_1 = R_2$, then $B = 0$ and $dA/dT_{1m} = 0$, $dA/dT_{2m} = 0$. On the other hand, if $Q_1 < Q_2$ and $R_1 < R_2$, then $B < 0$,

$$
dA/dT_{1m} = \beta_T(1 - \sigma)NP_2(P_{1m}/T_{1m})B\,|J| > 0, \tag{5.49}
$$

and

$$
dA/dT_{2m} = -\beta_T(1 - \sigma)NP_1(P_{2m}/T_{2m})B\,|J| < 0. \tag{5.50}
$$

These results have the following interpretation. Typically, central cities have a lower occupancy rate than the suburbs $(Q_1 < Q_2)$ and lower rent levels than the suburbs ($R_1 < R_2$). In this situation, if we increase city travel time for any one mode m, the city becomes less attractive relative to the suburbs, some households move to the suburbs (i.e., relocate from the low rent area to the high rent area), city rents decrease, suburban rents increase, and thus aggregate rent increases. The opposite occurs if the suburban travel times are increased. This causes some households to move to the city (i.e., from the high rent area to the low rent area), city rents increase, suburban rents decrease, but aggregate rent decreases.

Furthermore, solving the simultaneous system (5.45), we can also derive the change in the city and suburban rent levels as a function of city and suburban travel time improvements. These results for the city rent level are

$$dR_1/dT_{1m} = \beta_T(1 - \sigma)NS_2Q_2(1 - Q_2)P_2(P_{1m}/T_{1m})|J| < 0 \qquad (5.51)$$

and

$$dR_1/dT_{2m} = -\beta_T(1 - \sigma)NS_2Q_2(1 - Q_2)P_1(P_{2m}/T_{2m})|J| > 0. \quad (5.52)$$

The first of these states that city rents will decrease if city travel times are increased because some households will attempt to move to the suburbs: to curb this outmigration, city rents must be lowered. If suburban travel times are increased, some households will attempt to move into the city, thus driving up city rents. The results for dR_2/dT_{2m} and dR_2/dT_{1m} are symmetric with the above results.

Next, suppose that instead of improving the travel time of one zone while keeping the other zone's travel time constant, we assume a linear relationship between average zonal travel times and average zonal distances D_i. Thus

$$T_{im} = \text{const} + K_m D_i \qquad (5.53)$$

and

$$dT_{im} = D_i \, dK_m, \qquad i = 1, 2 \quad \text{and each } m. \qquad (5.54)$$

Substituting (6.54) into (6.49), we get

$$\frac{dA}{dK_m} = \beta_T(1 - \sigma)NP_1NP_2 \left(\frac{P_{m|1}}{T_{1m}/D_1} - \frac{P_{m|2}}{T_{2m}/D_2} \right) B|J|. \qquad (5.55)$$

In this case, dA/dK_m represents the change in aggregate rents as a function of a change in the unit travel time K_m for mode m. Now suppose that m respresents the auto mode. The suburban area will generate a higher proportion of auto trips. Thus typically, $P_{m|2} > P_{m|1}$. It is also the case that $T_{2m}/D_2 < T_{1m}/D_1$. This means that the term in the bracket in (5.55) is negative and, assuming $Q_1 < Q_2$ and $R_1 < R_2$, $B < 0$. All of this implies $dA/dK_m < 0$, which states that under these typical conditions, unit travel time improvements will increase aggregate rents.

3.7. A Measure of Consumer Welfare

Since the equilibrium model developed in this study is applicable to policy issues, a direct concern is the derivation of an "applied welfare economic" measure of consumer benefit. A recent paper by Small and Rosen (1981) and an older paper by Williams (1977) have investigated the formation of consumer benefit measures from discrete choice models based on utility maximization. Both articles conclude that "consumer surplus" *can*, under some conditions, be computed approximately as the area to the left of the demand curves, as in the traditional case. To apply these results to our case, we must first view our consumer choice problem as the choice of one of I zones, each zone corresponding to a different "good"—a housing–commuting bundle. A "generalized utility" measure of each zone j is

$$W_j = U_j'(\overline{X}_j) + (1 - \sigma) \log \sum_m \exp[U'(R_j + C_{jm}, T_{jm}, \overline{X}_{jm})], \quad (5.56)$$

where $\overline{X}_j$ is a vector of zone-specific attributes that are fixed; R_j, C_{jm}, T_{jm} are rent, travel cost, and travel time by mode m to zone j; and $\overline{X}_{jm}$ is a vector of zone- and mode-specific attributes that are also fixed. When $\sigma = 0$, i.e., the logit model is not nested, the "generalized utility" of each zone–mode combination can be separated, becoming

$$W_{jm} = U_j'(\overline{X}_j) + U_{jm}'(R_j + C_{jm}, T_{jm}, \overline{X}_{jm}), \quad (5.57)$$

which is precisely the mean utility of alternative (i, m) estimated subject to the aggregation error in the data. Small and Rosen (1981) derive their consumer surplus measure for the case of $\sigma = 0$ by making three specific assumptions. Translated to our case, these assumptions are (a) that the marginal utility of income be approximately independent of the price ($R_j + C_{jm}$) and travel time (T_{im}) of the alternatives; (b) that income effects from quality changes (in our case, travel time changes) be negligible (which means that the compensated demand function be approximated by the Marshallian demand function), and (c) that the choice probability for each choice alternative approach zero as the price of that alternative approaches infinity, i.e., $\lim_{R_i \to \infty} P_{im}(\overline{R}) = 0$. These assumptions imply the consumer surplus measure—which is equivalent to the area to the left of the demand curves, given a change in "rent plus travel cost" from an initial level ($R_j^0 + C_{jm}^0$) to a final level ($R_j^f + C_{jm}^f$)—

$$\Delta S = -\frac{1}{\omega} \int_{\overline{W}^0}^{\overline{W}^f} \sum_{j,n} P_{jn}(\overline{W}) \, dW_{jn}, \quad (5.58)$$

where ω is the marginal utility of income; $\overline{W}^0$, the initial generalized utility measure; and $\overline{W}^f$, the final or postpolicy generalized utility measure, with

ΔS the measure of the expected per household utility change, i.e., the average consumer surplus measure. Small and Rosen (1981) and Williams (1977) have demonstrated that for the logit model, the surplus measure (5.58) becomes

$$\Delta S = -\frac{1}{\omega} \log \frac{\sum_{jm} \exp(W_{jm}^{\mathrm{f}})}{\sum_{jm} \exp(W_{jm}^{0})}. \tag{5.59}$$

The Jacobian matrix $J = (\partial P_{im}/\partial W_{jn})$ being symmetric, the measure ΔS applies to cases in which "rent plus travel cost" and "travel time" are simultaneously altered in all zones because the line integral needed to derive it is unique (i.e., path independent).

In this study, we adopt this measure of consumer surplus for the general case in which the two attributes "rent plus travel cost" and "travel time" are simultaneously altered in all zones because of exogenous policy inputs, which alter travel cost and travel time, and endogenous equilibration, which alters rent. Furthermore, we adopt the same consumer surplus measure for the nested logit models ($\sigma \neq 0$), in which integration occurs over the "generalized utility measure" (5.56). Empirical experience demonstrates that these consumer surplus measures thus computed from (5.58) with $\omega = 1$ are approximate ordinal measures of the benefits of policy changes. Several policies that differ in the magnitudes of the exogenous policy input can be compared meaningfully by examining the sign and magnitude change in the respective ΔS's. Since simulations are performed with CBD and non-CBD population segments, two separate measures of welfare, ΔS^{C} and $\Delta S^{\mathcal{C}}$, corresponding to the CBD and non-CBD segments, can be computed for each policy.

4. COMPARISON OF ALTERNATIVE MODELS AND SENSITIVITY ANALYSIS ON ESTIMATED COEFFICIENTS

Tables 4.7 and 4.8 of Chapter 4 list the estimated coefficients for two CBD and two non-CBD models. Coupling each CBD model with each non-CBD model, we have four possible representations of the demand side. For the supply side, we choose the fourth model in Table 4.9. Because the four possible model combinations differ in specification, an empirical comparison of their equilibrium performance is needed to demonstrate the effects of specification on model predictions and on the policy conclusions resulting from these predictions.

The simulations to be reported in this section will focus on comparative static analyses of the effects of exogenous changes in travel time and travel cost. Before simulation is performed, each of the four demand models and the supply-side model are adjusted for specification error, as explained in Section

TABLE 5.4

Key Estimated Coefficients and Elasticities for the Four Model Combinations

	Coefficients					
	Inclusive value $1 - \sigma$		Rent plus travel cost β_{R+C}		Travel time β_T	
Model[a]	CBD	Non-CBD	CBD	Non-CBD	CBD	Non-CBD
SS	1.000	1.000	−0.265	−0.099	−1.619	−0.211
SN	1.000	0.045	−0.265	−5.461	−1.619	−0.910
NS	0.277	1.000	−1.488	−0.099	−2.392	−0.211
NN	0.277	0.045	−1.488	−5.461	−2.392	−0.910
	Elasticities					
	Rent		Travel cost		Travel time	
SS	−0.202	−0.082	−0.061	−0.017	−1.612	−0.210
SN	−0.202	−0.205	−0.061	−0.256	−1.612	−0.251
NS	−0.314	−0.082	−0.246	−0.017	−1.694	−0.210
NN	−0.314	−0.205	−0.246	−0.256	−1.694	−0.251

[a] SS: CBD and non-CBD models are not nested; SN: CBD model is not nested, non-CBD model is nested; NS: CBD model is nested, non-CBD model is not nested; NN: CBD and non-CBD models are nested.

3.2 of this chapter. Each simulation solves for a new equilibrium keeping the specification errors for each zone–mode pair constant and assuming exogenous changes in travel time and travel cost.

Since travel time and travel cost are our two chief policy instruments, each demand model is distinguished by three coefficients. These are the inclusive value coefficient $1 - \sigma$; the coefficient of the logarithm of rent plus cost, β_{R+C}, and the coefficient of the logarithm of travel time, β_T. Table 5.4 lists these coefficients for each model pair and reports the rent, travel cost, and travel time elasticities of demand for each model pair.

It is seen from the table that the choice of model type is important in determining the estimated elasticities. Travel time elasticities are the most robust across model type but they differ greatly for the CBD and non-CBD populations. Conversely, travel cost elasticities differ greatly by model type and less for the CBD and non-CBD populations. The rent elasticity is relatively stable across model type for the CBD population, but sensitive to model type for the non-CBD population. These patterns in the elasticities imply that the four models may yield possibly quite different predictions and policy conclusions. To investigate this sensitivity of predictions to model type, four hypothetical scenarios were selected and simulated by each model. These scenarios, for which results are reported in Table 5.5, are (1) a 50%

increase in all CBD and non-CBD automobile commuting costs, (2) a 50% increase in all CBD auto commuting costs, (3) a 20% decrease in all CBD automobile commuting times, and (4) a 50% decrease in all bus and rapid transit CBD commuting costs.

It can be seen from Table 5.5 that the predictions of the four models can differ substantially, but a definite pattern does not always exist with respect to rent changes. Changes in the aggregate demand of each travel mode are very sensitive to the specification of the relevant demand model. A 20% decrease in all CBD auto travel times (scenario 3) leads to twice as large changes in CBD mode demands when the CBD model is nested compared to when it is not nested, even though the nested and nonnested CBD models have nearly identical travel time elasticities (see Table 5.4). Conversely, the choice of the non-CBD model has a negligible impact on the CBD modal choices, but the choice of the CBD model has a much more noticeable effect on the mode choices of non-CBD commuters.

The CBD and non-CBD demand models are linked through the "rent" variable. To give an example of the effect of this link, consider the fourth scenario, in which the bus and rapid transit travel costs for CBD commuters are halved. Because most bus and transit commuting to the CBD occurs from within the city of Chicago and some surrounding suburbs, this scenario favors the city, and households show a tendency to relocate to the city and to switch from auto and commuter rail to bus and rapid transit. The number of suburban households actually relocating into the city is very small because city rents generally increase to maintain approximately the current equilibrium distribution of households, suburban rents decline, and, as shown in Table 5.5, the overall rent change is negative. Because suburban rents generally decrease as a result of the decisions of CBD households, non-CBD households receive an income "subsidy," and a very small number of them are able to afford switching to the superior automobile mode from the inferior bus mode.

While the effect of each scenario on CBD and non-CBD mode demands is predictable and consistent, aggregate rent changes are more difficult to generalize and more dependent on model type and coefficient estimates. Under the first scenario, all auto costs are increased by 50%, and while this favors the city, and city rents increase with suburban rents decreasing, a nonnested CBD model predicts a positive metropolitan rent increase, whereas a nested CBD model predicts a metropolitan rent decrease. It can also be seen from the second scenario (50% increase in all CBD auto commuting costs) that aggregate rent changes due to certain scenarios can be difficult to predict and are sensitive to model type both in sign and in magnitude.

The consumer surplus changes are well behaved and predictable from aggregate rent changes and from exogenous changes of each scenario. In

TABLE 5.5

Aggregate Responses to Four Simulation Scenarios Applied to Each of the Models

	Aggregate rent change (%)			Aggregate mode demand changes (%)						Consumer surplus change	
				CBD				Non-CBD			
	City	Suburbs	Total	Auto	Rail	Transit	Bus	Auto	Bus	CBD	Non-CBD
				(1) 50% Increase in All Auto Costs							
SS	0.481	−0.269	0.047	−2.87	1.67	1.66	1.73	−0.22	1.32	−0.0185	−0.0131
SN	1.596	−1.045	0.067	−2.86	1.95	1.62	1.54	−13.94	82.17	−0.0195	−0.0300
NS	0.368	−0.469	−0.116	−14.93	8.30	8.62	9.31	−0.22	1.32	−0.0271	−0.0128
NN	1.396	−1.108	−0.054	−14.79	8.78	8.50	8.86	−13.54	82.49	−0.0283	−0.0298
				(2) 50% Increase in All CBD Auto Costs							
SS	−0.003	0.017	0.009	−2.88	1.66	1.68	1.75	−0.001	0.005	−0.0178	0.0001
SN	0.071	0.062	0.066	−2.92	1.70	1.70	1.74	−0.020	0.150	−0.0178	0.0001
NS	0.005	−0.157	−0.089	−14.98	8.28	8.68	9.36	0.003	−0.002	−0.0261	0.0003
NN	0.086	−0.006	0.033	−15.00	8.34	8.71	9.31	−0.030	0.170	−0.0261	0.0003
				(3) 20% Decrease in All CBD Auto Travel Times							
SS	−0.195	1.087	0.547	16.24	−9.53	−9.46	−9.70	−0.014	0.086	0.1071	−0.0007
SN	−0.397	0.354	0.038	16.48	−9.74	−9.63	−9.78	−0.090	0.540	0.1067	−0.0006
NS	−0.034	0.527	0.291	32.18	−18.17	−18.94	−19.60	−0.006	0.035	0.0651	−0.0004
NN	−0.154	0.184	0.042	32.35	−18.33	−19.05	−19.64	−0.030	0.160	0.0650	−0.0004
				(4) 50% Decrease in All Bus and Rapid Transit CBD Commuting Costs							
SS	0.598	−0.914	−0.277	−0.81	−0.53	1.01	0.86	0.010	−0.070	0.0082	0.0001
SN	0.394	−0.497	−0.122	−0.83	−0.66	1.08	0.86	0.100	−0.610	0.0083	0.0001
NS	0.720	−1.231	−0.409	−4.36	−1.14	4.82	3.50	0.020	−0.100	0.0129	0.0002
NN	0.517	−0.715	−0.196	−4.40	−1.40	4.96	3.65	0.130	−0.810	0.0130	0.0002

the first scenario, for example, auto costs are increased by 50%, but models SS and SN differ their aggregate rent predictions. Model SN, which predicts a bigger rent increase, also predicts a bigger consumer surplus reduction for the CBD population.

It should be noted that comparison of consumer surplus changes *across different models* is not meaningful since the utility functions used in the models are different. Keeping model type constant, however, the welfare ranking of the four scenarios is stable for each of the four models. For CBD commuters, a 20% reduction in automobile travel times is the most preferred scenario, followed by a 50% decrease in CBD bus and transit fares (both of these scenarios increase welfare), followed by a 50% increase in CBD auto costs, followed by a 50% increase in *all* auto costs (both of these scenarios decrease welfare). Conversely, for non-CBD commuters the most preferred scenario is the 50% increase in CBD auto costs followed by a 50% decrease in CBD bus and transit costs (both of these scenarios increase the welfare of non-CBD commuters, albeit very slightly). A decrease in CBD auto travel times decreases the welfare of non-CBD commuters by encouraging city commuters to suburbanize and thus driving up suburban "rents" in those places where most non-CBD commuters reside. Finally, a reduction in all auto costs by 50% has the strongest negative impact on the welfare of non-CBD commuters.

The results of Table 5.5 are not conclusive in aiding us in the selection of a model specification to be applied to policy analysis. Models SS and SN predict CBD and non-CBD mode demand changes that are much smaller than those predicted by models NS and NN. Rent changes predicted by the same models also differ, but not as much as the mode demand changes do. It is important to note that differences in equilibrium predictions are of a different order of magnitude compared to differences in estimated elasticities. Thus, drawing policy conclusions from elasticities alone, a widespread practice among applied econometricians and travel demand modelers, can be seriously misleading because the equilibrating interactions between exogenous policy instruments and endogenous variables remains uncaptured unless equilibrium simulations, such as those reported here, are performed. To give an example of this, consider the elasticities of Table 4.7 in Chapter 4. It could be concluded from these results that a 10% increase in commuting costs would reduce CBD travel demand by auto by about 1.05–4.45%, depending on the type of model employed. From the equilibrium results reported in Table 5.5, the same reductions can be estimated to be 0.57–2.96%. Thus the equilibrium simulations help us correct a potential error of about 100% resulting from the neglect of equilibrium interactions. Table 4.7 in Chapter 4 also implies CBD automobile travel time elasticities that suggest that a 10% decrease in auto CBD travel times will raise CBD auto demand by about 16–18%, depending on the type of model employed. The corresponding equilibrium predictions from Table 5.5 are about 8–16%, again implying a potential error of up to 100%.

Knowing the rough magnitude of such potential error that can arise from neglecting equilibrium interactions is, of course, very helpful, but the fact still remains that demand models of different specification result in different equilibrium predictions, and the range of such predictions is substantial. To select the "best" model, judgment remains to be exercised. In the case at hand, a prudent choice may be to select models SN and NN or SS and NS primarily because our interest is to test policies related to the CBD oriented transportation system. Having to experiment with both nested (N) and nonnested (S) CBD model specifications provides some insurance against drawing faulty conclusions about CBD oriented policies.

Another issue in the preliminary evaluation of these equilibrium models is the degree to which the policy conclusions are sensitive to changes in the estimated coefficients β_{R+C}, β_T, and σ, i.e., the extent to which potential estimation error has an impact on equilibrium predictions. To investigate this possibility, we present some results in Table 5.6. Each of the four scenarios listed at the bottom of the table were tested five times. Each test is a different equilibrium simulation in which one estimated coefficient is perturbed by 20%, as described at the bottom of the table.

It can be seen from this sensitivity analysis that model output is by and large insensitive to $\pm 20\%$ perturbations in the estimated coefficients β_{R+C} and β_T, but substantially more sensitive to $\pm 20\%$ perturbations in σ, which measures the degree of intrazonal similarity among the unobserved attributes of the travel modes. The extent of this sensitivity varies from scenario to scenario, and this underscores the importance of accurately estimating the models' coefficients. Some policy conclusions can be in error, depending on how accurately a specific coefficient is estimated. As an example of this, consider scenario 4. If the correct value of σ is 0.723 but it is overestimated by 20% and found to be 0.868, the aggregate rent change can be predicted to be about two-thirds its correct value, as can the non-CBD bus ridership. The same perturbation in σ, however, leads to smaller changes when other scenarios are considered.

All factors considered, our choice for the equilibrium simulations of the next sections is model NN. There are several reasons for this decision. First, and most importantly, the nested formulation allows for correlated unobserved attributes and thus does not exhibit the IIA property. The resulting demand structures are not subject to the limitations discussed in Section 3.5. Second, the zonal rent distributions and rent changes predicted by the NN model are more reasonable than those of the SN or SS models. Third, even

TABLE 5.6

Sensitivity Analysis on the Estimated Coefficients of the Nested CBD Model Coupled with the Nested Non-CBD Model

			Aggregate mode demand change (%)						
Aggregate rent change (%)			CBD					Non-CBD	
City	Suburbs	Total	Auto	Rail	Transit	Bus		Auto	Bus
			(1) CBD auto costs up 50%						
(a) 0.086	−0.006	0.033	−15.00	8.34	8.71	9.31		−0.030	0.170
(b) 0.081	−0.030	0.017	−17.84	9.91	10.35	11.08		−0.032	0.192
(c) 0.086	−0.006	0.033	−14.99	8.34	8.71	9.32		−0.028	0.171
(d) 0.074	0.045	0.057	−14.85	8.64	8.18	9.26		−0.013	0.082
(e) 0.066	−0.059	−0.007	−15.11	8.45	8.77	9.35		−0.042	0.254
			(2) CBD bus and rapid transit costs down 50%						
(a) 0.517	−0.715	−0.916	−4.40	−1.40	4.96	3.65		0.130	−0.810
(b) 0.569	−0.822	−0.236	−5.26	−1.62	5.92	4.33		0.148	−0.899
(c) 0.517	−0.715	−0.196	−4.40	−1.39	4.95	3.65		0.133	−0.813
(d) 0.312	−0.381	−0.089	−4.40	−1.12	4.83	3.53		0.081	−0.495
(e) 0.632	−0.969	−0.295	−4.41	−1.60	5.04	3.74		0.165	−1.003
			(3) CBD auto times down 20%						
(a) −0.154	0.184	0.042	32.35	−18.33	−19.05	−19.64		−0.030	0.160
(b) −0.125	0.195	0.059	32.31	−19.02	−18.30	−19.62		−0.021	0.130
(c) −0.183	0.210	0.045	38.96	−22.95	−22.08	−23.64		−0.033	0.202
(d) −0.131	0.064	−0.018	32.09	−18.96	−18.03	−19.55		−0.016	0.098
(e) −0.155	0.306	0.112	32.54	−18.57	−19.11	−19.70		−0.034	0.203
			(4) CBD bus and rapid transit times down 20%						
(a) 3.018	−3.607	−0.817	−21.19	−7.39	21.03	20.21		0.488	−2.974
(b) 2.749	−3.450	−0.839	−21.15	−7.10	20.90	20.05		0.451	−2.749
(c) 3.637	−4.380	−1.004	−25.13	−8.98	25.09	24.02		0.579	−3.527
(d) 1.948	−1.964	−0.317	−20.98	−5.95	20.30	19.44		0.315	−1.917
(e) 3.631	−4.971	−1.348	−21.37	−8.41	21.59	20.78		0.584	−3.558

(a) $\beta_{R+C} = -1.488$, $\beta_T = -2.392$, $\sigma = 0.723$; estimated. (b) $\beta_{R+C} = -1.786$, $\beta_T = -2.392$, $\sigma = 0.723$; β_{R+C} 20% up. (c) $\beta_{R+C} = -1.488$, $\beta_T = -2.870$, $\sigma = 0.723$; β_T 20% up. (d) $\beta_{R+C} = -1.488$, $\beta_T = -2.392$, $\sigma = 0.868$; σ 20% up. (e) $\beta_{R+C} = -1.488$, $\beta_T = -2.392$, $\sigma = 0.578$; σ 20% down.

though the results of Table 5.5 imply that the NN model probably over-estimates the effect of automobile travel time reductions, this is a minor shortcoming because we can adjust the estimated travel time coefficient to correct this estimation error and bring the predictions into better agreement with reality.

5. INVESTIGATION OF GAS AND PARKING TAX POLICIES TO FINANCE PUBLIC TRANSIT IN THE 1980s

An important policy concern for the 1980s is the potential for financing public transportation systems by levying appropriate gasoline, parking, or the less efficient income and housing taxes. To investigate these issues, we made appropriate adjustments to the 1970 data in order to obtain a data set roughly representative of the 1981 (current) situation. The accuracy of these adjustments cannot be conclusively validated since the 1980 census is not available at the present time. There is no question, however, that the adjustments are qualitatively correct and probably quantitatively sound, if somewhat incomplete.

Several important changes have occurred during the 1970s. First, the price of gasoline in the Chicago area increased from 38¢ per gallon in 1970 to $1.40 per gallon in early 1981. The consumer price index for incomes rose, as well, from 135.4 in 1970 to 294.1 in 1981. Thus in real terms, the price of gasoline over the decade has only just more than doubled. Second, transit and bus fares have gone from 45¢ to 80¢ per ride, while the transfer fare paid to gain bus access to rail transit has remained at 10¢. In real terms, therefore, the cost of public transportation has decreased. The same is true for the suburban commuter rail lines, which doubled their fares in money terms, thus keeping them nearly constant in real terms. Parking costs in downtown Chicago (the CBD) have increased from about $2.80 a day on the average to about $5.20 a day, thus declining slightly in real terms. All of the above data are used to update our 1970 zone-to-zone costs to the 1981 base situation.

Another important updating assumption concerns the shrinking market share of the CBD employment. We assumed, somewhat arbitrarily, that by 1981 the number of jobs in the CBD decreased from 20% of the metropolitan area in 1970 to 15%, and that the aggregate number of jobs in the SMSA remained constant even though some decrease may have taken place during the decade. It was also assumed that the distribution of the non-CBD jobs among the non-CBD employment locations remained as in 1970. Auto travel times to the CBD from each zone were decreased by 5%, while non-CBD travel times were increased by 1% in order to provide a semblance of the changes in traffic congestion that followed the job redistribution assumptions. Transit, bus, and commuter rail travel times remain the same as in 1970.

Changes in the housing stock are quite difficult to determine since good data on the metropolitan distribution of vacant land and the geographical pattern of housing starts is not available. Considering these difficulties, we decided not to change the 1970 housing stock *and* its distribution. We did assume, however, that the average age of housing increased by 10 years in every zone. The resulting data set probably bears a strong resemblance to the 1981 situation without being a complete or accurate representation of this situation.

The updated exogenous data were entered into the simulation model and the new equilibrium calculated from it. Comparing the 1981 situation to the 1970 situation, we found that aggregate rents within the city of Chicago measured in 1970 dollars were 9.2% lower in the updated 1981 equilibrium. Suburban rents, on the other hand, increased by 6.7%, measured also in 1970 dollars. Aggregate metropolitan rents showed a 1% increase. Chicago vacancy rates increased slightly from 5.87% to 5.99%, while suburban vacancy rates declined slightly from 3.22% to 3.17%, with the SMSA rate remaining the same because of the assumption of an unchanged housing stock. CBD auto market shares declined slightly from 35% to 33.4%, as did suburban rail ridership, which went from 17.0% to 15.7%. Bus and transit ridership to the CBD absorbed these declines. Non-CBD bus ridership showed a small increase caused by a shift of the declining auto passengers. Gasoline consumption in automobile commuting declined by 2.2% SMSA-wide. Thus, between 1970 and 1981, all aspects of the data with the exception of the city–suburban housing rent distribution showed only small changes. The consumer surplus measure for both CBD and non-CBD households showed a decline.

Total public transportation costs in the Chicago SMSA during 1981 are estimated at $834.4 million (see Table 5.2). This amounts to roughly $374 per household per year and roughly the same per dwelling unit. The $128 million deficit plus the $88.3 million Federal and miscellaneous subsidies amount to roughly $98 per household per year. It would take an income or housing tax of just under $100 per family or dwelling to eliminate all Federal subsidies and deficits in the current public transportation budget. It can be said without any hesitation that such a tax is very difficult to defend politically and has no economic efficiency rationale. As we discussed in Section 1, however, such a local income or housing tax would still be a great deal more efficient than the current method of Federal subsidization. It has been argued by Giannopoulos (1980) that urban public transit may be thought of as a public service similar to public power and water supply utilities operated for the benefit of the community. Giannopoulos has further argued that a local income tax scheme could replace fares, making urban transit entirely fare-free. Under this assumption, he computes the per household cost of the public transit system of Athens, Greece. If all public transit fares in Chicago were to be set to zero and the initial fare box revenues plus the federal subsidies and projected 1981 deficit were to be raised by a household tax, this tax would amount to about $245 per household per year. In some countries, fare-free transit is justified as a means of substantially boosting public transit ridership, but in the U.S. the travel cost elasticity of ridership demand is too low to achieve such results.

To examine the more efficient finance alternatives of gasoline and parking taxes, we used our simulation model and compared the results to hand calculations based on the assumption that all travel demand elasticities are zero. First, we assumed that a per gallon gas tax would be applied to all auto travel (work and nonwork) and that the level of this tax would be set to raise an annual $216.3 million, which would cover the projected 1981 deficit plus the Federal subsidies. While our model is able to predict the adjustments in work trip gasoline consumption and gas tax revenues, the nonwork gasoline consumption was obtained from a Chicago Area Transportation Study report (1980), and a nonwork trip, gas consumption, short term price elasticity of -0.3% for gas consumption in nonwork trips was assumed, following the study by Burright and Enns (1975).* The simulation model predicts that the needed gas tax is about 21¢ per gallon in 1980 dollars, representing a 14.2% increase in the gross price of gasoline at the pump. Automobile commuting declined by only 0.985%. The same tax calculated by hand under the assumption that all travel demand elasticities are zero is found to be 19.8¢, which is very close to the simulation result of 21¢. As a counterpolicy, we examined the possibility of covering the $216.3 million deficit by appropriately raising rush hour public transportation fares. Doubling all current rapid transit, bus, and commuter rail fares covers this deficit. Rapid transit, bus, and commuter rail CBD riderships decline by approximately 5% each, while suburban transit ridership drops by 29%. The resulting decrease in the consumer surplus of the CBD commuters is more than ten times the welfare decrease caused by the gas tax policy. Thus current deficits can be covered either by a 21¢ per gallon tax applied to all automobile gasoline purchases or a doubling of rush hour bus transit fares to $1.60 and a raising of commuter rail fares to an average of $3.50 per ride.

To investigate the benefits of fare-free transit, we perform several simulations in which bus and rapid transit fares are set equal to zero but gas and parking taxes are set at such levels that they raise the same revenue initially obtained from fares. In one of these simulations, fares are set equal to zero and a gas tax of 48¢ per gallon covers the initial fare revenue from all bus and rapid transit commuting. Automobile commuting declines by 10.48%. Alternatively, if fares are set equal to zero, a $3.26 per day tax on CBD rush

---

* Changes in gasoline consumption are estimated from data on travel times and costs using engineering relationships between average travel speed and fuel consumption based on a recent study by the Chicago Area Transportation Study (1980). It is assumed that the gas consumption efficiency of the average automobile remains unchanged.

hour parking and a 56¢ per day tax on non-CBD rush hour parking is sufficient to cover all initial bus and transit fare revenues. Automobile commuting to the CBD declines by 16.5%, and to non-CBD destinations by 10.2%. Under both of these policies, consumer welfare increases because the positive effect from setting fares to zero dominates the negative effect from the gas or rush hour parking taxes. Under the gas-tax–free-fares policy, CBD commuter welfare increases twenty times more than under the paking-tax–free-fares policy. It should be noted that since our model does not separately identify the demand functions of commuter groups by income, the distribution of this welfare increase by income cannot be detected, but it is rather obvious. Any auto-tax–free-fare policy would reduce the welfare of automobile commuters (the higher income groups), while increasing the welfare of transit and bus commuters (the lower income groups). In a model without income segmentation such as ours, the welfare increase of the transit and bus commuters dominates: while a fare-free transit policy greatly benefits public transportation users, a sizable gas or rush hour parking tax imposes only a small burden on automobile commuters.

6. ANALYSIS OF RAIL PROJECTS PROPOSED FOR CHICAGO'S SOUTHWEST CORRIDOR

The Southwest corridor of the Chicago SMSA does not, at the current time, have rail transit service connecting its residential neighborhoods with the Central Business District. Figure 5.2 shows the zone map of this corridor, which consists of 57 suburban and 148 city residential zones, with 40 non-residential zones that contain no housing. The northern and eastern edges of the corridor are near existing rail transit lines, and express bus service serves the central area along Archer Avenue. Commuter rail service exists in the suburban part of the corridor.

Various elevated, surface, and subway rail alternatives have been proposed for the Southwest corridor, and the planning, programming and budgeting agencies of the region have been engaged in a multiyear, multiagency, Federally funded study aimed at selecting the best transit project for the corridor (see Krueger *et al.*, 1980).

The building of a fixed-guideway rail line in the Southwest corridor is a highly controversial issue since the costs of such projects are exorbitant and since the corridor is currently served with efficient bus lines that provide commuting to the CBD. Although light rail and exclusive bus lanes are probably the more cost effective of the alternatives proposed, we will confine our attention to three proposed heavy rail projects. Data on the characteristics and alignments of the rail and busway alternatives are not complete,

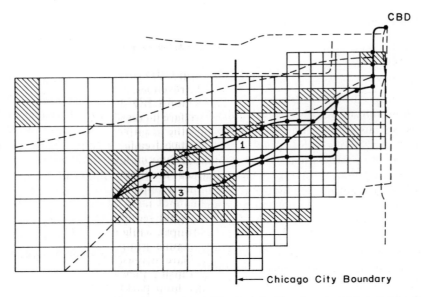

Fig. 5.2. Alignments and station locations of the three heavy rail projects proposed for the Southwest corridor. (1) Gulf Mobile & Ohio project (GM & O); (2) Archer Avenue project; (3) Indiana Harbor Belt project (IHB); ————, existing transit line; —•—•—, proposed transit project; —•—, proposed transit station; ▨, nonresidential zone excluded from simulation.

and most of the interest in the value capture issue revolves around heavy rail systems. The projects we will examine are the Archer Avenue line (to be built on Archer Avenue, mostly as a subway), the GM&O line (to be built at-grade on the right-of-way of the Gulf Mobile and Ohio freight railroad), and the IHB line (to be built as part subway, part at-grade, and part elevated on the right-of-way of the Indiana Harbor Belt freight railroad). The alignments and proposed station locations of each of these projects is shown in Fig. 5.2.

In order to evaluate the impacts of these projects, we must first be able to estimate the access cost and travel time changes introduced by each. To do so, we adapted a model developed and estimated for Chicago by Sajovec and Tahir (1976). This model classifies the vicinity of a transit station into three areas. The first area consists of all zones within $\frac{1}{4}$ mile of a transit station. Transit commuters within this area are assumed to walk to the nearest station. The second area consists of the zones within $\frac{1}{4}$–1 mile of a transit station. Transit commuters within this area are assumed to make a binary choice between walking to the nearest station and taking a feeder bus. The probability of taking a bus for a random transit commuter of zone i is given as the binary logit model

$$P_{bi} = \exp(V_i)/[1 + \exp(V_i)], \tag{5.60}$$

where

$$V_i = -2.60 + 0.132D_i - 0.157S_i - 0.044F, \tag{5.61}$$

where D_i is the street distance from the centroid of zone i to the transit station in hundreds of feet; S_i, the street distance from the centroid of zone i to the nearest bus stop in hundreds of feet; and F, the feeder bus fare. The third area consists of zones beyond 1 mile from the transit station; transit commuters in this area are assumed to make a binary choice between driving to the nearest station or taking the feeder bus. The probability of taking the bus for a random commuter of zone i is binary logit as in (5.60), where V_i is given as

$$V_i = 2.74 - 0.0022\Delta_i - 0.043\Gamma_i - 0.716\Pi_i - 0.041S_i, \tag{5.62}$$

where Δ_i is the difference between bus and auto access times in seconds; Γ_i, the difference between bus and auto out-of-pocket access cost in cents; Π_i, a dummy variable that equals zero if parking is not available at the transit station and equals one if parking is available; and S_i, the street distance from the zone centroid to the nearest bus stop in hundreds of feet.

The expected cost of access to the nearest station is computed as

$$(\text{expected access cost}) = c_{bi}P_{bi} + c_{ai}P_{ai}, \tag{5.63}$$

where c_{bi} and c_{ai} are the costs of access by bus and auto and P_{bi}, P_{ai}, the expected access choice probabilities, with $P_{bi} = P_{ai} = 0$ if zone i is within $\frac{1}{4}$ mile of the station and $P_{ai} = 0$ if zone i is within $\frac{1}{4}$–1 mile of the station. The expected access time to the nearest station is computed as

$$(\text{expected access time}) = t_{wi}P_{wi} + t_{bi}P_{bi} + t_{ai}P_{ai}, \tag{5.64}$$

where t_{wi}, t_{bi}, and t_{ai} are the travel times of access by walking, bus, and auto, respectively, and P_{wi}, P_{bi}, and P_{ai} are the walk, bus, and auto access probabilities, with $P_{wi} = 1(P_{bi} = P_{ai} = 0)$ if the zone is within $\frac{1}{4}$ mile, $P_{ai} = 0$ if the zone is within $\frac{1}{4}$–1 mile, and $P_{wi} = 0$ if the zone is beyond 1 mile. Walking speed is assumed to be 3 miles/hr, bus waiting time is taken to be 5 min, and overall bus speed is 12 miles/h, with 1 min allowed for the time needed to enter the rapid transit station from a bus stop and 2 min from a parking lot *at* the station. In the standard policy simulations, feeder bus stations are assumed to be at $\frac{1}{3}$ mile from the average residence, and the time of access from home to the nearest bus stop is taken to be 6.6 min. The feeder bus access fare is 10¢, the auto operating cost is 10¢/mile, and the cost of all day parking at the transit station is 25¢. All cost figures are for 1970. The new transit projects are assumed to operate at 40-mile/h running speed, with

1-min dwell time at each transit station. Combining (5.63) and (5.64) with the station-to-CBD costs and times, we obtain the expected out-of-pocket cost and travel time from each zone, through the nearest station on the proposed project to the CBD.

The existing economic and travel conditions within the Southwest corridor are shown in Table 5.7, while Table 5.8 lists the comparison between the travel times and costs of the existing rapid transit service, the existing bus service, and the new (proposed) rapid transit projects. It can be seen from this table that the proposed projects will improve existing zone-to-CBD travel times by about 6–7 min per trip for the "average" zone and by about 20–23 min per trip as a maximum. Travel cost savings are just under 20¢ per trip and about $1.00 at the maximum. The travel times of the new projects are roughly equivalent to the travel times provided by the current CBD express bus service, while the average cost saving of the new projects compared to the existing bus service is about 8–10¢ per trip. The existing bus service is 4 min faster and 13.6¢ cheaper than the current rapid transit service for the average zone.

Not all of the 205 zones in the Southwest corridor report trips by rapid transit in 1970. Eighty-nine of these zones are located away from the existing transit lines that neighbor the corridor, and each of these zones reports zero rapid transit trips. The problem of determining the alternative-specific constant part of these zones' transit utility was discussed in Section 3.2. In order to do so, we examined the remaining 116 zones, all of which report some trips by auto *and* rapid transit. We first computed the alternative-specific constants (specification errors), as explained in Section 3.2. Letting G_{ia} and G_{it} be the specification errors in the automobile and rapid transit utilities of zone i, we estimated the regression

$$G_{it} = -0.344 + 0.823 G_{ia}, \qquad R^2 = 0.488, \qquad (5.65)$$
$$\phantom{G_{it} = }(0.094)\quad(0.079)$$

from the 116 zones that report both auto and transit trips. The mean value of the independent variable G_{ia} is 0.2173, while the mean of G_{it} is -0.1657. The numbers in parentheses are the standard errors of the regression constant and its slope coefficient. The estimated regression (5.65) can be used to predict the unobserved value of the transit constants G_{it} from the values of the G_{ia} for those 89 zones that report auto trips but no transit trips. These predicted values of the G_{it} are then entered into the CBD demand model. Through this adjustment, the equilibrium model is able to generate rapid transit trips from those zones which in the initial 1970 situation do not report any transit trips.

The basic policy simulations that we will discuss revolve around the following theme: Suppose that either one of the three projects depicted in

TABLE 5.7

Aggregate Data Descriptive of the 1981 Situation in the Southwest Corridor Study Area Updated from the 1970 Data[a]

Housing

	Rent ($/yr)	Housing stock	Vacant units	Vacancy rate (%)
City	232,506,706 (53.5%)	165,604 (66.1%)	8,382 (81.4%)	4.82
Suburban	202,400,397 (46.5%)	84,745 (33.9%)	1,917 (18.6%)	2.21
Total	434,907,103 (100%)	250,349 (100%)	10,299 (100%)	3.95

Work trips[b]

	Auto	Commuter rail	Rapid transit	Bus	Other	Total
CBD	20,442 (38.6%)	5,689 (10.7%)	4,894 (9.2%)	20,502 (38.6%)	1,464 (2.8%)	52,991 (18.8%)
Non-CBD	159,196 (69.4%)	1,575 (0.7%)	2,132 (0.9%)	37,196 (16.2%)	29,193 (12.7%)	229,292 (81.2%)
Total	179,638 (63.6%)	7,264 (2.6%)	7,026 (2.5%)	57,698 (20.4%)	30,657 (10.9%)	282,283 (100%)

Travel time and cost for work trips[c]

	Auto	Commuter rail	Rapid transit	Bus	Total
CBD travel time	957,842	270,167	206,895	830,690	2,265,594
Non-CBD travel time	5,858,183	[d]	[d]	1,243,073	[d]
CBD travel cost	19,471,295	2,739,071	1,607,423	4,637,050	28,454,839
Non-CBD travel cost	146,705,281	[d]	[d]	4,637,050	[d]

[a] See Fig. 5.1.
[b] Daily one-way.
[c] Daily, one-way times (min); annual two-way costs($).
[d] Not available.

TABLE 5.8

Comparison of One-Way Zone-to-CBD Travel Times and Costs for the Three Proposed Projects

Proposed project		Travel time (min)			Travel cost (cents)		
		a	b	c	a	b	c
Archer	Avg[d]	4.06	−0.30	−6.94	13.62	7.79	−19.08
	Max[e]	22.70	12.92	−23.62	38.30	15.88	−101.76
	Min[e]	−21.60	−12.62	0.00	5.00	0.00	0.00
GM&O	Avg[d]	4.06	0.41	−5.89	13.62	9.18	−17.60
	Max[e]	22.70	15.54	−20.19	38.30	19.95	−101.76
	Min[e]	−21.60	−13.96	0.00	5.00	0.00	0.00
IHB	Avg[d]	4.06	0.37	−6.24	13.62	7.59	−19.13
	Max[e]	22.70	15.35	−23.19	38.30	18.00	−101.76
	Min[e]	−21.60	−16.49	0.00	5.00	−2.42	0.00

[a] (Existing transit time or cost) − (existing bus time or cost).

[b] (Proposed project transit time or cost) − (existing bus time or cost).

[c] (Proposed project transit time or cost) − (existing transit time or cost).

[d] Avg: *a*, *b*, average of 158 zones that had both rapid transit and bus service in 1970; *c*, average of all zones.

[e] Max, Min: maximum and minimum differences.

Fig. 5.2 or a modification of these were to have been built in 1970; what would its effect on metropolitan equilibrium be? To answer these questions, we employ the nested CBD and non-CBD (NN) models.

It can be seen from Fig. 5.3 that for the GM&O project, the maximum annual rent increase is $247 annually, whereas for the IHB project, it is $200 annually. These rent increases are about $17–$21 per month on the average within these zones, and these are maximum increases within the corridor. It is also seen that the zones with the largest increases are generally located adjacent to the proposed transit stations. As one moves away from these stations, one generally encounters smaller increases. Substantially away from the proposed stations, rents will decrease, but the maximum decrease encountered within the Southwest corridor is $8 annually, an insignificant amount. As one would expect, outside the corridor rent decreases are even smaller. The predicted magnitudes of these rent changes have very encouraging policy implications. First, if a value capture policy, discussed in Section 1, is to be implemented, the annualized lump sum tax to be paid by the average property owner is not large. This makes a value capture policy more acceptable politically than the gas and parking tax policies discussed in Section 5. Second, where rents decrease, the change is so small as to be negligible. If

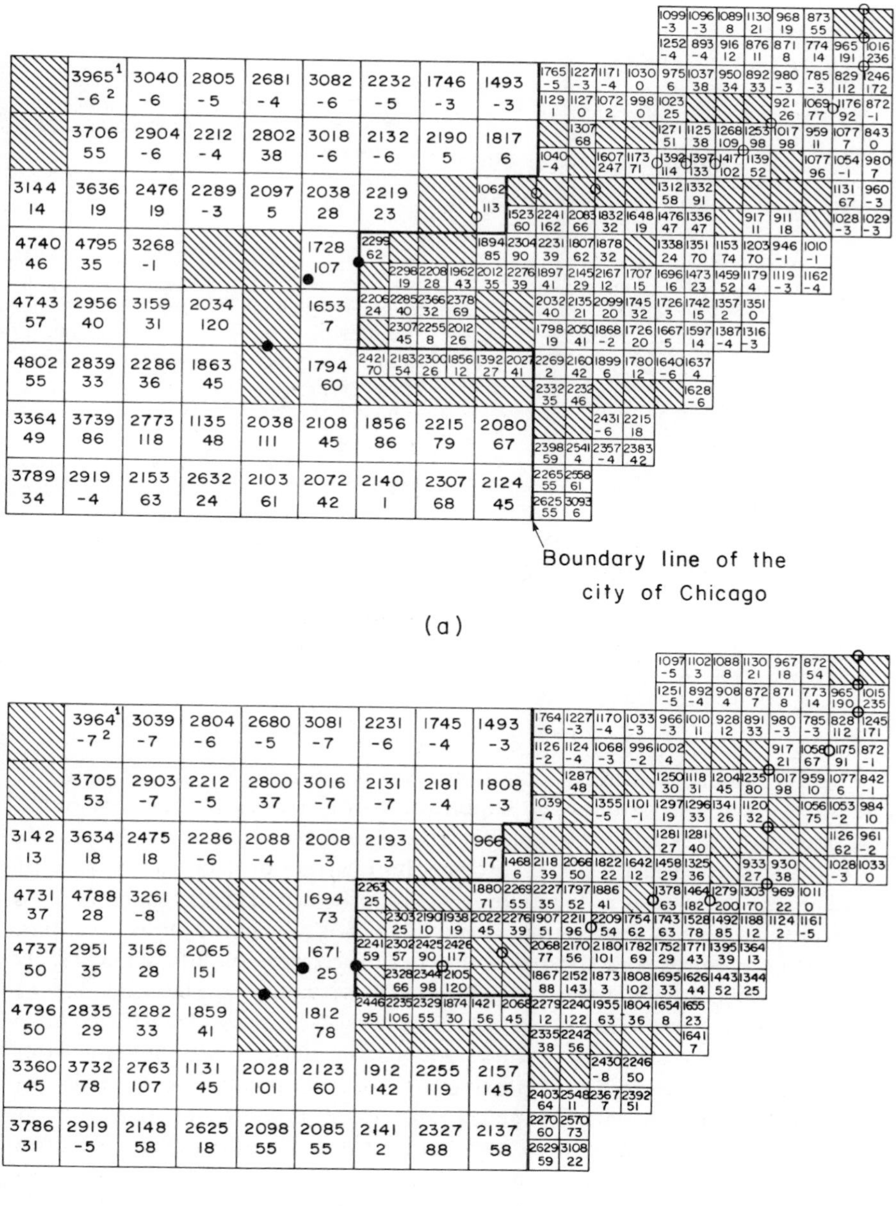

Boundary line of the
city of Chicago

(a)

(b)

Fig. 5.3. Average zonal rent changes due to the GM&O (a) and IHB (b) projects predicted by the NN model. (1) Equilibrium zonal average rent ($/yr); (2) zonal average rent change ($/yr); ○, transit station without parking; ●, transit station with parking; ▨, nonresidential zone excluded from simulation.

TABLE 5.9

List and Description of Fifteen Hypothetical Policies Tested

Policy	Description
1.	Remove all CBD bus service in the Southwest corridor.
2.	Introduce the Archer Avenue subway.[a]
3.	Introduce the IHB project.[a]
4.	Introduce the GM&O project.[a]
5.	Introduce the GM&O and remove all CBD bus service in the Southwest corridor.
6.	Increase average distance to the nearest GM&O feeder bus stop from $\frac{1}{3}$ mile to $\frac{1}{2}$ mile.
7.	Increase the GM&O running speed by 20%.
8.	Close all parking lots at the last three GM&O stations.
9.	Open parking lots at the two westernmost city stations on the GM&O.
10.	Close every other GM&O station.
11.	Close the last two (suburban) GM&O stations.
12.	Introduce the GM&O, but set transit and bus CBD fares equal to zero for all transit and bus service to CBD.
13.	Introduce the GM&O, and double gas price by setting a gas tax.
14.	Introduce the GM&O, and double CBD parking cost by setting a parking tax.
15.	Introduce the GM&O, and move 5% of the CBD employment to non-CBD employment locations.

[a] See Fig. 5.2.

property owners in these areas do not receive tax rebates, they are very unlikely to voice political objections. What remains to be examined is whether a value capture policy would succeed in raising a large part of the total cost of the rail investment. To investigate this, we first computed the construction costs of the three rail projects in current dollars and discounted these to 1970. To obtain these construction costs, we utilized the unit costs and detailed project descriptions provided by analysts in the Chicago region agencies (see Permut and Zimring, 1975; Krueger *et al.*, 1980). The GM&O project, which is planned as an at-grade construction, would cost $254.3 million; the Archer Avenue line, which is mostly a subway, $497.9 million; and the IHB, $511.4 million. Since construction cost is the biggest part of each project's total cost, and considering the exorbitant costs involved, we selected the GM&O, which is the least expensive, for further policy analysis. In all, fifteen policies have been designed and tested, and these are described in Table 5.9. The first policy is for reference purposes. Under this policy, all CBD bus service in the Southwest corridor is terminated, and no rail project is introduced. Policies 2–4 introduce each of the three rail projects without disturbing existing bus service. Policies 5–11 all deal with building the GM&O project in conjunction with assumed modifications in the system characteristics of this project, or under the assumption that the existing CBD bus service is terminated (policy 5). Finally, policies 12–15 introduce the GM&O project in standard form (as in policy 4) with assumed exogenous conditions regarding fares, gas, and parking taxes, and CBD employment. Table 5.10 summarizes the metropolitan rent changes, model split changes, and consumer surplus changes due to each policy, while Table 5.11 summarizes the within-corridor rent change, the modal split changes, and the number of employees who move their domiciles in or out of the Southwest corridor.

We will discuss the metropolitanwide and corridor-specific results of Tables 5.10 and 5.11, focusing on each one of the fifteen policies and hypothetical scenarios. Considering the first policy, the removal of all CBD bus service in the Southwest corridor causes about 4800 CBD employees to relocate outside of the corridor. Aggregate rents within the Chicago portion of the corridor decline by 21.3% and increase by 0.12% in the suburban portion. Corridorwide aggregate rents decline by 11.3%, while metropolitanwide aggregate rents increase by 0.053%, which amounts to a surplus of about $2.34 million a year. The annual aggregate rent deficit within the Southwest corridor is about $49 million a year. The cost of operating the Southwest corridor CBD bus service (removed in this policy) is nearly $15 million a year (Chicago Transit Authority, April 1980). Considering the corridor alone, the deficit created by the removal of the bus service to the CBD is more than three times the cost of the CBD bus service. The area outside the corridor makes up for this deficit via very thinly spread, small rent increases. This result suggests that a tax on housing amounting to 5% or less of aggregate housing values may in some cases be sufficient to expand bus services or pay for existing bus services. As we shall see from the other policies, the results for rail transit are not nearly as strong, primarily because of the higher construction costs for rail systems.

Policy 5 consists of removing the CBD bus service as in policy 1 *and* introducing the GM&O heavy rail transit line shown in Fig. 5.2. Doing this increases the metropolitan surplus to $3.9 million a year. The annual capital and operating cost of the proposed rail line is estimated to be $36 million, and the saving from removing the bus service is about $15 million. Thus the net cost of policy 5 amounts to $21 million annually, and the metropolitan rent surplus is only 18.6% of this net cost.

Policies 2, 3, and 4 consist of introducing the three proposed heavy rail projects (Archer, IHB, and GM&O) shown in Fig. 2. The rent changes within the Southwest corridor caused by two of these projects (IHB and GM&O) have already been illustrated in Fig. 5.3. Tables 5.10 and 5.11 show that while the metropolitan city and suburban rent changes caused by the three projects differ somewhat, aggregate metropolitan changes do not differ by much, and aggregate rent changes within the city and suburban parts of the corridor are

TABLE 5.10

Metropolitan Results for Policies 1–15 in 1970

| Policy[a] | Rent change (%) | | | Mode demand change (%) | | | | | | Consumer surplus | |
| | City | Suburb | Total | CBD | | | | Non-CBD | | CBD[b] | Non-CBD[c] |
				Auto	Rail	Transit	Bus	Auto	Bus		
1	−0.859	0.716	0.053	9.60	1.54	4.08	−18.36	−0.66	4.04	19.0	130
2	0.033	−0.128	−0.060	−1.05	−0.32	4.50	−1.70	0.02	−0.15	2.9	−1.6
3	0.027	−0.115	−0.055	−1.01	−0.30	4.24	−1.57	0.02	−0.14	2.8	−1.7
4	0.003	−0.089	−0.051	−0.84	−0.29	3.59	−1.32	0.02	−0.15	2.3	−0.74
5	−0.716	0.673	0.088	6.82	1.04	10.07	−18.53	−0.48	2.90	14.0	84
6	−0.0005	−0.084	−0.049	−0.82	−0.29	3.48	−1.28	0.02	−0.14	2.2	−0.76
7	0.003	−0.103	−0.058	−0.98	−0.35	4.17	−1.52	0.03	−0.16	2.7	−0.98
8	0.004	−0.091	−0.051	−0.83	−0.28	3.55	−1.32	0.02	−0.15	2.3	−0.64
9	0.004	−0.091	−0.051	−0.85	−0.29	3.63	−1.34	0.02	−0.15	2.3	−0.77
10	−0.006	−0.070	−0.040	−0.84	−0.33	3.48	−1.21	0.02	−0.11	2.3	−2.0
11	0.007	−0.09	−0.050	−0.82	−0.28	3.52	−1.31	0.02	−0.15	2.3	−0.6
12	2.46	−3.87	−1.20	−9.09	−2.12	12.25	5.44	−8.73	53.18	27.0	750
13	0.24	−0.26	−0.05	−3.43	0.87	5.26	0.35	−1.57	9.58	−4.3	−4.2
14	−0.26	0.29	0.06	−17.5	7.14	14.02	9.74	−0.08	0.47	−25.0	14.0
15	−14.13	11.59	0.76	−30.58	−30.18	−21.68	−23.96	4.29	23.63	44.0	−450

[a] See Table 5.9 for description of policies.

[b] ($\times 10^{-3}$).

[c] ($\times 10^{-5}$).

TABLE 5.11

Southwest Corridor Study Area Results for Policies 1–15 in 1970

Policy[a]	Rent change (%)			Mode demand change (%)						Employee change[b]	
				CBD				Non-CBD			
	City	Suburb	Total	Auto	Rail	Transit	Bus	Auto	Bus	CBD	Non-CBD
1	-21.31	0.12	-11.33	62.71	3.52	53.93	-100	-5.79	36.99	-4,844	4,536
2	2.92	0.70	1.89	-6.45	-2.07	78.31	-8.5	0.33	-3.13	657	-634
3	2.73	0.73	1.80	-6.23	-1.91	73.79	-7.8	0.31	-2.96	622	-601
4	2.14	0.72	1.48	-5.21	-2.12	62.45	-6.6	0.31	-2.66	516	-499
5	-17.15	0.94	-8.74	43.86	0.96	159.39	-100	-4.25	27.45	-3,681	3,438
6	2.05	0.74	1.44	-5.08	-2.13	60.64	-6.37	0.29	-2.56	502	-486
7	2.51	0.88	1.75	-6.07	-2.51	72.56	-7.59	0.34	-3.04	611	-589
8	2.13	0.69	1.46	-5.15	-2.01	61.84	-6.58	0.31	-2.65	510	-494
9	2.18	0.72	1.50	-5.26	-2.13	63.15	-6.69	0.31	-2.68	522	-505
10	2.00	0.93	1.50	-5.25	-2.60	60.53	-6.01	0.24	-2.36	509	-494
11	2.12	0.64	1.44	-5.08	-1.96	61.27	-6.56	0.31	-2.65	504	-488
12	5.74	-2.52	1.90	-14.71	-4.29	81.15	-0.25	-13.46	56.01	668	-595
13	2.13	0.62	1.42	-7.70	-0.83	65.56	-4.85	-2.44	8.89	593	-581
14	1.55	0.85	1.22	-23.56	5.45	81.73	4.44	0.16	-1.75	404	-402
15	-5.19	8.99	1.41	-34.01	-31.48	17.07	-31.37	5.45	15.31	-14,341	14,376

[a] See Table 5.9 for description of policies.

[b] Number of employees who relocate into or move out of the Southwest corridor study area.

very similar, as are changes in modal split. The number of new one-way rail transit CBD commuters diverted from auto, commuter rail, and bus are between three and four thousand. These are highest (3832 commuters) for the Archer Avenue subway project, which is strategically aligned, and lowest (3057 commuters) for the GM&O project, which is the least strategically aligned but the cheapest to construct.

It is noteworthy that each of these transit projects decreases metropolitan aggregate rents by about $2.25–$2.65 million annually. Within the corridor, however, rents increase by about $6.44 million for the GM&O project to $8.22 million for the Archer Avenue project. Changes in zonal average rents outside the corridor are generally very small and negative and, as discussed earlier, very unlikely to generate any political opposition if not rebated to the property owners.

Policies 6–11 are selected physical or engineering design refinements for the basic proposed form of the GM&O project. To see the differential impact of these refinements, we should compare the results of the relevant policy to policy 4. It is rather easily verified from Tables 5.10 and 5.11 that the differential impacts of these policies on rents and modal splits are rather small and deviate only slightly from the results of policy 4. For example, aggregate rent increases in the city part of the corridor vary from 2.00 to 2.51%, with the base policy 4 showing an increase of only 2.14%. In the suburban part of the corridor, rent increases vary from 0.64 to 0.93% compared to the 0.72% of the base policy, while in the entire corridor the aggregate rent increase is between 1.44 and 1.75%, compared to the 1.48% of the base policy. In the case of the entire SMSA, rent changes are between -0.040 and -0.058%. For the SMSA suburbs, changes are between -0.07 and -0.103%, and for the city of Chicago they are between -0.0005 and $+0.007\%$.

The policy of increasing train running speeds by 20% (policy 7) has the strongest positive impact on corridorwide rent change, but it results in an increase of only $1.174 million annually compared to policy 4. Policies 9 and 10 also increase rents within the corridor, but by only $87,000 annually. In the case of policy 9, the rent increase comes from increasing the number of transit stations with parking lots from the last three on the GM&O line to the last five. In the case of policy 10, the increase in rents comes from closing every other station on the GM&O. This policy has two opposite effects. One is to contribute to a decrease in travel times by eliminating station dwell times for the closed stations; the other is to contribute to an increase in travel times by lengthening the time needed to access the stations. Another effect arises from the fact that the number of transit stations within $\frac{1}{2}$, $\frac{1}{2}$–1, 1, and 2 miles directly enter the preferences of the commuters. The combined outcomes of these three effects are only a 3% decrease in transit patronage and a small increase in rents within the corridor. This increase arises from the fact that the positive improvement in travel times due to less station-dwelling time dominates the negative effect due to the closing of stations. In contrast to policies 9 and 10, policy 11, which closes the last two stations on the GM&O, decreases aggregate rents by $87,000 annually and transit patronage on the GM&O by about 1.9%. This occurs because the closing of the last two stations lengthens the trips of the suburban residents. Finally, policies 6 and 8 also decrease rents within the corridor by roughly $174,000 and $87,000 annually, respectively. This is an expected result since policy 6 increases the distance to the nearest feeder bus station from $\frac{1}{3}$ to $\frac{1}{2}$ mile, while policy 8 closes all of the parking lots on the GM&O line. All of these results support the notion that the initial alignment of transit lines is much more important than *marginal* changes in the engineering design and physical characteristics of a given alignment.

We now turn to policies 12, 13, and 14. In these policies, the base GM&O line is introduced in conjunction with systemwide changes in fares, gas taxes, and parking taxes. Policy 12 sets all transit and bus fares for CBD rush hour commuting equal to zero. This increases CBD rents by 2.46%, and decreases suburban rents by 3.87% and metropolitan rents by 1.20%. Within the corridor, city rents are increased by 5.74%, and suburban rents are decreased by 2.52%, causing a corridor surplus of 1.90%. The within-corridor aggregate effects of a gas tax and parking tax are similar but less pronounced. In fact, these policies increase the cost of automobile commuting and thus lower the within-corridor rent increase from 1.48% to 1.42% and 1.22%. The three policies differ substantially in their modal split changes, as seen from Tables 5.10 and 5.11. Compared to policy 4, the patronage of the new transit line is 5–31% higher under policies 12–14.

Policy 15 is the introduction of the GM&O line under the hypothetical scenario that 5% of the CBD employment is moved to non-CBD employment locations, with the relative frequency distribution of this employment among the non-CBD locations remaining constant. It should be recalled that such a hypothetical change assumes that the relocated employees change their preferences from those of the CBD commuters to those of the non-CBD commuters since the utility coefficients for the two commuter groups differ substantially. Because of this, policy 15 consists of two confounded effects: a preference change and an employment decentralization. The combined effect within the corridor is that city rents decline, suburban rents increase, and there is a corridor wide increase of 1.41% compared to the 1.48% of the base GM&O policy 4. The SMSA-wide result (Table 5.10) is that there is a rent surplus of 0.76%, compared to the deficit of 0.051% in the case of policy 4. This is as expected since the average travel times and costs of non-CBD commuters is lower than that of the CBD commuters. Other things being equal, moving an employee from the CBD to an employment location outside of the CBD increases that employee's "rent paying ability."

Having discussed each of the fifteen policies, we now turn to an examination of the financial viability of transit projects under each policy. These results are summarized in Table 5.12, which lists the new rapid transit CBD commuters generated by each policy, the annual operating cost of the proposed project plus its associated feeder bus service, and the annualized capital cost, which consists of the construction cost (for stations and guideway) plus the cost of the necessary rolling stock.

To perform these cost calculations, we relied on the reports by Permut and Zimring (1975), Krueger *et al.* (1980), and the Chicago Transit Authority (April, 1980). The last report estimates the annual operating cost of bus and transit service as follows:

$$\binom{\text{annual bus}}{\text{operating cost}} = \$26.45 \binom{\text{annual}}{\text{vehicle hours}} + \$1.15 \binom{\text{annual}}{\text{vehicle miles}}$$

$$+ \$12,300 \binom{\text{peak period}}{\text{vehicles}} + \$0.020 \binom{\text{annual revenue}}{\text{passengers}}$$

$$\binom{\text{annual rail}}{\text{operating cost}} = \$30.39 \binom{\text{annual}}{\text{vehicle hours}} + \$1.32 \binom{\text{annual}}{\text{vehicle miles}}$$

$$+ \$9,700 \binom{\text{peak period}}{\text{vehicles}} + \$0.020 \binom{\text{annual revenue}}{\text{passengers}}.$$

Since our model predicts only peak period CBD passengers, the entire system's revenue passengers are obtained roughly by multiplying the CBD daily peak period passengers by two (a rule of thumb roughly valid for Chicago). Annual passengers, including weekend travelers, are obtained by multiplying daily passengers by 290. Vehicle hours, vehicle miles, and peak period vehicles are obtained from the assumed headway and other characteristics of the feeder bus and rail transit systems. Construction costs are estimated using transit station costs by type of station and type of guideway construction by type, such as subway, at-grade, and elevated, using per mile costs from Permut and Zimring (1975) and Krueger *et al.* (1980). Rolling stock costs are computed from unit prices for transit cars and feeder bus vehicles. Capital costs are then annualized using a 35-yr assumed project life and a 15% interest rate. Table 5.12 also shows the annual aggregate rent surplus generated from within the corridor; the annual fare revenue of each project; and the ratios of fare revenue to annual operating cost, rent surplus (or value captured) to total (operating plus annualized capital) cost, and value captured plus fare revenue to total annual cost. For the GM&O project, the percent

TABLE 5.12

Estimated Costs and Cost Recovery Ratios for Policies 2–4 and 6–14 in 1970[a]

Policy[b]	New passengers (one-way work trips to CBD)	Annual operating cost	Annual capital plus operating cost	Annual value captured	Annual fare revenue	Annual fare revenue to operating cost ratio	Annual value captured to total cost ratio	Annual value captured plus fare revenue to total cost ratio
2	3,832	9,993.2	54,453.3	8,211.0	2,440.4	0.244	0.151	0.196
3	3,611	10,371.0	55,831.3	7,810.0	2,299.6	0.222	0.139	0.181
4	3,057	9,828.9	36,212.9	6,446.0	1,946.8	0.198	0.178	0.232
6	2,968	9,389.9	35,226.4	6,278.0	1,890.1	0.201	0.178	0.232
7	3,551	9,338.4	35,152.9	7,626.0	2,261.4	0.242	0.217	0.281
8	3,026	9,828.6	36,212.6	6,355.0	1,927.1	0.196	0.175	0.229
9	3,090	9,829.3	36,212.3	6,523.0	1,967.8	0.200	0.180	0.234
10	2,962	9,088.3	32,800.4	6,527.0	1,886.3	0.208	0.199	0.257
11	2,998	8,556.3	32,976.5	6,243.0	1,909.2	0.223	0.189	0.247
12	3,971	9,839.3	36,223.3	8,242.0	—	—	0.228	0.228
13	3,208	9,830.6	36,214.4	6,191.0	2,042.9	0.208	0.171	0.227
14	4,000	9,839.6	36,223.6	5,319.0	2,547.4	0.259	0.147	0.217

[a] All dollar valued items in thousands in 1970 dollars.
[b] See Table 5.9 for description of policies.

of the total cost raised by value capture ranges from 14.7% to 22.8%, while the percent of the total cost raised by value capture *and* fare revenue ranges from 21.7% to 25.7%. For policies 13 and 14, however, the revenues raised by the gas and parking taxes are significant. In the case of policy 13, the gas tax revenue generated from Southwest corridor CBD commuters alone ($1.5 million) raises the percent of the total cost recouped from 22.7% to 26.9%. For policy 14, the parking tax revenue generated by the corridor's CBD commuters raises the percent of the total cost recouped from 21.7% to a dramatic high of 51.9%.

It is important to recall that the results reported in Tables 5.10–5.12 deal with the introduction of each policy in a 1970 environment. How much are the results changed if the same policies are to be implemented in 1981? To investigate the answer to this question, the fifteen policies of Table 5.9 were reevaluated using the 1981 updated data set profiled in Table 5.7. As one would expect, the changes that have taken place between 1970 and 1981 have weakened the financial viability of the transit projects and associated policies. Without reporting the results in detail, we will state that the ratio of value captured to total annual cost for the GM&O project declined from 17.8–22.8% to 9.7–13.8%. The percent of total cost raised by value captured and fare revenue declined from 21.7–25.7% to 9.6–17.9%. Finally, for policies 13 and 14, the percent of total cost captured declined from 26.9% to 19.2% and from 51.9% to 35.5%, respectively. These changes represent a serious erosion over the decade in the ability of rail transit systems to pay for their own costs.

Before accepting the quantitative results of this section as accurate policy statements, we owe it to our sense of empirical wisdom to consider a sensitivity analysis on the estimated coefficients. The results of such a sensitivity analysis based on the 1970 situation are shown in Table 5.13. Four variations of the GM&O base policy are examined. In one of these, the estimated travel time coefficient of the CBD model is divided by four, which is roughly equivalent to dividing the travel time elasticity of demand by four. In the second sensitivity analysis, the coefficient of rent plus travel cost is halved; and in the third, the travel time coefficient is divided by four *and* the coefficient of rent plus travel cost is halved. Finally, in the fourth sensitivity analysis, the coefficients for the number of transit stations within $\frac{1}{2}$ mile, $\frac{1}{2}$–1 mile, and more than 1 mile are set equal to zero, which is the equivalent of dropping these attributes from the utility function.

It is seen from Table 5.13 that the halving of the coefficient of rent plus cost changes the results of the base policy only very slightly. The effect of dividing the travel time coefficient by four is much more profound: aggregate rent change within the corridor and SMSA-wide is roughly divided by four,

TABLE 5.13

Sensitivity Analysis on the Coefficients of the CBD Demand Model and the GM&O Base Policy Results for 1970[a]

| | Rent change (%) | | | Mode demand change (%) | | | | | | | Employee change | |
| | | | | CBD | | | | Non-CBD | | | | |
	City	Suburbs	Total	Auto	Rail	Transit	Bus	Auto	Bus	CBD	Non-CBD
				Metropolitan							
1	0.003	−0.089	−0.051	−0.84	−0.29	3.59	−1.32	0.02	−0.15	—	—
2	0.0079	−0.028	−0.013	−0.18	−0.055	0.77	−0.29	0.01	−0.06	—	—
3	0.0035	−0.074	−0.041	−0.65	−0.26	2.72	−0.96	0.02	−0.13	—	—
4	0.0090	−0.032	−0.015	−0.18	−0.058	0.75	−0.27	0.01	−0.07	—	—
5	−0.0066	−0.034	−0.022	−0.56	−0.22	2.31	−0.80	0.01	−0.06	—	—
				Southwest corridor							
1	2.14	0.72	1.48	−5.21	−2.12	62.45	−6.60	0.31	−2.66	516	−499
2	0.55	0.08	0.33	−1.20	−0.33	13.47	−1.43	0.11	−0.78	101	−112
3	2.07	0.68	1.42	−4.02	−1.85	47.93	−4.60	0.29	−2.48	475	−461
4	0.67	0.07	0.39	−1.16	−0.29	13.15	−1.31	0.14	−0.93	123	−133
5	1.24	0.67	0.97	−3.59	−1.82	40.21	−3.96	0.14	−1.45	320	−319

[a] (1) GM&O base policy; (2) divide "travel time coefficient" by four; (3) divide "rent plus travel cost coefficient" by two; (4) divide "travel time coefficient" by four *and* "rent plus travel cost" coefficient by two; (5) set all coefficients for the number of transit stations within $\frac{1}{2}$ mile, $\frac{1}{2}$–1 mile, and more than 1 mile equal to zero.

and mode split changes are correspondingly reduced. Dividing this co-efficient by four lowers the ratio of value captured plus fare revenue to total annual cost from 23.17% to a mere 5.09%, whereas halving the rent plus travel time coefficient lowers the same ratio from 23.17% to 21.19%. The effect of setting the coefficients of "the number of stations" equal to zero is to reduce SMSA-wide aggregate rent changes to 43% and within-corridor aggregate rents to 65% of the GM&O base policy. The ratio of value captured plus fare revenue to total cost is reduced from 23.17% to 15.16%.

The sensitivity of the policy conclusions to the estimated travel time coefficient is especially notable. The implication of this sensitivity is that *if* our estimated coefficient is substantially overestimated, the policy results are also substantially inflated. It was discussed in Chapter 5, however, that our estimated travel time elasticity is the least sensitive to estimation method, sampling, and model specification. Furthermore, our estimated travel time elasticity is very similar to that estimated by other analysts who have em-ployed similar specifications. If the specification of travel time is changed by the separate introduction of in-vehicle and out-of-vehicle times, we may find some change, perhaps significant, in the policy results.

7. POLICY IMPLICATIONS AND CAVEATS

The empirical policy simulations of this chapter demonstrated the nature of a package of housing taxes, gasoline taxes, parking taxes, and transit fares necessary to make metropolitan public transit systems financially viable. The analysis has been exploratory and predictive in nature: we have sought to cultivate insight about the relative strength of the alternative financing schemes rather than attempting to find *optimal* financing plans. The purpose of this section is to review and appropriately qualify these findings, bringing judgment and several caveats to bear on them.

A very encouraging finding is that under 1970 conditions, roughly 14–18% of the annualized cost of a CBD oriented heavy rail transit system (such as the GM&O project) can be recouped via lump sum value capture taxation of housing alone within a special assessment corridor surrounding the rail project. We will now argue that assuming the estimated coefficients are free of error, this 14–18% is probably a lower bound. The reasons for this are as follows:

First, the above estimate can be increased somewhat by optimizing the boundary of the special assessment district within which lump sum housing taxes and rebates are to be implemented. Examining Fig. 5.3, we can see that the corridor definition can be extended southward and reduced on the north side. If this is done, more housing with positive rent changes comes into the tax district, while the housing that is excluded has only small negative rent changes. The precise boundary definition is a political matter. It should be handled in a way that maximizes the positive rent surplus while excluding those areas where the estimated rent rebates are so small as to be politically negligible. The results of our analysis show that this can be easily achieved.

Second, our simulation model could be extended to include explicitly the travel behavior of employees located in specific non-CBD job centers within the Southwest corridor. The travel time and cost savings of such commuters who would use the transit system would further enhance the increase in housing values around the proposed transit projects.

Third, the model can be extended to include explicitly the shopping and other nonwork trips generated by the transit project and the resulting appreciation in the value of commercial floor space within the Southwest corridor. Value capture taxes applied to the commercial properties would substantially add to the total value capture potential of the project.

Fourth, the Southwest corridor and, indeed, any other corridor in a mature metropolis contains substantial amounts of vacant land. Some of this is situated in suburban areas ripe for development and some in the central city in abandoned and dilapidated neighborhoods. Value capture taxes assessed on the vacant land within the corridor would also add to total value capture revenues generated by the project.

It may be conjectured, on the basis of the four arguments above, that the actual value capture revenues of a heavy rail project such as the GM&O may be not 14–18% but certainly 20–25%, and perhaps even 30–35%.

We have also seen the importance of judicious project design as a means of keeping down the capital cost. In our case, this was achieved by selecting the GM&O over the more expensive Archer and IHB projects, which require subway or elevated construction. An even less expensive type of public transit, not examined in this study, is that of exclusive bus lanes. Such alternatives to heavy rail cost about 5–8 times less to construct. To set up an exclusive bus lane, the median or a working lane of an existing expressway is reserved for buses only. Although exclusive bus lanes must be situated on major highways and are thus less accessible to potential transit riders, and although the comfort and level of service of bus commuting is generally worse than that of fixed rail, the great capital cost saving of exclusive bus lanes can result in value capture revenues of over 50–60% of total cost. If one adds to this fare revenues and moderate gas and parking taxes, properly designed exclusive bus lanes can easily succeed in paying for their own costs entirely.

Finally, we can consider the possibility of extending the current model into a long run equilibrium framework in which new housing construction and price changes are simultaneously predicted by location. This, too, should enhance the value capture potential of transit projects by including the tax revenues from newly constructed dwellings, especially if zoning regulations and public land development policies are coordinated with the construction of the transit project in a way that maximizes total value capture revenue.

The purpose of this chapter was to develop a prototypical integrated analysis of the equilibrium allocation of households to dwellings, travel modes, and residential locations. Although this prototypical model is not a complete general equilibrium formulation because it treats the housing and travel markets in isolation, it is sufficiently detailed to provide a strong lower bound for the financial viability of CBD oriented public transit investments. It can be concluded from the analysis that public transit systems in the 1980s *can* be financed without any federal or state subsidies. It appears that value capture taxes on real estate are a substantial but declining part of the total local contribution. To design and implement systems that break even, one must combine a judicious choice of the type of transit with substantial gas and/or parking taxes and appropriate fare increases, coupled with value capture taxes on real estate. It goes without saying, however, that the configuration of a transit system that *does* break even in this way is substantially different from the existing configuration. Heavy rail extensions to existing systems are difficult to justify. Wherever possible, public transit agencies may be well advised to disinvest in or curtail rail service, replacing it with carefully planned and relatively inexpensive bus systems.

The transportation planning problem that emerges from this chapter is that of optimal investment–disinvestment planning and programming for locally financed metropolitan transit systems. In this problem, one seeks to find transit system and fare–tax structures that maximize a measure of consumer welfare or system performance while paying for the system's operating and capital costs. The current equilibrium model or a more general equilibrium extension of it has a central place within such a complex planning and programming framework. Solving these problems is beyond the scope of the present book, but the developments herein do bring the solutions within comfortable reach.

CHAPTER 6

TOWARD COMPLETE MODELS
OF THE URBAN ECONOMY

The theoretical, empirical, and policy-analytic developments reported in this book are but a small step in the direction of the ultimate objective: that of complete policy-analytic models of the urban economy based on economic theory and econometrics. The rationale and justification of this objective was discussed in the introduction. In this chapter, an effort is made to briefly sketch an agenda of modeling tasks remaining to be accomplished in order to approach the ultimate objective.

The central focus of the chapter is the extension of the discrete stochastic choice models developed in this book in three directions: (a) general equilibrium or multisector market equilibrium models, (b) general equilibrium models with endogenously specified public sectors, and (c) dynamic models. Immediate and long term obstacles in the development of these models are discussed, and extensions that can be achieved in the short run are described in some detail.

The last three sections discuss problems in the computability of large scale policy analytic urban models, overview the need for a holistic approach to urban public policy analysis, and summarize in brief the contribution of this book.

243

1. GENERAL EQUILIBRIUM

The model developed and estimated in Chapter 4 and applied in Chapter 5 examines partial equilibrium in the housing market while ignoring the important longer term interactions between the housing and land sectors and between the housing and employment (labor) markets. Even within this single-sector partial equilibrium model, the representation of housing demand is rather incomplete, as data limitations have forced us to pool renters and homeowners into one group while ignoring the different behavioral patterns of these two groups. One obvious direction for future research is the separate estimation of the demand for home ownership by developing models of tenure choice and the separation of housing supply into owner and renter occupied units. Because the market adjustments implied by a tenure choice model cannot be adequately addressed within static models, this problem will be discussed more extensively in the section that deals with dynamics.

Extension of the model of Chapter 5 to include a land sector is quite straightforward. To achieve this, each zone within the model can be divided into two parts. The first part consists of the existing housing in that zone; each landlord decides whether to rent or keep vacant his dwelling at the going rent, as in the model of Chapter 5. The second part of the zone consists of the vacant land in that zone; each landowner must decide whether to sell the land to a developer or to withhold it from development. Each developer in turn must determine the dwelling type or residential density of the land to be developed. Such a model will predict the rent for existing and new dwellings in each zone, the price of the vacant land in each zone, and the number and type of new dwellings built in each zone, as well as the amount of land that will remain vacant in each zone.

A more ambitious extension of the current model is to introduce the interactions between housing and employment by making the employment sector endogenous. The obvious way to achieve this is by providing an improved version of the Lowry population–employment interaction framework. To do so, one must first estimate demand models of joint residential location–commuting travel mode and shopping destination choice. Given an employee's job location, such a model would determine the residential location and commuting mode of the employee as well as the probabilities of that employee visiting each of various shopping destinations. It would thus be possible to use this model to compute not only the demand for housing at each location but also the demand for shopping employment at each location. Rents for housing and shopping floor space, land prices, and labor wages are an integral part of this model and would be adjusted to balance the demand and supply in each zone for both the vacant land and the existing building stock in that zone. The location of basic (manufacturing) employment could be given exogenously as was the case in the original Lowry model, but this need not be the case because the location of basic employment could become endogenous, as in the linear programming models of Mills. In fact, if such a model could be developed, it would correspond to a probabilistic and nonlinear generalization of Mills' linear programming model. The structure of such a model is quite complex, and it must first be determined whether a unique equilibrium solution exists. The required proof may indeed be a very difficult one. If such a model *can* be developed, it would complete in one giant sweep the integration of Lowry's framework with urban economic theory by bringing both behavioral and systemic consistency to Lowry's largely intuitive and ad hoc treatment of population–employment interactions.

The above extensions of the current model, introducing a vacant land sector and internalizing population–employment interactions, would result in the ultimate general equilibrium model of land, housing, and labor markets. The appeal of the Lowry model to urban modelers and urban planners stemmed from three characteristics of the initial formulation. First, this model described the interactions between the spatial distributions of employment and population in an intuitive way. Second, the Lowry model utilized a very crude probabilistic (or proportional) spatial distribution procedure. Third, it provided a formulation that was operational on the computer. If the crude probabilistic procedures of the Lowry model can be replaced with behaviorally meaningful choice functions derived from utility and profit maximization and the resulting model can be shown to be computationally efficient, a powerful policy tool suitable to long term general equilibrium analysis will have emerged.

2. MODELS WITH ENDOGENOUS PUBLIC SECTORS

The partial equilibrium model of Chapter 5 and its general equilibrium extensions described in the previous section can be extended further by endogenizing aspects of the public sector. These extensions are necessary if the impact of government policies on market equilibria are to be effectively and accurately analyzed. What are the salient features of such extended models with endogenous public sectors? It is indeed the case that there is not a single public sector but a multiplicity of public sectors, since each municipality within a metropolitan area operates as an independent government with its own fiscal budget and policy instruments. In the Chicago SMSA, for example, there are over 300 suburban municipalities, unincorporated areas, and the central city of Chicago, which is the largest local government in the SMSA. A model that recognizes this multiplicity of public sectors would subscribe to Tiebout's (1956) theory of local governments.

Such a model should contain at least one equation for each municipality. This equation should balance the municipality's local property tax and other revenues plus any external subsidies from state and local government applied against the public service provision costs of the municipality. The equilibrium property tax rates and the levels of other policy instruments should be determined endogenously by simultaneous solution of these public sector equations while at the same time solving all equations needed to determine general market equilibrium. The demand side of such a model should explicitly include consumers' and firms' choices of the municipality where these consumers and firms will locate as well as determining all other choices required for market equilibrium. The above framework would thus determine the *fiscal equilibrium* of the public municipalities simultaneously with the *market equilibrium* of the land, housing, and employment markets. While many public services such as police and fire protection, education, and local recreation are locally supplied and financed, many other types of public services—in particular, highways, public transit systems, water supply, and waste treatment systems—are supplied at a larger scale and rely on inter-municipality financing schemes administered by metropolitan agencies whose authority goes across several municipalities. To include these public services, the extended public sector models should represent each agency with one or more equations describing the balance between the revenues and the costs of that agency.

Combining all of the above considerations into one model implies a rather complex mathematical structure in which the market equilibrium of the land, housing, and employment sectors is determined simultaneously with the fiscal equilibrium of the interdependent local municipalities and the metropolitan public agencies. Such a complex model is still an equilibrium model of the public and private sectors taken together. A further extension would embed such an equilibrium model into an overall public sector optimization model in order to explore socially optimal plans and allocation decisions. Such an optimization model may represent the point of view of state or federal governments, which control various policy instruments and subsidization programs, through which they influence metropolitan resource allocations.

Ultimately, in order to correctly and consistently model the policy making of state and federal governments, it will be necessary to link the various metropolitan models into a supermodel structure that would be used to explore the intermetropolitan interactions resulting from various state and Federal policies

It would appear that the development of large scale urban simultation models with endogenous public sectors should be of profound importance in urban economic modeling. Without such a model, fundamental policies dealing with pricing, taxation, land zoning, and subsidized public systems cannot be consistently analyzed.

One "public sector" of particular importance and great complexity is the urban transportation system. Urban economists have been generally content with rather simple and geographically symmetric representations of the transportation system, such as the grid pattern in Mills' linear programming model. In contrast, transportation planners have dealt with more realistic representations of the transportation system as a *network* or several networks representing different modes of travel. The mathematical complexity of networks becomes clear when one considers the combinatorial problems that arise when all the links of the network must be jointly examined and manipulated. A very important task in the development of public sector models is the introduction of network representations of the transportation system into general equilibrium models of the urban economy.

3. DYNAMICS

It is generally recognized that successful urban policy analysis requires the development of dynamic models suited for exploring the intertemporal effects of public decisions. The main obstacle in the way of dynamic modeling is the lack of adequate data that would enable the successful estimation of such multiperiod dynamic disequilibrium models. The large scale data sets needed to estimate the equilibrium models discussed above may, in some cases, be available for one point in time but are generally unavailable for several consecutive years. It is actually doubtful that successful dynamic disequilibrium models can be estimated without comprehensive data sets available for at least five or ten years.

Conceptually, the development of dynamic models does not pose as great a difficulty as that posed by data limitations. It may indeed be the case that dynamic disequilibrium models are mathematically and computationally simpler than static general equilibrium models. This may be the case because in dynamic models, the equations of one time period are sequentially linked to those of the next and previous periods. Simulating the events of one time period may not require the simultaneous solution of equations but simply the recursive extrapolation of prices, demands, and supplies from previous time periods, based on expectation and growth equations. While a static model may find an equilibrium solution at great expense by computing the fixed point of numerous simultaneous equations, an equivalent dynamic model may find the same equilibrium by simulating an extended time span at approximately the same cost. Thus simulated, the dynamic model will provide information for a longer period, determining not only the ultimate equilibrium path but also the actual path the urban economy follows in adjusting toward this equilibrium path.

Policy analysis with dynamic models requires a much higher level of sophistication. Comparative dynamics must be used to simulate the path of the urban economy under various assumptions about the values of the exogenous parameters and functions. Clearly, the policy options that need to be examined by a decision maker are greatly varied and much more complex when the model is dynamic.

Urban economists can begin the task of the theoretical development of dynamic disequilibrium modeling by drawing on the existing single market and multimarket disequilibrium theories. One task that has not been accomplished by theoretical economists and econometricians is the development of disequilibrium models in which the demand and supply equations are given as stochastic choice models. The econometrics of nonlinear disequilibrium models are not yet well developed, and they need to be studied carefully in the future. It would appear, however, that even if such developments *do* take place, data limitations will prevent the design of complete and consistent disequilibrium models for some time to come.

One interesting aspect of dynamic models is the treatment of tenure choice and residential location choice within such models. In static partial equilibrium models such as those of this book, each household is identified by its employment location and is assumed to choose a residential location, given the employment location. As long as households are treated as renters, it is not necessary to identify their current residential location separately from their newly chosen location. Once tenure choice is introduced in a dynamic model, it then becomes necessary to identify homeowners with their *current* residential location in order to correctly model their choice of their *new* residential location. The reason for this is that homeowners who move will typically sell their current home and buy a new one. How much they can pay for their new home depends on how much they receive or expect to receive for their current home. At the same time, the household's wealth is adjusted by the capital gain or loss experienced in the transaction and move. It the urban model consists of I residential home ownership zones or submarkets, there are precisely $I \times I$ possible moves or relocations for the homeowner population at each time period. The dynamic model would determine the probability that a home owning household, which is in zone i at time t, will relocate to zone j at time $t + 1$. These transitions from one zone or housing submarket to another can be modeled as a Markovian or semi-Markovian stochastic transition process, the steady state behavior of which can be examined to derive equilibrium path spatial housing price adjustments from one time period to another. Although such a zone-to-zone transition process is necessary in a dynamic model with home ownership, it can greatly increase the computational cost and can greatly complicate the dimensionality of the model. Because of the proliferation of states and transition possibilities, the number of homeowners in any given state may be quite small, thus reducing the reliability of the expected demand calculations. Typically, when this reliability is greatly reduced, it may become advisable to formulate the model as a Monte Carlo microsimulation process, in which the decisions of each household are separately modeled through a probabilistic process. The market dynamics of microsimulation models can be quite complex and have not been adequately examined. The use of microsimulation in dynamic models remains an interesting area for future research.

4. THE HOLISTIC SOLUTION TO PUBLIC POLICY ANALYSIS

It may be inquired why the development of multisectoral, complete models with endogenous public sectors should be pursued with the zeal suggested in the preceding sections. The reason for pursuing the development of complete, multisectoral models is that the exercise of public policy making with partial and incomplete models may be ultimately inconsistent and counterproductive.

Strictly speaking, one cannot pursue the making of public transportation policy while ignoring the effects of these policies on the housing, employment, land, and public sectors. If one does so, one can conceivably propose a policy or plan the unaccounted costs of which greatly exceed its accounted benefits. To put this another way, errors in what is left out of the model may overwhelm what is included in the model. Developers of partial and incomplete models will frequently qualify the significance of the missing parts of their models and will claim that the quantitative errors introduced because of the missing aspects are not significant. In many cases they may be right, but the extent to which their judgments are justified cannot be put to a conclusive test unless complete models of the urban economy are developed and tested empirically. This ultimate successful development of holistic models can be accomplished by the development of partial models in the short run to be combined into more general multisectoral models in the longer run.

5. THE COMPUTABILITY OF LARGE SCALE MODELS

The computational expense required in solving large scale models of the kind proposed in this chapter can easily become impractical and insurmountable. The long term solution to this difficulty rests with the rapid ongoing development of increasingly advanced computers. Yet the combinatorial complexity that arises from discrete urban investment decisions is so great that may realistic policy problems are infinitely beyond the scope of the most efficient computers.

The typical illustration of the combinatorial hopelessness is as follows: Consider a public investment problem that consists of finding the best combination of projects to be selected out of 100 proposed facilities or public projects. The number of possible combinations in this combinatorial problem is 2^{100}. If each of these combinations could be evaluated in 1 sec of computer time, thanks to a very efficient urban simulation model, to evaluate all of the combinations would require 4.0196937×10^{22} yr! Such combinatorial complexity poses an ultimate challenge that brings us to question the fundamental rationale of aiming to find "optimal plans." It is rather "fairly good" or approximately optimal plans that we must seek and be content with.

It is precisely because only a very small number of possible plans can be evaluated that we must focus on good predictive models. If such models are available, we can safely say that the few alternatives that we can analyze, we can analyze and understand well. The benefits from a detailed and complete analysis of a single plan or policy are much greater than the benefits from a tiny and crude search in an ocean of all possible plans.

The computational problems associated with predictive models are also quite impressive but of a different nature. In these models, the key computational issue is that of aggregation. It is generally recognized that microsimulation models in which each market participant is separately represented are potentially the most accurate but are the most expensive computationally. From this fact arises the need to experiment with aggregative models, such as those of the preceding chapter, in which zones, submarkets, and the like, the units of analysis, reflect the existence of a certain degree of aggregation error. Disaggregation of such aggregative models can be carried to great extremes short of microsimulation; but disaggregation is generally useless unless it is accompanied with commensurate increases in the data that are needed to distinguish and differentiate the smaller aggregation units from one another. Thus the choice of a proper degree of disaggregation requires the striking of a delicate balance between computational and predictive accuracy on the one hand and computational and data collection cost on the other.

6. THE CONTRIBUTION OF THIS WORK

In the context of the research directions discussed in this chapter, the contribution of this work may seem small indeed. It is more appropriate to judge this work by comparing it to the state of the art than to expected future accomplishments. In this light, the research reported in this book has achieved the following. First, it has demonstrated that stochastic utility-maximizing and stochastic profit-maximizing models of renter and landlord behavior can be combined into a partial equilibrium model of the rental housing market that exhibits a unique solution. This was done by taking advantage of the convenient computational structure of the multinomial logit and nested logit models. Second, it has demonstrated that multinomial logit and nested logit models of household, commuter, and landlord behavior can be meaningfully and accurately estimated using small spatial aggregation units and relative frequency data of commuters' choices of modes and residential locations. It appears from all indications that the aggregation errors introduced by using such zones are quite small and that they do not seriously bias the results compared to the many other sources of bias that are ever present in disaggregate or aggregate estimation. Third, it has demonstrated that the resulting partial equilibrium model of the rental housing market combines the problem of mode choice prediction (a traditional concern of the travel demand analyst within transportation planning) with the problem of rental housing market equilibrium and residential location choice prediction (a traditional concern within urban economics and urban modeling). In this way, the gap separating urban economics, transportation planning, and urban modeling is closed, and an economic urban model capable of doing transportation planning is established. Since this model relies on multinomial logit and nested logit models, it is indeed entirely comprehensible to the transportation planner and does not require extensive retraining of scholars working in this subdiscipline. Fourth, the model described above is a prototypical policy-analytic tool that expands the concerns of transportation planners to include an array of policies dealing with the impact of transportation improvements, investments, and disinvestments on property values, population mobility within and across municipalities, and housing vacancies. In this way, the model enables more comprehensive evaluation and analysis of transportation policies and system changes. Finally, the prototypical model described above can be extended to include general equilibrium considerations, an internalized public sector, and a dynamic structure. The research reported in this book does not show *how* these developments can be achieved, but the basic structure of the partial equilibrium model that has been developed and tested certainly contains all the necessary insights and thus brings a vast array of more complex models within reach. It has been argued in the Introduction that once such comprehensive models are developed, the accuracy and scope of urban economic analysis will become greatly enhanced and pushed forward.

REFERENCES

Alonso, W. (1964). "Location and Land Use." Harvard Univ. Press, Cambridge, Massachusetts.

Amemiya, T. (1978). On a two step estimation of a multivariate logit model, *J. Econometrics* **8**, 13–21.

Anas, A. (1975). The empirical calibration and testing of a simulation model of residential location, *Environ. and Planning A* **7**, 899–920.

Anas, A. (1978a). Dynamics of urban residential growth, *J. Urban Econom.* **5** (1), 66–87.

Anas, A. (1978b). Mathematical programming models of urban redevelopment: An extension of the Herbert-Stevens model, paper presented at the *Conf. Urban Transport., Planning and the Dynam. Land Use, Northwestern Univ., June 2–4*.

Anas, A. (1979). The impact of transit investment on housing values: A simulation experiment, *Environ. and Planning A* **11**, 239–255.

Anas, A. (1980a). Evaluating the effects of transportation—land use policies on housing values and household welfare, *Environ. and Planning A* **12**, 747–764.

Anas, A. (1980b). A probabilistic approach to the structure of rental housing markets, *J. Urban Econ.* **7**, 225–247.

Anas, A. (1981a). The estimation of multinomial logit models of joint location and travel mode choice from aggregated data, *J. Regional Sci.* **21**(2), 223–242.

Anas, A. (1982). Discrete choice theory, information theory and the multinomial logit and gravity models, "*Transportation Research*" (in press).

Anas, A., and Lee, G. Y. (1982). The potential for a value capture policy to finance rapid transit projects in Chicago's Southwest Corridor: An empirical simulation analysis, *in* "Research in Urban Economics," (J. V. Henderson, ed.), pp. 171–202.

Anas, A., and Moses, L. N. (1976). Mode choice, transport structure and urban land use, *J. Urban. Econom.* **6**, 228–246.

Atherton, T. J., and Ben-Akiva, M. E. (1976). Transferability and updating of disaggregate travel demand models, *Transportation Res. Record* (610), 12–18.

Atherton, T. J., Suhrbier, J. H., and Jessiman, W. A. (1975). The Use of Disaggregate Travel Demand Models to Analyze Carpooling Incentives. Unpublished report, October.

253

Ben-Akiva, M. (1973). The Structure of Passenger Travel Demand Models, Ph.D. dissertation, MIT, Department of Civil Engineering, Cambridge, Massachusetts.

Ben-Akiva, M. (1974). Alternative travel behavior structures, *Transportation Res. Record* **526**, 26–41.

Bouthelier, F., and Daganzo, C. F. (1979). Aggregation with multinomial probit and estimation of disaggregate models with aggregated data, *Transportation Res.* **13B**, 133–146.

Boyce, D. E., and Allen, B. (1973). Impact of Rapid Transit on Suburban Residential Property Values and Land Development. Department of Regional Science, Univ. of Pennsylvania, Philadelphia, Pennsylvania.

Burright, B. K., and Enns, J. H. (1975). Econometric Models of the Demand for Fuel. The Rand Corporation, Santa Monica, California.

Callies, D., Sharpe, C., and William, D. (1976). Value capture gives the public an added payoff, *Planning* **42**(9), 22–23.

Cambridge Systematics, Inc. (1977). Tests of Transferability and Validation of Disaggregate Behavioral Demand Models for Evaluating the Energy Conservation Potential of Alternative Transportation Policies in Nine Cities. Report for the Office of Energy Conservation, Federal Energy Administration, April.

Capozza, D. R. (1973). Subways and land use, *Environ. and Planning* **5**, 555–577.

Charles River Associates (1967). A Model of Urban Passenger Travel Demand for the San Francisco Metropolitan Area. Cambridge, Massachusetts.

Chicago Area Transportation Study (1980). Personal Travel Energy Consumption: Accounting Methods and Case Study for the Chicago Metropolitan Area.

Chicago Transit Authority (1980). Estimates of Heavy Rail Operating Costs: Southwest Transit Study. General Operations Division, Operations Planning Department, April.

Clark, C. (1961). The greatest of a finite set of random variables, *Oper. Res.* **9**, 145–162.

Committee Print 96–7 (1979). Urban Rail Transit: How Can Its Development and Growth Shaping Potential Be Realized?" Subcommittee on the City of the Committee on Banking, Finance and Urban Affairs, U.S. House of Representatives, 96th Congress, First Session. U.S. Government Printing Office, Washington, D.C.

Cosslett, S. R. (1978). Efficient Estimation of Discrete-Choice Models from Choice Based Samples. Ph.D. dissertation, University of California at Berkeley.

Daganzo, C. F., and Sheffi, Y. (1977). On stochastic models of traffic assignment, *Transportation Sci.* **11**, 253–274.

deLeeuw, F., and Struyk, R. J. (1975). The Web of Urban Housing: Analyzing Policy with a Simulation Model. The Urban Institute, Washington, D.C.

Dewees, D. N. (1976). The effect of a subway on residential property values in Toronto, *J. Urban Econom.* **3**(4), 357–369.

Dixit, A. (1973). The optimum factory town, *Bell J. Econom. Management Sci.* **4**, 637–651.

Domencich, T., and McFadden, D. (1975). "Urban Travel Demand: A Behavioral Analysis." North-Holland Publ., Amsterdam.

Federal Register (1976). Major Urban Mass Transportation Investments, Vol. 41, No. 185. Department of Transportation, Urban Mass Transportation Administration, Washington, D.C., September 22.

Federal Register (1978). Policy Toward Rail Transit, Vol. 43, No. 45. Department of Transportation, Urban Mass Transportation Administration, Washington, D.C., March 7.

Federal Register (1979). Urban Initiatives Program: Guidelines, Vol. 44, No. 70. Department of Transportation, Urban Mass Transportation Administration, Washington, D.C., April 10.

Forrester, J. W. (1968). "Urban Dynamics." MIT Press, Cambridge, Massachusetts.

Fujita, M. (1976). Spatial patterns of urban growth: Optimum and market, *J. Urban Econom* **3**(3), 209–241.

Galster, G. C. (1977). A bid-rènt analysis of housing market discrimination, *Amer. Econom. Rev.* **67**(2), 144–155.

Giannopoulos, G. A. (1980). Fare-free public transit potential in Athens, Greece, *Traffic Quart.* **34**(2), 313–327.

Goldner, W. (1968). Projective Land Use Model (PLUM): A Model for the Spatial Allocation of Activities and Land Uses in a Metropolitan Region, BATSC Tech. Rep. 219. Bay Area Transportation Study Commission.

Gómez-Ibanéz, J. A., and Fauth, G. R. (1980). Using demand elasticities from disaggregate mode choice models, *Transportation* **9**, 105–124.

Hagman, D., and Misczynski, D. (eds.) (1978). "Windfalls for Wipeouts: Land Value Capture and Compensation." American Society of Planning Officials, Chicago, Illinois.

Haring, J. E., Slobko, T., and Chapman, J. (1976). The impact of alternative transportation systems on urban structure, *J. Urban Econom.* **3**, 14–20.

Harris, B. (1968). Quantitative models of urban development: Their role in metropolitan Policy-Making, *In* "Issues in Urban Economics" (H. S. Perloff and L. Wingo, Jr., eds.), Johns Hopkins Univ. Press, Baltimore, Maryland.

Harris, B., Nathanson, J., and Rosenburg, L. (1966). Research on An Equilibrium Model of Metropolitan Housing and Locational Choice. Interim Report, Univ. of Pennsylvania, Philadelphia, Pennsylvania.

Hartwick, P. G., and Hartwick, J. M. (1974). Efficient resource allocation in a multinucleated city with intermediate goods, *Quart. J. Econom.* **88**, 340–352.

Hausman, J. A., and Wise, D. A. (1978). A conditional probit model for qualitative choice: Discrete decisions recognizing interdependence and heterogeneous preferences, *Econometrica* **46**(2), 403–426.

Henderson, J. M., and Quandt, R. E. (1958). "Microeconomic Theory: A Mathematical Approach." McGraw-Hill, New York.

Henderson, J. V. (1975). Congestion and optimum city size. *J. Urban Econom.* **2**(1), 48–62.

Herbert, J. D., and Stevens, B. H. (1960). A model for the distribution of residential activity in urban areas, *J. Regional Sci.* **2**, 21–36.

Horowitz, J. (1980). The accuracy of the multinomial logit model as an approximation to the multinomial probit model of travel demand. *Transportation Res.* **14B**(4), 331–342.

Ingram, G., Kain, J., and Ginn, J. R. *et al.* (1972). "The National Bureau of Economic Research, Detroit Prototype, Urban Simulation Model." Columbia Univ. Press, New York and the NBER

Kain, J. F., Apgar, W. C., Jr., and Ginn, J. R. (1976). Simulation of the Market Effects of Housing Allowances, Vol. I, Description of the NBER Urban Simulation Model, Research Report R77-2. John F. Kennedy School of Government, Harvard Univ.

Kim, T. J. (1979). Alternative transportation modes in an urban land use model: A general equilibrium approach, *J. Urban Econom.* **6**(2).

Koppelman, F. S. (1976). Guidelines for aggregate travel prediction using disaggregate choice models, *Transportation Res. Record* 19–24.

Krueger, C., Heramb, C., Kunze, B., and Gallery, M. (1980). Southwest Transit Study, Phase I Report: Preliminary Alternatives Analysis. City of Chicago, Department of Public Works, Bureau of Transportation Planning and Programming.

Lancaster, K. J. (1966). A new approach to consumer theory, *J. Polit. Econom.* **74**, 132–157.

Lerman, S. R. (1977). Location, housing and automobile ownership and mode to work: A joint choice model, *Transportation Res. Record* (610).

Lerman, S. R., Damm, D., Lerner-Lam, E., and Young, J. (1977). The Effect of the Washington METRO on Urban Property Values, Center for Transportation Studies Report No. 77-18. MIT, Cambridge, Massachusetts.

Leven, C. L. (1978). "The Mature Metropolis." Heath, Lexington, Massachusetts.

Lowry, I. S. (1964). "A Model of Metropolis." Rand Corporation.

Luce, R. D. (1959). "Individual Choice Behavior." Wiley, New York.

Manski, C. F., and Lerman, S. R. (1977). The estimation of choice probabilities from choice-based samples, *Econometrica* **45**(8), 1977–1988.

McFadden, D. (1973). Conditional logit analysis and qualitative choice behavior, *In* "Frontiers in Econometrics" (P. Zarembka, ed.). Academic Press, New York.

McFadden, D. (1977). Quantitative Methods for Analyzing Travel Behavior of Individuals: Some Recent Developments, Working paper No. 7704. Urban Travel Demand Forecasting Project, Institute of Transportation Studies, Univ. of California, Berkeley, California.

McFadden, D. (1978). Modelling the choice of residential location, *In* "Spatial Interaction Theory and Planning Models" (A. Karlqvist *et al.*, eds.). North Holland Publ. Amsterdam.

McFadden, D., and Reid, F. (1975). Aggregate travel demand forecasting from disaggregated behavioral models, *Transportation Res. Record* **534**, 24–37.

McFadden, D. *et al.* (1979). Forecasting Travel Demand in Small Areas Using Disaggregate Behavioral Models: A Case Study, Vol. XI. The Urban Travel Demand Forecasting Project Final Report Series.

Metropolitan Housing and Planning Council (1980). Regional Transportation Authority: Future Financing, Structure and Operations. Chicago, Illinois, December.

Miller, E. J., and Lerman, S. R. (1979). Disaggregate Modeling of Retail Firm's Decisions: A Case Study of Clothing Retailers. Paper presented at the 26th North American Meeting of the Regional Science Association, November 9–11, Los Angeles, California.

Mills, E. S. (1967). An aggregative model of resource allocation in a metropolitan area, *Amer. Econom. Rev.* **57**, 197–210.

Mills, E. S. (1972a). "Studies in the Structure of the Urban Economy." Johns Hopkins Press, Baltimore.

Mills, E. S. (1972b). Markets and efficient resource allocation in urban areas, *Swedish J. Econom.* **74**, 100–113.

Mills, E. S., and deFerranti, D. M. (1971). Market choices and optimum city size, *Amer. Econom. Rev. Papers Proc.* **61**, 340–345.

Mohring, H., and Harwitz, M. (1962). "Highway Benefits: An Analytical Framework." Northwestern Univ. Press, Evanston, Illinois.

Mudge, R. (1972). The Impact of Transportation Savings on Suburban Residential Property Values. Ph.D. dissertation, Univ. of Pennsylvania, Philadelphia, Pennsylvania.

Muth, R. F. (1969). "Cities and Housing." Univ. of Chicago Press, Chicago, Illinois.

Muth, R. F. (1975). Numerical solution of urban residential land use models, *J. Urban Econom.* **2**(4), 307–332.

Permut, H., and Zimring, M. (1975). Capital and Operating Costs for the Expansion of the Chicago Rapid Transit System. Technical rep., Regional Transportation Authority, Chicago, Illinois.

Putman, S. H. (1974). Preliminary results from an integrated transportation and land use package, *Transportation* **3**, 193–224.

Putman, S. H. (1979). "Urban Residential Location Models." Martinus Nijhoff Publ.

Quigley, J. (1976). Housing demand in the short run: An analysis of polytomous choice, *In* "Explorations in Economic Research" (S. D. Winter, ed.), Vol. 3, No. 1, pp. 76–102.

Reif, B. (1973). "Models in Urban and Regional Planning." Intext Educational Publ., New York.

Sajovec, J., and Tahir, N. (1976). Development of Disaggregate Behavioral Mode Choice Models for Feeder Bus Access to Transit Stations. M.S. Thesis, Northwestern University, Evanston, Illinois.

Sharpe, C. (1974). A Value Capture Policy, Volumes I–IV, Technical Report TST-75-82-85. United States Dept. of Transportation, Washington, D.C.

Sheffi, Y. (1978). Transportation Networks Equilibrium with Discrete Choice Models. Ph.D. dissertation, MIT, Department of Civil Engineering, Cambridge, Massachusetts.

Small, K. A., and Rosen, H. S. (1981). Applied welfare economics with discrete choice models, *Econometrica* **49**(1), 105–130.

Solow, R. M. (1972). Congestion, density and the use of land in transportation, *Swedish J. Econom.* **74**, 161–173.

Solow, R. M., and Vickrey, W. S. (1971). Land use in a long narrow city, *J. Econom. Theory* **3**, 430–447.

Strotz, R. H. (1957). The empirical implications of a utility tree, *Econometrica* **25**, 269–280.

Strotz, R. H. (1965). Urban transportation parables, *In* "The Public Economy of Urban Communities" (J. Margolis, ed.), pp. 127–169. Johns Hopkins Press, Baltimore, Maryland.

Talvittie, A. (1973). Aggregate travel demand analysis with disaggregate or aggregate travel demand models, *Transportation Res. Forum* 583–603.

Talvittie, A., and Dehgani, Y. (1979). Comparison of observed and coded network travel time and cost measurements, *Transportation Res. Record* **723**, 46–51.

Tiebout, C. (1956). A pure theory of local public expenditure, *J. Political Economy*

Train, K. E. (1976). A Post-BART Model of Mode Choice: Some Specification Tests, Working Paper No. 7620. Urban Travel Demand Forecasting Project, Univ. of California at Berkeley, Berkeley, California.

Train, K. E. (1977). The Urban Travel Demand Project Post-BART Codebook, Working Paper No. 7707. Urban Travel Demand Forecasting Project, Univ. of California, Berkeley, California.

Train, K. E. (1978). Sensitivity of parameter estimates to data specification in mode choice models. *Transportation* **7**, 301–309.

Vickrey, W. (1965). Pricing as a tool in the coordination of local transportation, *In* "Transportation Economics" (J. Meyer, ed.), National Bureau of Economic Research, New York.

von Thünen, J. H. (1826). "Der Isolierte Staat in Beziehung auf Landwirtschaft und Nationalökonomie." Hamburg.

Warner, S. (1962). "Stochastic Choice of Mode in Urban Travel: A Study in Binary Choice." Northwestern Univ. Press, Evanston, Illinois.

Wheaton, W. C. (1972). Income and Urban Location. Ph.D. dissertation, Univ. of Pennsylvania, Department of Cith and Regional Planning.

Wheaton, W. C. (1974). Linear programming and locational equilibrium: The Herbert-Stevens model revisited, *J. Urban Econom.* **1**(1), 278–287.

Wheaton, W. C. (1977a). A bid rent approach to housing demand, *J. Urban Econom.* **4**(2), 200–217.

Wheaton, W. C. (1977b). Income and urban residence: An analysis of consumer demand for location. *Amer. Econom. Rev.* **67**(4), 620–631.

Wheaton, W. C. (1978). private correspondence.

Williams, H. C. W. L. (1977). On the formation of travel demand models and economic evaluation measures of user benefit, *Environ. and Planning A* **9**, 285–344.

Wilson, A. G. (1967). A statistical theory of spatial distribution models, *Transportation Res.* **1**, 253–269.

INDEX

259